The Vision of Christine de Pizan

Library of Medieval Women　　　　　　　　　ISSN 1369–9652

Series Editor:　Jane Chance

The Library of Medieval Women aims to make available, in an English translation, significant works by, for, and about medieval women, from the age of the Church Fathers to the sixteenth century. The series encompasses many forms of writing, from poetry, visions, biography and autobiography, and letters to sermons, treatises and encyclopedias; the subject matter is equally diverse: theology and mysticism, classical mythology, medicine and science, history, hagiography, and instructions for anchoresses. Each text is presented with an introduction setting the material in context and a guide to further reading.

We welcome suggestions for future titles in the series. Proposals or queries may be sent directly to the editor or publisher at the addresses given below; all submissions will receive prompt and informed consideration.

Professor Jane Chance. E-mail: jchance@rice.edu

Boydell & Brewer Limited, PO Box 9, Woodbridge, Suffolk, IP12 3DF, UK. E-mail: boydell@boydell.co.uk. Website: www.boydell.co.uk

Previously published titles in this series appear at the back of this book

The Vision of Christine de Pizan

Translated from the French by

Glenda McLeod
Charity Cannon Willard

with Notes and Interpretive Essay by

Glenda McLeod
Gainesville College

D.S. BREWER

First published 2005
D. S. Brewer, Cambridge

Reprinted in paperback and transferred to digital printing 2012

ISBN 978–1–84384–058–9 hardback
ISBN 978–1–84384–298–9 paperback

D. S. Brewer is an imprint of Boydell & Brewer Ltd
PO Box 9, Woodbridge, Suffolk IP12 3DF, UK
and of Boydell & Brewer Inc.
668 Mount Hope Ave, Rochester, NY 14620-2731, USA
website: www.boydellandbrewer.com

A CIP catalogue record for this book is available
from the British Library

This publication is printed on acid-free paper

Contents

Preface   vii

Acknowledgements   ix

Abbreviations   x

Introduction   1

The *Vision* of Christine de Pizan

Gloss on the First Part of this Present Volume   10
Book One   18
Book Two   53
Book Three   88

Interpretive Essay   135

Select Bibliography   159

Index   175

This book is dedicated to Charity Canon Willard (1914–2005). Her scholarship, toughness, good will, and generosity of spirit inspired and encouraged all whose lives she touched.

Preface

Christine de Pizan (1365-ca. 1430) is one of the most fascinating and prolific of the women writers of medieval Europe or indeed of any time. Her range was broad; she wrote courtly and pastoral love poems, allegorical histories, manuals of warfare and government, defenses of women, and commentaries on contemporary politics. Moreover unlike many medieval women writers, she was a secular and public figure who concerned herself not only with the position of women in society but also with court life and politics in late medieval France. Her works touch upon the Babylonian captivity, the Hundred Years War, and the civil wars that engulfed France at the end of her life. She discusses the plight of women in medieval society as well as her own difficulties as a widow and writer. Most fascinating is her experimentation with different ways to legitimate her speaking on a number of issues not usually open to feminine commentary. Without her voice, we would be much the poorer not only in the legacy of women writers but in the general legacy of her era.

Among her works, the *Vision* (1405–1406) occupies an important place, as scholars have long recognized. Stylistically, it represents her last experiment with allegory, a form she had written about in the debate on the *Roman de la Rose* and later utilized in six book-length works. Like many of her writings, it speaks to public events, in this case a growing political crisis generated by the madness of King Charles VI and the ensuing rivalries for control of the king-dom. Of greatest interest to many modern readers is its narrative of Christine's development as a writer, an account replete with interesting insights into a medieval woman's life story. In all of these roles—as a political commentary and allegory and a professional autobiography—the *Vision* continues to speak to us. It is thus worthwhile to make an out-of-print translation of this text available again.

The translation that follows has been reworked in the light of a recently issued edition of the original text. Despite its public themes, the *Vision* exists in only three known manuscripts: Brussels, Bibliothèque royale, 10309; Paris, B.N. f. fr. 1176; and ex-Phillips 128. For this translation we have relied upon Liliane Dulac and Christine Reno's *Le Livre de l'advision Cristine* published by

Champion in 2001, which is based on ex-Phillips 128. Ex-Phillips includes revisions in Christine's own hand and a unique copy of a preface interpreting Book I's allegory. Aside from the preface, it was not consulted for the earlier version of this translation. Additionally, Dulac and Reno's generous and meticulous scholarship has opened the door to many aspects of this difficult text.

The translation was completed by Charity Canon Willard and Glenda McLeod; McLeod wrote the endnotes. The opening introduction was written by Willard, the closing interpretive essay and annotated bibliography by McLeod. The translation draws from an earlier translation by McLeod published by Garland Press in 1993 as the *Vision*.

We hope that this translation will make this remarkable work by a remarkable woman better known. The last of Christine's book-length allegories, it sheds a great deal of light on her life and the times in which she lived.

Glenda McLeod

Acknowledgements

In this, as in any scholarly project, the debts owed are many. For moral support, encouragement, endless patience, and scholarly consultation, I would especially like to thank Katharina Wilson and Jane Chance, the editor of the series in which this book appears. It is particularly pleasing to express Professor Willard's and my gratitude to Liliane Dulac and Christine Reno for kindly sharing their manuscript of *L'Advision Cristine* with us before its publication in 2001. Caroline Palmer, editorial director at Boydell and Brewer, was unfailingly helpful and patient in response to my many queries. Finally, I would like to thank Charity Willard for her assistance with this translation. Without her generosity, warmth, and meticulous care, this volume would not have been possible.

Glenda McLeod

Abbreviations

Advision	Christine Reno and Liliane Dulac. *Le Livre de l'advision Cristine*. Études Christiniennes 4. Paris: Champion, 2001.
Christine de Pizan: A Casebook	*Christine de Pizan: A Casebook*. Ed. Barbara K. Altmann and Deborah L. McGrady. New York and London: Routledge, 2003.
CMA	Thomas Aquinas. *Commentary on the Metaphysics of Aristotle*. Trans. John P. Rowan. Library of Living Catholic Thought. 2 vols. Chicago: Regnery, 1961.
Consolation	*The Consolation of Philosophy*. Transl. Victor Watts. London: Penguin, 1999.
Contexts and Continuities	*Contexts and Continuities Proceedings of the IVth International Colloquium on Christine de Pizan Glasgow 21–27 July 2000 published in honor of Liliane Dulac*. Eds. Angus J. Kennedy with Rosalind Brown-Grant, James C. Laidlaw, and Catherine M. Müller. Glasgow University Medieval French Texts and Studies I. 3 volumes. Glasgow: Glasgow University Press, 2002.
Macrobius	*Commentary on the Dream of Scipio*. Trans. William Stahl. Records of Civilization, Sources and Studies 48. New York: Columbia University Press, 1990.
PL	*Patrologiae cursus completus, series latina*. Ed. Abbé Jacques-Paul Migne. 221 volumes. Paris: 1844–64.
PMLA	*Publications of the Modern Language Association*
SATF	Société des Anciens Textes Français

Note: Works appearing in the Select Bibliography have been cited in abbreviated form; full publication details are given there.

Introduction

Charity Cannon Willard

Translating the writings of Christine de Pizan is by no means a new venture. Translations were even undertaken during her lifetime, beginning with Thomas Hoccleve's English version of her first long poem "L'Epître au Dieu d'Amour" ("The Letter to the God of Love"). William Caxton later translated and printed "The Moral Proverbes of Christyne" (1478) and *The Book of Fayttes of Armes and Chyvalrye* (1489) that turned out to be his second best-selling book.[1] As P.G.C. Campbell showed in his study of sources, her earliest long work, *L'Epître d'Othéa*, written in both poetry and prose, although never translated, circulated in England in a number of manuscript copies. Her *Livre des Trois Vertus* (*Book of the Three Virtues*) was translated into Portuguese and was one of the first books to be published in that country,[2] and recently a manuscript copy of the *Faits d'Armes et de Chevalerie* in German translation has come to light in a private collection in Switzerland. Curiously, her autobiographical *Vision* has not been translated into English until the present day.

These details, however, call attention to the achievement of this remarkable woman, born in the fourteenth century (1364) and living until around 1430. The date of her death is uncertain, but she is referred to in the past tense in 1434. Of course the most significant aspect of her life is that in a day when it was not considered desirable or necessary to educate women, she made of herself an educated person and a significant writer.

To be sure, the circumstances of her birth and early years were unusual.[3] She was born in Venice, where her father was for a time an official of the Republic. Thomas of Pizzano was no ordinary man. A graduate of the University of Bologna with training in Medicine and

---

[1] See William Caxton, *The Book of Fayttes of Arms and of Chyvalerye*, ed. A.T.P. Byles (London: Oxford University Press, 1932).
[2] See C. C. Willard, "A Portuguese Translation of Christine de Pizan's *Livre de Trois Vertus.*" *PMLA* 78 (1963): 459–64.
[3] For a detailed study of her life and writings, see Willard, *Christine de Pizan: Her Life and Works.*

Astrology (a usual combination in the fourteenth century), he taught at the University for a time before accepting the position in Venice, arranged through a friend of university days, Thomas of Mondino, whose daughter he subsequently married.

This was a time when Venice was noted not only for expanding maritime ventures, which undoubtedly contributed to an interest in the stars that would guide its ships, but also for an outstanding intellectual and artistic life. Thomas of Pizzano might well have known both Petrarch and Boccaccio who were there while he was in residence. Furthermore, his professional reputation was such that at one and the same time he was invited to the courts of both the Emperor of Austria and the King of France. It was the French court that attracted Thomas and after a period of trying out the situation offered there, he decided to stay and sent for his family to join him. Christine recalls with pleasure in the *Vision* their reception by Charles V on their arrival in Paris. Thomas enjoyed the favor of the King, and Christine spent her early years in the shadow of the most cultivated court in the Europe of its day.

At that time it was the custom of Italian families of the early Renaissance to educate girls with their brothers. Thus it is probable that Christine was instructed during her early years with her two brothers. It is even possible that she learned a little Latin, and it is evident that her father exercised an important influence on her intellectual formation. It is also quite possible that he had an extensive library, for there is a record of Charles V having given him some books and his contemporaries in Italy are known to have had collections. Later portraits of Christine in a book-lined office suggest that at least some of those books might have come from her father.

Unfortunately, following the customs of the day, Christine's education was cut short, for at the age of fifteen she was married to Master Etienne Du Castel, a promising young man of a good Picard family that still exists in France today. In 1380, the year of the marriage, he was appointed a royal secretary, a position that offered a promising future. His situation also suggests his association with other young men in the royal chancellery, who would become France's first humanists, for they read Petrarch and Boccaccio and corresponded with such Italian humanists as Coluccio Salutati. Christine thus continued to be in contact with educated men.

As was to be expected, the early years of the marriage were dominated by domestic concerns, including the birth of three children, a daughter and two sons. Christine would later refer to this as the happiest time of her life. The future seemed bright, in spite of her father's failing health and his death around 1387; Etienne Du Castel then became the head of the whole family and fortunes continued to prosper for another ten years. Then he died unexpectedly as he was accompanying the King on a mission to Beauvais, perhaps as a result of one of the epidemics of plague that swept over Europe repeatedly in the second half of the fourteenth century. Thus at the age of twenty-five Christine found herself a widow, responsible not only for her children, but also for her widowed mother and a niece left in Paris when her two brothers returned to Italy to claim family property there.

In common with many widows, she suffered from the devious ways of men who had charge of her finances. In spite of lawsuits it was years before she received money due to her husband from the government. These misfortunes are described in the *Vision*. Widowhood and its frustrations are, not surprisingly, a persistent theme in Christine's writings. Ten years of sorrow and struggle were to pass between the loss of her husband and her emergence as a courtly poet. Little is known of how she made a living, but she may have copied manuscripts for a workshop, as it is possible that she learned the book-hand identified as hers in some of the manuscripts of her writings from helping her husband. Royal secretaries are known to have had assistants and sometimes an office in their homes where they prepared letters and documents for official purposes. This would further explain Christine's portraits in the little study to which she refers on several occasions. Women were known to have copied manuscripts in this period and the best manuscripts of her writings and her seeming association with her illustrators would suggest an involvement in the Parisian book trade.

It may have been to console herself for her unhappy life that Christine began to write poetry. Her first collection *Cent Ballades* (*One Hundred Ballads*) appears to have been completed in 1399. In it, she expresses her grief for the loss of her husband, but it is also evident that she was making an effort to continue her education, reading Ovid's *Metamorphoses* and the *Consolation* of Boethius, which would be an important source for her *Vision*. As has been suggested, she had undoubtedly inherited books from her father, but her husband had probably added to the library as well. Christine is also known to have had access to the extensive Royal Library in the Louvre, where a friend of her husband's family, Giles Malet, was the principal librarian.

Her early poetry would also seem to have grown out of associations with the Orleans court, where the duchess, Valentina Visconti, was also Italian, with Malet the official head of her household. The Orleans court in the early fifteenth century had a taste for poetic competitions that may have inspired Christine, for it is to the Duke of Orleans that she dedicated several of her early works, notably *L'Epître d'Othéa* (*The Letter of Othea to Hector*) composed around 1400. To judge from the number of copies that still exist, it was one of her most successful works. In a combination of poetry and prose, she offers advice to a young knight, pretending the epistle is addressed to Hector by the goddess Othéa. It is based primarily on legends from antiquity, especially the Trojan war. She also addressed one of her longer poems, *Le Débat de Deux Amants* (*The Debate of Two Lovers*), to the Duke of Orleans, as well as several shorter poems. *Le Débat de Deux Amants* sets forth her disapproval of so-called "courtly love," inspired in large measure by her partici- pation in a debate with former colleagues of her husband over the merits of Jean de Meun's continuation of the popular *Roman de la Rose* (*Romance of the Rose*) with its unflattering account of such love.

Her enduring interest in study, however, is well reflected in another long poem, *Le Chemin de Long Estude* (*The Long Road of Learning*), written in 1402. Here she describes an imaginary voyage, not only across Europe and the Middle East but up into the Heavens to the Court of Reason. It is evident that she had been inspired by Dante here, but these imaginary travels also reflect an interesting knowledge of the geography of her day, at a time of important devel- opments. In the Court of Reason Christine discusses with Queen Reason and four companions—Wisdom, Nobility, Chivalry and Wealth—the qualities needed in a ruler to deal with the problems of a troubled world. In the end, these goddesses urge Christine to take their advice back to the world, for it is the duty of writers to give such advice. One sees here an outlook that would be developed fur- ther in the *Vision*.

It was perhaps at the Orleans court that Christine met John Montague, Earl of Salisbury, who was in France on a diplomatic mis- sion. A poet himself, as well as an admirer of Christine's poetry, he offered a place in his household in England to Christine's son, Jean, now thirteen years old. Unfortunately this promising opportunity for the young man turned out badly, for political events in England brought about Montague's death, and it was with considerable diffi- culty that Christine achieved her son's return to France; although King Henry IV offered her a place at his court, she had no desire to accept it.

His eventual return probably brought about a break with the Orleans court. Although she wrote a poem asking the Duke to give her son a place in his household, it brought no result. (It was at the court of Burgundy that he was finally given employment.) Christine's disappointment in the Duke of Orleans is understandable, but in 1403 she had already expressed her admiration for the court of Philip the Bold, Duke of Burgundy. At the end of that year she had offered the Duke of Burgundy a copy of another long poem, the *Mutacion de Fortune (The Mutation of Fortune)*, which led to his commissioning her to write a biography of his brother, King Charles V. Unfortunately the Duke did not live to see the biography completed, but Christine was rewarded for her work by his son, John the Fearless.

It is possible, even probable, that this change in sponsorship was a factor in Christine's change from composing poetry to writing prose. Burgundian interests were more inclined toward history, education of the young and political reform than to poetry. Their influence is evident in Christine's subsequent writings, which would make a significant contribution to the extensive Burgundian library.[4]

The biography of Charles V was perhaps influential in turning Christine's attention to her own autobiography, although this was also obviously inspired by her concern for the contemporary problems of France. Possibly it was directed to John the Fearless in the hope that her own troubles as well as her concern for the troubles of France would attract his interest. Undoubtedly one of the first copies was presented to him (Brussels, Bibl. Roy. Ms. 10309). Although there are only three known manuscripts of this work (see the preface to this volume), it has attracted considerable interest in later times, perhaps even more than most of Christine's other writings.

The date of composition, 1405, also suggests that she might well have been inspired by a sermon, *Vivat Rex*, preached by Jean Gerson, provost of the University of Paris, at the royal court in 1405.[5] Both Gerson and Christine were greatly concerned about the situation of the French dauphin, Louis of Guyenne, son of a mentally deficient father and a frivolous mother. The *Vision* also reflects Christine's continuing program of study. Her principal sources here are Dante's *Divine Comedy*, notably in her vision of the Holy Trinity at the end, the *Grandes Chroniques de France*, attributed to the chancellor of

---

[4]   See Georges Doutrepont, *La littérature française à la cour des ducs de Bourgogne* (Paris: Librairie Champion, 1909).

[5]   See Louis Mourin, *Jean Gerson: Prédicateur Français* (Bruges: Rijksuniversiteit to Gent, 1952).

France, Pierre d'Ogremont, and the commentary of Saint Thomas on Aristotle's *Metaphysics*. Dame Philosophy would seem to have been inspired by the *Consolation* of Boethius.

For most of the rest of her career as a writer, then, Christine produced mainly works in prose. In 1405 she devoted herself to the *Livre de la Cité des Dames (Book of the City of Ladies)*, undoubtedly inspired to some degree by Boccaccio's *De Claris Mulieribus*, which had been recently translated into French, but primarily devoted to showing the valuable contributions of women to society. A sort of sequel was her *Book of Three Virtues (Livre des Trois Vertus)*, dedicated to Marguerite de Bourgogne, now married to the Duke of Guyenne, undertaking to instruct women about the useful role they could play in contemporary society if they observed certain rules of conduct. It is notable that she concerned herself with women from all classes of society, and the book presents an unusually interesting view of the situation of women in the French society of her day.

Christine's other preoccupation, however, continued to be the problems disturbing France. In 1405 she directed a letter to the queen, Isabeau of Bavaria, reminding her of her duty to use her influence to settle difficulties between the contentious dukes of Orleans and Burgundy, but unfortunately the queen was not capable of or interested in dealing with the problem; indeed the situation worsened to the point where the Duke of Burgundy arranged to have his rival assassinated in November 1407.

Shortly before this, Christine had devoted her *Livre du Corps de Policie (Book of the Body Politic)* to the Duke of Guyenne offering him some needed instruction in the art of government, although the book's three parts offered advice not only to rulers, but also to the military and to the common people. Then in 1409 it was to the Duke of Berry, the King's uncle, to whom she appealed for intercession in France's endless troubles.[6]

At about that time, however, the Duke of Burgundy had managed to acquire influence over the queen and was designated to supervise the military training of the Duke of Guyenne. It was certainly true that he was the best expert available on military matters, once having been captured by the Turks at the Battle of Nicopolis and been their prisoner for several years. He almost alone among his royal contemporaries had experienced serious warfare. It was undoubtedly this Duke who directed Christine to write the *Fait d'Armes et de*

---

[6]   See Kennedy, ed. "*La Lamentacion sur les maux de la France de Christine de Pizan.*"

Chevalerie (*Deeds of Arms and of Chivalry*) for the young prince. He also saw to it that Louis was given some practical experience in government, having him appointed the governor of Creil, north of Paris. But just as the young prince was showing some aptitude for these duties a popular uprising occurred in Paris which once more threw everything into confusion. These was renewed contention between the Duke of Burgundy and supporters of the house of Orleans, now dominated by the young Duke's father-in-law, the Count of Armagnac. It was at this time that Christine wrote her already mentioned letter to the Duke of Berry, reflecting the terror felt by Parisians at the prospect of greater civil strife. Fortunately, a truce, the Treaty of Bicêtre, was achieved in 1412, due at least in part to the Duke of Guyenne's efforts, but also to the lack of provisions and money on both sides. This truce also encouraged the Armagnacs to undertake negotiations with the English.

It was during the lull in hostilities that Christine began to write her *Livre de la Paix (Book of Peace)* inspired in large measure by her hope that the dauphin would be a force in solving France's problems. Unfortunately, before the book was finished, in the spring of 1413, there was an other uprising of Parisian merchants, artisans and laborers, headed by the corporation of butchers and called the Cabochien revolt after one of the leaders. Even the efforts of John the Fearless and the University of Paris were unable to contain the violence that erupted. There was, however, a temporary truce in the late summer that allowed Christine to finish her book, which gives a vivid account of the violence that had occurred in the streets. Unfortunately the Armagnacs, now favored by the dauphin, soon renewed hostilities and the Burgundians were driven from Paris. It was this sad state of affairs that encouraged the English to undertake a new invasion of France, leading ultimately to the French defeat at Agincourt in November 1415. It is interesting to note that, contrary to Shakespeare's presentation of that battle, the Duke of Guyenne was not present. The disaster was followed only a few weeks later, however, by Louis de Guyenne's unexpected death. France was indeed in a sorry plight with a demented king and no heir to the throne.

Christine's reaction to Agincourt and the accompanying misfortunes is expressed in her *Epistre de la Vie Humaine (Letter Concerning Human Life)*, dedicated to Marie de Berry, Duchess of Bourbon, who had not only lost a number of relatives in the battle, but whose husband and son-in-law were prisoners in England, where they both would perish in captivity. Christine speaks to the women bereaved by the disaster with great understanding and compassion. Indeed, she seems to speak to the widows of all wars, telling them that they have no choice but to cultivate patience and hope for their husbands' salvation. Her psychology is timeless and universal. She shows an evolution from the personal grief expressed in her early poetry, reflecting her extensive reading and the relief provided to her by her writing as well as her recent experience. The epistle shows a most appealing humanity.

One of Henry V's ploys in his plan to take possession of France was his questioning of the legitimacy of the remaining possible heir to the French throne, the future Charles VII. This prince and his court were obliged to flee from Paris, and as Christine's son Jean was now a royal secretary he, too, was obliged to leave. This circumstance and the general upheaval in the city made it unsafe for Christine and many others to remain there. It is probable that she found refuge in the royal Abbey of Poissy, where her daughter had been a member of the Community for some years. Accommodations for lay people are known to have been available there. During her years of exile we hear her voice only in the *Heures de la Contemplation de Nostre Seigneur* (*Hours of the Contemplation of Our Lord*) possibly inspired by the death of her son in 1426. This poem expresses less personal sorrow than compassion for the suffering of all women in times of loss. Again, it shows a significant development from the revelation of her own misfortunes in her early poetry and in her *Vision* to a sympathetic understanding of the sorrows of womankind in general.

Happily, Christine's career as a writer does not end on this sorrowful note. She was to live to see the triumph of Joan of Arc at Orleans in 1429 and the coronation of Charles VII, and to write the first poem in celebration of the young woman who brought about this change in France's fortunes. In this poem, dated July 31, 1429, Christine not only celebrates these events but also expresses the hope that good Frenchmen will show loyalty to their king so that the country may return once more to peace and prosperity. This poem represents her final effort on behalf of France. As previously expressed in the *Chemin de Long Estude* she firmly believed that it was the role of poets and philosophers to remind kings as well as others of their patriotic duties. These were her last official words and the date of her death is uncertain, but, as has been noted, Guillibert de Metz, recording his memories of Paris in 1434, speaks of her in the past tense.[7]

---

[7]   See Solente, "Christine de Pisan." *Histoire littéraire de la France*, Vol. 40. Paris: Imprimerie Nationale et Klincksieck, 1974. 335–442.

An impressive number of her descendants are still living in Paris today[8] and her writings are preserved in numerous very handsome manuscripts.

Taken as a whole, Christine de Pizan's writings cover a remarkable variety of subject matter, from personal grief at the loss of her husband to commentary on the serious problems of France, along with advice to its rulers on dealing with them. They also evolved from describing personal grief to compassion for all women who had suffered comparable loss. And of course she terminated her career by writing of the great savior of France, Joan of Arc, admonishing her contemporaries to take her accomplishments seriously, which the Parisians did not seem to be sufficiently prepared to do. The *Vision* reveals a remarkable step in this evolution.

Christine de Pizan wrote at a time when neither French spelling nor grammar had been established in modern terms, so that even the early printed texts can provide complications for the modern reader. It is therefore a great advantage to have a translation of her *Vision* in modern English, permitting readers to understand clearly the thoughts of this remarkable woman.

---

[8] Colonel Jean Du Castel of the French Army, a descendant of Christine de Pizan, told me that there are eighty persons in his generation in the family (pers. comm.).

Gloss on the First Part of this Present Volume

[T]his is written] to open the way to explain matters described by means of figures in the first part of this book, which appears somewhat obscure, in the event that someone in the future might want to understand how to interpret it more fully, or after the manner of poets, by whom often, under the figure of metaphor or veiled speech, are hidden much secret knowledge and pure truths. And in such poetic speech, one can often have many meanings; and then poetry is beautiful and subtle when it can present several meanings and when one can take it different ways.[1]

And to touch briefly upon all this, without explaining each specifically, how figures in this said part can be taken, so that one can by explaining the most obscure matters more easily understand them and the meaning of the work, the dream can be taken for thought, the pilgrimage for human life. The large figure about which at the beginning of this said book it speaks, can be taken for the whole world, or heaven, earth, and the abyss. His name, which he carries written on his forehead, "Chaos," that can be interpreted at its beginning, as the ancient poets named the mass that God formed, from which He made heaven, earth, and all things, "chaos," or confusion, which still prevails in the world. The two openings that he has, through which he was fed and purged, can be understood as the birth of all corporeal things and also as the death of all living creatures. The sorrowful countenance that he bears is self-explanatory.

Likewise, this said image can be taken for each individual human being according to the manner of language of the philosophers who called man the image of the microcosm. He is great in regard to creation because formed by God. He has his head in heaven; this is his spirit which comes from there and must strive for there. The stars with which his head is adorned are the virtues of the soul, such as understanding, knowledge, memory, and the others. His belly represents the

---

[1] For another translation of this preface and a commentary on its debt to Boccaccio's poetics, see Reno, "The Preface to the *Avision-Christine* in ex-Phillipps 128." Brown-Grant, *Christine de Pizan and the Moral Defence of Women* 93–100 offers an interpretation that applies the standards of the commentary to the whole of *Advision*.

exterior operations necessary to his life. His feet, which pace the depths, represent hell, to which he will fall if he is not careful. He has two conduits; these are the two natures, earthly and heavenly, or body and soul. Sometimes he bears a sorrowful countenance; this indicates the tribulations that he frequently experiences. And in this fashion at greater length it can be explained.

Similarly, the body of this image can be taken for the kingdom of France, which is large and forms a single body [politic]. His head, which is in the heavens, represents the Catholic faith, which from the early days has flourished and grown and been more honored in this realm than in any other spot. The stars around his head can signify the noble princes and barons. He has two openings, which signify the temporal and the spiritual. He paces the abysses, which indicate the abyss of the Scriptures and the sciences that are studied in schools, on which his fair government was founded.

The book in the second chapter declares that a large, crowned shadow was appointed to feed the great image and completely surrounded him; which said shadow can be taken for Nature, which we can call a shadow. Although we call her "Nature," and have given her this name, we nonetheless do not see her as a material body. She can be said to be crowned by the dignity of her authority. She feeds the world, which she contains; all this we can see by the generations which naturally succeed one another, by which the world, or the human and other living species, are preserved. The four different materials from which she creates her food can be related to the four elements of which all things are composed. The tools in which she places the said mixture are the bodies of strange forms which she generates, such as people, beasts, and even trees and plants. The birth of all living things is sufficiently evident for the sound understanding from the text.

Likewise, this shadow can be interpreted as human life, which passes like a shadow. And yet she nourishes each man as long as he is alive on earth. But with what does she feed him? With bitterness, like bile; with foolish pleasure, like honey; with heaviness, like lead; with lightness, like feathers. The mouth in which she places this mixture is his thought, in which she has various utensils, that is different ways of thinking. She lets them cook a certain length of time and then pulls them out, but not all together; [thus] signifying his operations which variously leap out from him and fall on the earth through the various works that he does.

Likewise, with regard to the fact that the kingdom of France can be taken for the said shadow, she can again signify the Catholic faith, which has been from its early days the nourisher of this realm. And there is no doubt that France would have fallen long ago if God had not protected her because of her Catholic faith. For I do not believe that in any other region is the Church better served, thanks be to God, than she is in this realm, and this anyone can know who travels through other lands. Faith congeals and puts together four very different materials which she places to cook in the mouth of the said figure of France for her nourishment, which are bile, honey, lead, and feathers. The mouth of the image is the Church; bile is remorse of conscience; honey, the hope of divine mercy; lead, the fear of hell; feathers, life that soon passes away. The different tools are men of various callings, by whom the Catholic faith, which puts them in the belly of the Church, gives birth to good works of many kinds.

By what Christine says in the third chapter—that her spirit by the hands of the shadow was cast into the mouth of the image, and then after a while was withdrawn in a small body that fell into the belly of the said figure and was fed by the servant of the said shadow until it could sustain itself and move about—can be clearly understood as the birth and first nourishment both of her and similarly of all human creatures.

Likewise, this can be interpreted morally with regard to each man: the large figure, which we understand to be man, by his aspiration, that is his desires, attracts habit, which falls into the hands of the shadow, which we take to be human life. This life takes this habit and lets it cook in perseverance, from which arise small bodies, these are different works. Thereafter comes the shadow's servant who nourishes these bodies: that is Sensuality who nourishes and strengthens delight in perseverance until man is confirmed in habit.

Likewise, with regard to the kingdom of France, this can thus reveal the shadow, which we take for Faith: it took France and put her in the mouth of the Church and left her to cook until she was delivered into the belly of the earth, or the heart of the earth, just as this noble realm is seated in the midst of the true faith. And this can signify how the faith was carried into France and then nourished by the handmaiden of Faith, which is Holy Theology, who fed France until she was strong enough to walk over and trample all heresies.

We have already said how the fiction of this book can be allegorized in three ways, that is to say, applied to the general world, which is the earth, also to the individual man, and then to the realm of France. Also in the manner that each might speak of his own existence, so we can take what Christine says in the fourth chapter, how, because of the cry of Fame she, as a child, was transported with her parents into the country of a noble crowned lady, she can say that the earth, in the time of her childhood, or her innocence—which signifies the time when the law was not yet given to the world—she was transported by the cry of Fame—which means the cry of the blessed prophets—to the law of God, in which all goodness is contained; but the great ruins she saw there can signify the many heresies that have existed. And this can signify the people of Israel, led into the Promised Land. Likewise, it can represent sinful man when he is drawn from the ignorance of sin to penitence by the voice of the Holy Scriptures or by the blessed sermons and thereafter arrives at the perfect life in which he discovers all beauties through devout meditations. And the ruins about which he speaks can be interpreted as the assaults of temptation in a just life.

Likewise, this same fourth chapter can signify how Christine, in the time of her childhood, was with her parents carried into France from the land of Lombardy where she was born—as she later explains more fully in the third part, in which country she saw the beautiful things, which she discusses in the literal sense, and also the ruins which had come through wars.

By the fifth chapter can be understood what the world or the earth would say after the law had endured for a time in perseverance, which said world or earth could rejoice in such a manner by saying that it was acquainted with the blessed Wisdom that had already made it the antygraph[2] of its adventures, that is that it was made the witness of its commandments, as we see the commandments of God established on earth.

Likewise, this can signify man, already entered into a state of virtue, who already tastes the sweetness of contemplation.

Likewise, this can signify how Christine was already an adult when she became aware of the customs of France, whereby she was able to speak of them.

In the sixth chapter, in which begins the complaint of the Crowned Lady, it must be interpreted that the earth could likewise complain to Dame Rectitude. And the earth begins its plaint with its earliest deeds, which is to say since the age which is called the Golden Age, when people lived freely and without avarice, and then how this time ended when people became covetous and as soon as

---

[2]   Antygraph comes from the Latin *antigraphus* for clerk or scribe. For differing commentaries on the use of this term see Laennec, "Christine Antygrafe;" Dulac and Reno, "The *Livre de l'advision Cristine*" 213, n. 29; and Reno and Dulac's edition of the French text, *Livre de l'advision Cristine* 147, n. V/11–VI/11.

Rapine entered the world, which can be understood by the ants who by their nature are greedy to amass. Nonetheless, virtue was not so completely destroyed by the greedy that some of it did not remain in the world in various places so that thereafter men were more virtuous than they first arrived. And in the story of these plants of gold which were transported can be understood many stories of the second age and of individuals who descended from the good sons of Adam, such as patriarchs, prophets, and other holy and worthy men.

Likewise, this can indicate the reasonable soul which complains to Reason saying how God had created it innocent and good and then how, through various mishaps, the virtues were taken away from it, but not so entirely that there does not still remain some sound growth, such as understanding and the other blessings.

Likewise, this can signify the imagining that Christine has that France is speaking to her and telling her complaint. And first, she tells her how her deeds arose in the beginning from the noble Trojans, whom Christine calls the tree of gold for their richness and nobility. The colony of ants who uprooted the tree are the Greeks who destroyed the Trojans. Why does she call them ants? Because there were so many of them, and also because the ancient Persians said the Greeks came first from ants. The grafts of the tree of gold which were planted in several places can be understood as several relatives of King Priam of Troy who were carried into different countries from which came several noble generations, such as the Romans and others; and even to France these Trojans came, from which are descended the French princes from one of the nephews of King Priam of Troy, as one can know from the chronicles which mention this.

The seventh chapter continues the previous one. In this manner, one can explain what the text says: that into this country was transported a graft from the crown of the aforesaid tree of gold, that grew so large. This can signify the lineage of Our Lady, and first Abraham and the other descendants; from whom the earth can rejoice in such noble seed which grew so that it surpassed all other plants: this was Jesus Christ who surpassed all things. The earth took its name from him and was called "Libera." Truly the earth was liberated by that noble plant, Jesus Christ, who freed man from the Enemy. They crowned the third shoot, the third person of the Trinity, Jesus Christ, King of heaven and earth, who bore fruit of great worth. And the rest of the chapter can be sufficiently understood by this proposal alone.

Likewise, all can reduced to and spoken of as the soul and human life, with regard to this perfection of virtue.

Likewise, as was said, this can signify the arrival of the kings of France, from whom she took her name, for some say it was from one of these said princes named Francio. Others say that they gave it this name "France" for the great freedom they established there. They crowned the third shoot after their arrival, this was the third prince who came by succession, who was named Pharamond and he was the first king of France, as it is told in the chronicles.

By what is told in the eighth chapter can be understood what the earth could have said in the early days of Christianity in speaking of the holy popes and the other blessed preachers and cultivators of the holy law. Therein are included many stories of pagans and miscreants converted to the Christian faith, and the conversion of Vespasian, the noble Emperor who greatly honored and spread the faith of God.

Likewise, this can refer to the meditations of the devout soul which can be France, who speaks of herself, and therein can be included the period which continues to good King Clovis, who was the first Christian king, a prince of great worth. And by what the text says about the living water that the good prince attracted can be understood the conversion of this Clovis and his goodness and worth.

What is contained in the ninth chapter can signify the time thereafter during which several Christian princes were filled with concupiscence and grave sins, and even the popes and high men of the Church, in whom were grave heresies, who established false sects and perverse beliefs; and therein can be included many stories of the time past.

Likewise, it can signify the tribulations of the human body and even the spirit.

Likewise, this can signify the perversity of several French kings, such as King Childeric who was exiled for his lustful ways, who then carried off the wife of the king who had welcomed him, as the chronicles relate; also the other kings who were lazy and lacking in virtue, and their most cruel successors married to women of great cruelty.

The tenth chapter, which says that from the pip of the fruit of the aforesaid tree sprang a noble plant that grew so, etc., this can signify the virtuous sons, such as the good holy popes and the other blessed Doctors, who thrived so that they destroyed the heresies and spread the Catholic faith. This can also be understood as Saint Paul the Apostle or Saint Augustine, or any other great extender of the Church and the Catholic faith. And what is said thereafter, that the virtues are declining and so forth, can be taken for some fraudulent men who came later, who were settled in high places, both in the papacy and other prelacies of the Holy Church and also in positions of temporal power by tyranny, and for successive generations who possessed these. And what is said afterwards can indicate the misfortunes that have often existed on earth in many ways because of foreign vexations.

Likewise, all this can refer to the individual man.

Likewise, in regard to France, this can indicate Charlemagne, King of France, who gloriously extended Christianity and from whom the fame of France still exists; and then Hugh Capet who was given the crown of France. This Hugh Capet came from a foreign line; and then the crown returned to the father, Saint Louis, a descendent of the line of Charlemagne; and everything since that time, the rebellions and misfortunes that visited France in many forms.

What is contained in the eleventh chapter can indicate the good pope Urban, who greatly repaired the Church and restored it to righteousness and peace.

Likewise, it can signify the good conscience addressed to God.

Likewise, in regard to France, it can indicate the good wise King Charles the fifth of that name, by whom the state of France was restored from its previous ruins.

The twelfth chapter which speaks of the two birds of prey that arose from the entrails of the aforementioned one can indicate the two occupying the papacy for around twenty-eight years.[3] The apparent praise said of one of them can be understood through the rhetorical figure called *antiphrasis*, which is the opposite of what is said. What is said of Fortune, who with her wind felled the noble falcon, can be understood as the ruin of the Church, which Church is so noble that it encircles the whole world, which is to say that it should encompass the whole world.

Likewise, it can signify the body and soul together.

Likewise, in regard to France, this can indicate King Charles, sixth of that name, who presently reigns, the good that exists in his noble conditions, and the pity of his illness and the time that it has taken from him; and with him our lord the Duke of Orleans, his brother.

By the thirteenth chapter, and what is said thereafter in the other chapters, can be understood the ancient prophecies of Merlin, the Sibyls, Joachim, and John concerning the plagues to come in the world, both in the kingdom of France and elsewhere, because of the sins rampant there, which is to say because of the pride of the

---

[3]   On Christine's treatment of the Schism, see Blumenfeld-Kosinski, "Christine de Pizan and the Political Life."

rich and powerful, and the lasciviousness, fraud, avarice, and lack of faith in the world.

And everything contained in the said ensuing chapters, if regarded aright, concurs and accords with the sayings of the prophets on the times to come, with which agrees the Holy Scripture; and whoever reads and understands them properly will find them similar and analogous.

Book One

Here Begins The Book of Christine's *Vision* Which Said Book is Divided into Three Parts

The first part speaks of the image of the world and the extraordinary things that she saw in it.
The second speaks of Dame Opinion and her shadow.
The third part speaks of the comfort of Philosophy.

I.1. Christine first tells how her spirit was transported

I had already passed halfway through the journey of my pilgrimage[1] when one day at eventide I found myself fatigued by the long road and desirous of shelter. As I had arrived here eager for slumber, after I had said grace and taken and received the nourishment necessary for human life, recommending myself to the author of all things I betook myself to a bed of troubled rest. Soon thereafter, my senses bound by the weight of sleep, an amazing vision overcame me in the sign of a strange prophecy; even though I am hardly Nebuchadnezzar, Scipio, or Joseph, the secrets of the Almighty are not denied the truly simple.[2]

It seemed to me that my spirit left my body, and in example, as happens many times in dreams, it seemed that my body was flying in mid-air; and then it seemed to me that by the force of many winds, my spirit was being carried into a shadowy country in which it came to rest in a valley, floating on many streams. There the figure of a man appeared before me, beautifully formed but immeasurably tall; for his head rose above the clouds, his feet trod the depths, and his belly enveloped the whole world. He had a bright, ruddy face; innumerable stars adorned the hair of his head. From the beauty of his eyes such brightness radiated that all was suffused with light, and their brilliance reflected even to the entrails of his body. The inhalation from his enormous mouth drew in so much wind and air that all filled with an agreeable coolness. Two main conduits had

---

[1] Christine is echoing line 1 of Dante's *Inferno*, Canto I.
[2] Christine is referring respectively to the dream interpretations found in Dan. 4, Macrobius' *Commentary on the Dream of Scipio*, and Gen. 37:5–11, 40:9–19, and 41:1–7 and 17–36.

this figure: one was the opening of his mouth, through which he was receiving his food; the other was beneath, through which he was purging and emptying himself. But the two differed in nature because everything entering through the upper passage by which he fed had to have a material and perishable body, but nothing mortal or tangible passed through the other conduit. The clothing of this creature was a beautiful linen cloth—rich, durable, and very cleverly embroidered in flourishes of every color.[3] On his forehead had been clearly printed the imprint of five letters—C.H.A.O.S.—which specified his name. Nothing about the statue was ill-favored, but at times he would appear sad, melancholy, and sorrowful, just like a man who feels and suffers various passions and pains throughout the many parts of his body, because of which, he uttered great moans and various cries of lamentation to God.

I.2. Wherein she relates how the aforesaid figure was being fed

Standing at the side of this image was a large, crowned shadowy figure shaped like a woman, as if this were the semblance of a powerful queen naturally fashioned without visible or tangible body.[4] She was so tall that she surrounded and overshadowed the entire body of the aforesaid image, whose feeding she was particularly appointed to oversee and such were her duties. All around her she had instruments of different shapes and stamps, exactly like the waffle irons in Paris or other, similar tools. And as this lady had not the sin of sloth within her, the necessary dispatch of various tasks was keeping her continuously busy; for she was endlessly mixing a mortar in which she put bile and honey, lead and feathers to congeal together. She would fill pitchers of various shapes with this material and afterwards pour small amounts of it into the aforesaid molds, which she would stop and seal well. All this she made not in one but in many different forms; she would put everything to cook and take form in the gigantic figure's mouth, which was so broad that it

---

[3] This cloth, a *dyapree*, was originally a silk cloth decorated with flowers, branches, or arabesques usually woven in golden thread, but by the fifteenth century could be a fine linen fabric in diamond patterns. Both are characterized by a shimmering quality. For a discussion of the possible sources of this figure in the works of Boethius, St. Augustine, and Alain de Lille, see *Advision* 145, n. I/15–37. For a discussion on the Thomist origins of this image, see Richards, "Somewhere between Destructive Glosses and Chaos" 44–45.

[4] This figure, Nature, also appears in Christine's *Mutation of Fortune*. See Huot 366–68 for a discussion of this scene and its relation to the figure of Nature in the *Romance of the Rose*.

resembled a great oven, heated as a tempered bath might be. There she would leave them for the time which, according to the differences and weights of the molds, was most appropriate for each. After the time when the wise directress knew the moment for her work's perfection had arrived, she would open the giant's mouth so skillfully that she had room to withdraw the materials that were done; the others she would leave to cook until their time was up. Small bodies, variously shaped in accordance with the imprints of the instruments, would then be taken from the molds. But an amazing thing would happen to them: for as soon as these tiny figures left their dies, then the large figure in whose mouth they had been cooked would greedily swallow them all into his belly in a single gulp. And thus neither night nor day would the work cease, continued at the hands of this lady for the nourishment of the great, insatiable body.

I.3. How Christine was swallowed into the body of this figure

My spirit, applying itself to the study of this wondrous phenomenon, was cast into that quarter; then the strength of this great form's breathing drew it toward him until it fell into the hands of the crowned lady. When she had placed all the molded material into the oven, she took my spirit and exactly as she was accustomed to do to give human bodies form, mixed it all together and left me to cook for a certain period of time until a small human shape was made for me. However, because she who had cast it wished it to be so rather than because of the mold, I was given the feminine sex. Just like the others, I was suddenly swallowed into the giant's belly. When I was thrown there, the lady's servant immediately arrived carrying ewers filled with a very sweet and pleasing liquid from which she courteously led me to drink; because of which virtue and continued application, my body grew taller and taller, stronger and stronger, and more and more vigorous. This wise woman would increase and augment the food in proportion to my strength until I could carry and feed my body by myself; because of it, my judgment was increasing and providing me with an understanding of the remarkable nature of the entrails of the belly of this image, through which I would walk on foot and which were made of pebbles, hard rocks, through mountains and valleys, woods, metals, and many different substances. The space enclosed by this image seemed long and wide, extending so far and wide that a man's lifetime might not serve to seek out all the many countries included within it.

I.4. How she was transported from one place to another

At that time when Fame, who had blown and was still blowing with all her trumpets and horns in the country where I was, had been shouting out what she had already made known both there and in all other lands—that is, she was recounting the worth, honor, the great nobility, and powerful dignity of a princess of great authority, who was crowned by a precious diadem with a royal scepter of great age and wealth, who was seated in the region which we call Phyrgia[5] and in all the universe had no equal in beauty, nobility, valor, and renown—then because of the cries of Fame and after conclusive messages confirmed these matters, my guardians left, desirous to serve such a princess. And so walking with them through this figure's entrails, crossing foreign countries, the high Alps, wild moors, deep forests, and fast-running rivers, I journeyed for many days until the light of the country I was approaching appeared to me from afar, bright in honors. And discerning her glory the better the nearer I approached, I finished my long journey in her principal city, which was called the second Athens. Thereupon with the labor of the long road accomplished, resting my weary limbs, I considered how—by what means—I might make the acquaintance of the said princess. But since I was still quite young, I knew not how to apply myself or learn the language, which differed from that of my parents; still, in accordance with my unskilled and still immature faculties, I was continually studying this lady's customs, manners, and conditions. And as I persevered in this way for several years, enlarging my memory, I was instructed in this lady's noble power and mastery, concerning whom I truthfully and (to avoid prolixity) briefly attest that I thought her land glorious in name, fertile in harvests, abundant in treasures, large and broad in circuit, and notably framed with large towns, strong cities, castles, villages, strongholds, and innumerable noble manors; [it had] powerful lordships and compassionate princes—kind not cruel, gentle in dealings with others, Catholic in faith, wise in government, and admirable in the fashion of a strong and powerful chivalry—as well as loyal subjects and obedient people. In this land I truly perceived all these conditions and many other benefits, which brevity permits me to discuss no further. But since no good fortune may exist without envy, it is true that I saw

---

[5] Phrygia is an alternative name for the region of Troy. Like other political writers in this period, Christine founded France's grandeur in part on the descent of its royal family from the royal princes of Troy. See Beaune.

there many areas vandalized on a large scale by envious foreigners, because of which it seemed to me that there had been and sometimes were great and terrible persecutions in this land.

I.5. The acquaintance which she wished to have of a certain lady wearing a crown

I was already fully grown when after much pursuit and many, varied adventures, I arrived at that which I was longing for. I had the full acquaintance of the renowned lady whose beauty, intelligence, and kindness I would be insufficient to describe. Thus I move on, saying only that I certainly never considered Fame a liar in the good reports given of her everywhere; actual experience, I saw, concurred with them. Now thanks be to God, I was so close a friend to this princess that she graciously favored me with the revelations of the secrets of her heart. And she feared not to do me, a woman, such an honor as to appoint me antigraphus[6] of her adventures of old, and she wished me to compose songs and speeches about them as she was already as informed about my feelings as about who I was.

I.6. The complaint of the crowned lady to Christine

Speaking then in such a manner, she said: "Dear friend, eager for the cultivation of my welfare, since in nature all loving hearts necessarily deserve to be loved, it is right that your worthy desire should be of use to you; and since it was desirous of my acquaintance, let its good wishes be granted. Friend, to whom God and Nature have conceded the gift of a love of study far beyond the common lot of woman, prepare parchment, quill, and ink, and write the words issuing from my breast; for I wish to reveal all to you, and I am pleased that you, following your wise good will, should henceforth present the written memories of my dignity. It is a thing well known that he who wishes to speak properly about himself should specify first his origins; I will begin, therefore, at the outset of my exploits.

"In the time of the second age,[7] when Neptune's line was reigning in the comfortable dwellings of the chivalric frontier, when because of the chosen girl stolen by the foreign shepherd, the heirs

---

[6] Antigraph comes from the Latin word *antigraphus* for scribe or clerk (see note 2 of gloss).

[7] The dating of Troy to the second age alludes to the common medieval practice of dividing history into six periods based on the six days of creation and the six ages of human life.

of ants came riding within wooden horses with armed force, by the shield of Deceit, they were victorious in the end.[8]

"Then from this earth was uprooted the golden tree,[9] which, according to the songs of the poets, the ancient gods had reserved for their glory, the grandeur of whose shadow extended all the way to distant lands. So I was at this time through inhospitable Fortune, who smiled on this swarm of revenge-hungry ants, burned, destroyed, and reduced to ashes. But despite the ants' wicked and frantic desire, there were several gardeners [who], eager for the worthy seed, seeing the noble plant's persecutions, through subtle skill and with their own hands gathered and carried away many branches and shoots culled from the high summit of that lordly, noble tree. As the god Pelagus[10] consented to this theft, he gave them a road and passage through his realm. They were thus transported, spreading throughout different countries where, because of their value, they were planted in many orchards and grafts were made, which were enclosed fast within thorny hedges to thwart the temptation of thieves. Despite Fortune's influences, the noble plant was revivified in several places, one shoot of which then grew so in the European frontier in the Latin lands that its grandeur cast a shadow over the whole world, and its first root increased beyond comparison."

I.7. Wherein the crowned lady speaks of her origin

"At the time of these aforesaid thefts, one shoot among others from the crown of this golden tree was carried to this land, which they planted in fertile soil in a noble orchard. This plant grew until I took my name from its beauty and was called Libera. Thereafter, through proliferation through cultivation, this noble shoot continually grew and increased always with great dignity, so that the plants, now stronger and more beautiful in their force, crowned the third offshoot of their arrival and, as was most appropriate, made him their

---

[8] Christine is referring to the Trojan War: the "chosen girl" is Helen, the "foreign shepherd" Paris, and the "heirs of the ants" the Greeks. See *Advision* 143, n. 170–74 where the Greeks' depiction as ants is traced to an etymology in Isidore of Seville's *Etymologiae* (IX.2.75).

[9] See *Advision* 148, n. VI/19 on this image of the French dynasty, apparently created by Christine.

[10] This name is not found in either of Christine's sources: *Grandes Chroniques* or *l'Histoire ancienne jusqu'a César*. In *Advision* 149, n. VI/28, Reno and Dulac suggest Christine translated it from the Latin word *pelagus* for sea.

king.[11] This one bore most worthy fruit, for it saved this land from many infirmities; and so, little by little, the fame of its nature grew through multiplying. Consequently the people were most felicitous gardeners of it for many years in this country. And thus I have told you about the root and cultivation of my name. And I tell you truthfully that although to the eye I may be and appear young, new, fresh, flourishing, and beautiful, more than a thousand years have now passed since my first birth."

I.8. The crowned lady speaks of her exploits

"The fame of my liberty having already spread to all places, noble governors and their children took me into their care, so I was long retained in their hands without foreign kind. O glorious God, if I told you all the adventures over the years I have encountered since the birth of my name until now, your lifetime would not suffice to hear it! So I tell you in brief that my guardians took great pains to increase my legacy's nobility, but as ignorance still held them in darkness, they knew not how to draw the sweet water to give my little roots and plants permanent drink; because of this, many vines and other stems—completely dry and barren—had to be uprooted and thrown on the fire. And thus this pestilence persisted until the arrival of the fifth son,[12] who by virtue of wise counsel attracted such light that the shadows of this deadly drought were expelled; in this way, he knew of the waterway, and the source from which water came with great abundance so that he himself nearly entirely lost and dried was watered and revived. He eagerly pursued so many matters through the wise doctors[13] that the abundant, living river filled the streams, brooks, and fountains to such extent that all my plants were watered and given life. Oh what a noble gardener was he, for he so increased and augmented the permanence of my legacy that he became the first witness of my salutary glory. In his hands, I grew and became pleasingly beautiful; and while he lasted for me, I was well defended and so sustained and supported that nothing whatsoever unfavorable overtook me."

I.9. More about the same topic

"Thereafter, I fell into the hands of negligent gardeners, because of which lapse, the glory of my orchards was turned to fallow land,

---

[11] Christine's gloss indicates this is Pharamond, the first king of France.
[12] Christine's gloss indicates this is Clovis, king of the Franks from 481–511, who converted to Christianity.
[13] That is the doctors of the Church.

filled with weeds and useless grains bearing no good fruit. And since the vice of fornication was bred in the bones of these men's heir,[14] his misdeeds made him an exile, and his paths carried him into a trustworthy border region that took pity on his wretchedness. Oh wicked sin of ingratitude, which invalidates and withdraws the merit and reward of kindnesses received and obliterates the memory of due compensation! Did you not cause him to forget all reason for fealty when you duplicitously allowed his treacherous she-beast to withdraw from [her] loyalty to her first bed? And on hearing the news of the reconciliation between the son of Venus and his persecutors through the sign of the half-dernier, he departed secretly from the greedy wife, crowned beyond the order of law twice. The presentation of this affair by this treacherous woman can signify the order of his vision.[15]

"After that man were born to his heirs murderous, greedy, faithless men, who made their relatives presents of death and murder; they were advised and deceived by the cruel, proud lionesses come from Spain and concubinage.[16] Their vengeance did not spare the one accused of spilling innocent blood before the just. She was pulled apart by horses."

I.10. Of the good and bad governments of the crowned lady

"Thereafter, a plant from a pippin of fruit from the aforesaid tree in my land grew so much that its branches, canopy, and crown extended far beyond all my territories.[17] The fruit it bore was most worthy, fragrant, and strong for God by special grace had given it the ability to expel evil spirits and it was most useful against the perpetual poison. Many countries were saved from irredeemable death because of it, for which Germany should do [it] honor; and it extended its strength beyond the Italian Alps as far as the land of Africa. Oh God,

---

[14] As Christine's gloss indicates, these stories refer to Childeric I, even though he was actually Clovis' father and not (as Christine indicates) his descendent.

[15] Christine also used this story in her *City of Ladies*. See the translation by Richards 107–08 or Brown-Grant 99.

[16] From the royal couple Childeric and Basine, Christine has skipped to the fourth- and fifth-century queens Brunehalt and Fredegund, wives of Sigebert and Chilperic I, who precipitated a series of deadly wars between their families. Brunehalt was tied to the tail of an unbroken horse, whose hooves cut her to shreds as it galloped away. See *Grandes Chroniques de France* I: 137–301 as cited by Towner 20–1, nn. 14–15.

[17] As indicated by Christine's gloss, this refers to Charlemagne, son of Pepin le Bref, and to the Carolingian line he founded.

how I was celebrated, flourished, and was exalted by the splendor and beauty of that plant, for despite the long time that has passed, it (like a thing eternal) still augments the brightness of my glory. From the issue of this I was cultivated for a time. But after its strength decreased, there came diligent gardeners of foreign origin, who boasted of greater strength than the proprietors; and through hypocritical, hidden guile, masked as apostolic judgment, they reserved my sovereign throne for themselves, their line possessing it through several descendants.[18] However, a frail, hidden shoot then sprang up from the ancient, celebrated root, even though it had been blocked among the thorns in the wasteland; the time for its growth having come, the green leaves of its grandeur appeared.[19]

"Then were the foreign seeds uprooted; the beautiful shoot, subjugating all the saplings of my courtyards, flourished in great honor. From its descendants sprang precious seed that eventually produced fruit dedicated to God and very agreeable.[20] Now the first gardeners were restored to their path and have continued even so despite the long time that has passed until the present. Oh my dearest friend, if I told you all the troubles that tormented me in the time of which we speak, you would marvel at how I have remained so lovely, for in order to plunder and rob me, there assembled many provinces and foreigners who desolated my land with a great army and burned my towns and manors; they would bring great destruction to my people and rob me many, many times. Likewise, I have been imperiled with loss, abduction, rape, and complete dishonor, despite the resistance of bands of my defenders, the people who fought against the fury of these. Do not believe that my cruel torments, often and variously renewed, ever stopped for long; I have not been stripped of everything by them at present, but I tell you that even since the time of your parents, I have been so mistreated by various problems that the perils of my adventures have not been greater since my birth. And everything considered, of not having entirely fallen into the trap of complete perdition I attribute the glory to almighty God alone, who

---

[18]   This refers to Hugh Capet who came to the French throne through the intrigues of Adalberon, Archbishop of Rheims; see also *Advision* 151, n. X/14–28 where the apostolic judgment is identified as being that of Ascelin, the archbishop of Laon.

[19]   This shoot is Louis VIII, who was frail and reigned only briefly after reestablishing the Carolingian line. As the allegory notes, he did reclaim a great deal of territory that had been lost to the English. See *Advision* 151, n. X/14–28.

[20]   The fruit is Saint Louis (1214–1270).

because of my Catholic faith preserved me just as He told St. Peter that his small boat would rock and not be lost. Oh Lord, how great the horrors of my troubles were! For enemies descended from subservient races[21] would come hard upon me; and Fortune, favoring them for a time, would consent to their victories against the crowns who defended me, against whom (despite their great, noble, and impeccable courage) she would permit undeserved adversities. During this time, the earthworms rebelled, rising up because of the hoofbeats of horses with the intention of dishonoring me to my face in the days when my leader was in the chains of my enemies, but the vultures came who made this abominable, poisonous mass of vermin their prey.[22] Oh, how troubled and dismayed I was then by the various afflictions because of which the brightness of my beauty—once so glorious, pleasing, and wholesome—seemed dead, for nothing came forth but cries, tears, and all the voices of lamentation. What could I tell you about them? Numerous were the sufferings that pierced me over and over, but their end will be told you."

I.11. Wherein the crowned lady speaks of a good governor that she had

"Since God opened the eye of His mercy upon me, the chastised one, just like a father who, tender toward His beloved daughter, wishes to stop the flails of her torturers and spread the oil of His mercy on the wounds of her afflictions, there then appeared the able physician, come by succession to my ancient inheritance, who, leaving aside idleness in his youth, in the palace of my nobleness received the crown of dignity.[23] Lady Wisdom, the venerable goddess of ordered things, came and refitted him like a dear son in the mantle of her properties. Then saying, 'Flee! Flee! you enemies of happiness! Let the remedies of restoration arrive!' he drew to himself all good while rejecting all things dishonorable. This one, seized by the sword of Justice, did not spare his mother's tools; rather, by their decree, he put the hands to work from his high summit. Thus

---

[21] Christine seems to be referring to early events in the Hundred Years' War with England; the most important English victories were at Crecy (1346) and Poitiers (1356).

[22] Christine is referring to the capture (and later ransom) of King John, who was seized in 1356 at the battle of Poitiers. The revolt of the earthworms—the chronicles' customary way of referring to the common people—probably refers to the La Jacquerie, which erupted in 1358. See, for example, Towner 23.

[23] This physician is Charles V, patron of Christine's father.

armed with useful courage, walking through these courtyards, gazing at corners now covered with thorny stems, he gave orders to his assistants for the repair of the ruins. Then were assembled by the hundreds and thousands companies of these people—loyal subjects not foreigners—who, with sharp swords of various sizes, began to destroy the fallow lands filled with strange seeds, unsuited to the nature of my men, who were customarily fruit-bearing gardeners. Then they began to destroy the useless herbs and renew the untilled earth where they provided and attracted good seeds. Thus continuing the proper cultivation of the land, they made room for the small grasses and the sweet little plants to rise above the secret place where they had been hidden beneath the thorns that choked all out as if perished in their strength. Whoever might have seen them growing, spreading, and filling these orchards with greenery and fragrant, fruit-bearing flowers, might have said that their fortune had greatly changed indeed. What should I tell you about him? He was by no means deceived by the shackles of currency, which governed not the distribution of his orders; nor did labor suppress the execution of this useful work, to whose achievement Fortune was not averse and which continued across the days of the useful gardener, who spared not his efforts. Oh glorious God, what a worker! How he renewed my joy! Past tribulations were now forgotten. My entire land, also freed of harmful things, began to rejoice and raise songs praising that noble person through whose diligence I was now recovering and convalescing. To speak briefly, he was so beneficial to me that I must still rejoice in the memory of his blessing; about him a long speech could not weary me! But alas, just as after calm weather there follow heavy rains, so I must now change the subject from my smiles to very bitter tears. Since the pursuit of Fortune cannot suffer my happiness for long, showing her envy of my good circumstances, when my glory was higher than it had been for most of my lifetime, she deprived me of the wise administrator. Alas, he left me in a bad situation, before the natural end of his voyage; and she sent me one who spares no living being to take and ravish him from me with no pity for my widowhood. Can you now understand the signs of Fortune's changes in me, who once laughed while speaking of my beloved? Now you see me with a troubled countenance, full of tears, regretting his strengths which disappeared for me much too soon. I was obliged to change the arrangement of my offices with astonishing mutations. Nevertheless, the light of his blessings remained on earth after him since, despite the blows from several hands, the radiance still endures on the most beautiful part of my face."

I.12. Of the two noble birds of prey

"From his entrails there arose a double number of small, golden butterflies, very elegant and very beautiful, who dared to boast as they with the swarms of wasps grew larger of being the guardians of me and my dwellings.[24] They formed their alliances and because of the ancient fame of their line, they were justifiably allowed to sit at the top of the highest saplings. Just like the reputed merit attributed to the phoenix, who first emerges from the ashes as a small worm then grows and improves until he is beautiful beyond all birds, these butterflies grew so in strength that their form changed into a species of the noblest birds of prey, but with the difference that a certain number of them were crowned on the head like the birds called hoopoes. In order to study their prey, these noble ones kept together and flew over my ditches and rivers; and well advised, they had no intention at all of completely destroying these haunts by eating them but, being adequately fed, passed them by. Oh Fortune, directress of all adversities, who prompted you to find a way to create a disturbance by the falcon, flying so high that the expectation of his attack would make all the greedy prey pounced on in his anger tremble before him? Whence did you procure the harmful wind with which you so savagely battered him as he was circling so proudly before he reached his prey? You threw him to the ground so abruptly with the blast of your gale that he continued laid out, not only the feathers but the whole body torn asunder.[25] Because of this he has always had to be fed since by strange hands. God! what a pity for such a noble bird, trained in all good habits, proud and brave in his flight, sweet in greeting, lively and pleasing in appearance, who had unhesitatingly defended all my marshes and rivers from every greedy bird and evil way! Thus, I greatly wept and grieved for him as a special loss, whose harm has not ceased but was renewed for me every day by sad deprivations."

I.13. Wherein the crowned lady speaks of the disputes that occurred to direct her

"After these events came furtive spirits, inhabitants of the forests, who said it was for them to divide up private and personal things.[26]

---

[24] The allegory here becomes a little confusing, but the two butterflies are clearly Charles V's sons: Charles VI and Louis, the Duke of Orleans. The wasps seem to be the uncles of the boys. See *Advision* 152, n. XII/1–5.

[25] An allusion to Charles VI's first psychotic episode in 1392, which occurred while the young king was on a mission against the Duke of Brittany.

[26] The following allegory has puzzled all of Christine's editors. Here Christine seems to depart from chronological order to discuss various popular revolts that

These made common use of private houses and appropriated them for themselves until even the wild beasts cried out against them.

"At that time, the cry of the chameleon awoke a reprehensible breed of humans who said they would suffer not the offensive clamor of female voices.[27] So they entered the homes of the birds of their forests and were there until given wings of flight; with these in several groups they even went to the badger caves of my forests. They gathered the acorns from oaks and put the poor people they found in the fire, and they found no opposition against their doing all this; rather, there was great displeasure in my lands.

"The error was multiplied by several misfortunes, for the time came when the waters rose so high that no field remained that was not entirely covered by them.[28] The fish, having leapt beyond their ditches, were then feeding in the planted fields, even devouring the roots of the grains after the green leaves of the grasses. All these things embodied the birth of pestilence.

"Oh, sweet, dear friend, up to the present, I have told you most of my adventures. But since I cannot say everything at once, the anguished speech concerning these matters has not yet ceased; rather, with a troubled countenance, I must now tell you of the distressing concealment of my present shadows, which precede the others if their perseverance should be long."

I.14. Wherein the annoyed lady complains about her children

"What greater perplexity can visit the heart of a mother than to see anger and strife engendered and continued to the point that arms of war are taken up and seized by alliances among her own legitimate children of loyal fathers, whose crimes mount so that they ignore the grief of their poor mother, who, compassionate of her offspring, plants herself between the two sides to separate their troops? But incited by mindless intentions, neither sparing nor sensible of her maternal honor, they do not divert their horses' hooves from her

actually happened soon after the death of Charles V, more than ten years before Charles VI's first fit of madness. See, for example, Towner 28–30 and *Advision* 153–4, n. XIII/1–16, both of which suggest at least part of the paragraph discusses the rebellions of the Maillotins in 1382. These riots were sparked by new taxes imposed by the Duke of Anjou to raise ransom money for Jeanne of Naples, whose kingdom he wished to inherit.

[27] Towner 29 notes that the riots began in Paris on March 1, 1382 when a tax collector tried to collect a new tax on comestibles from a woman vendor of watercress.

[28] Such a flood did occur in 1399; see Towner 30.

worthy person but release the multitude of their alliances upon her until they break and mangle her completely.[29]

"Romulus and his company were not so cruel when the fathers and relatives gathered in a great army to avenge that disgrace because of the disgraceful abduction of the Sabine daughters by these Romans. But when the queen and all these women, piteous of their husbands, fathers, and families, placed themselves with tears and cries between the gathering armies, their hair disheveled, beseeching them in the name of God to make peace, they were not trampled beneath the horse hooves of these strong and powerful knights; rather spared by reverence and heard with pity, their feminine voices made their loved ones make peace even on the field of battle. Oh friend, look, look upon the greatest of sorrows!"

I then saw this princess entirely covered in tears, and her beautiful face, usually fresh and blooming, was pale and gloomy as she said, "Alas! Alas! I am that bitter mother fallen into the circumstances I describe to you. Oh my beloved servant and good friend, companion of all my sorrows, you may not be of the fruit of my land, but your noble heart is not ungrateful for the benefits you have received here; weep with me out of true friendship, piteous to see the days of my tribulation. And so that experience may assure you of the truth of my stories—my beauty notwithstanding—behold and consider first and foremost the wounds of my sides and limbs."

The venerable princess then raised part of her gown and showed me her naked sides, saying, "Behold." Then my gaze turned in that direction; I saw the white and tender sides blackened and beaten by the force and trampling of the crowds and collapsed in places as far as the entrails not cut by the blow of the sword. Then completely disconcerted in consideration of the new, piteous, and dishonorable circumstance that such wounds might be procured so venerable a mother by her children, I told her, "Cover them, lady, in the name of God!" Like a weak woman, filled with astonished pity, faint and covered in tears, when I could speak, I tried as best I could to comfort the distressed one saying, "Noble and venerable lady, for God's sake I beg you, abate your woeful tears, trust in His mercy, which has never failed you, and banish for a while the thoughts that lead you here with such weeping. If it please you to honor me, your poor

---

[29] Libera is referring to the political tensions and civil strife occurring at the time of the *Vision*'s composition. These struggles are discussed in detail in the book-length study by Guenée.

unworthy servant, so that in speaking you might forget your troubles, please explain to me the chain of causes for these dissensions. It must not be strange to speak about your children's faults to me, your familiar and intimate friend."

And she said to me, "Ah, dear friend, if I would censure those whom I create, I would dishonor my own work. So I tell you I accuse no one of maliciously contrived evil nor of being moved to this action by scorn or hatred of me. It is indeed true that considering that I am the bed of their being and that the light of their glory comes from me, they should have curbed the attacks that harm me so. And of the birth of the root of ill feeling now planted between them, I will speak to you.

"After shares of my estate in accordance with the customs of Athens were provided each of my begotten children, the mightiest declared that the guardianship of his younger brother belonged to him;[30] and since the settlement was not denied him, they cried out against him, whereby, their voices having been heard, they assembled the family of the ward in council.

"My children then convened and utterly denied the eldest's opinion. This cause assembled the flails of my persecutors, which have spared me not, as was shown you. That torment, continuing today among my laborers, withers and desiccates the green leaves and the liquors of my fruits, drains my fountains, diminishes my reputation, and torments me cruelly. And what is most distressing to me is the fear of worse—that without medicine, my wounds may become ulcerated and incurable."

I.15. Wherein she tells how the virtues in the world are imprisoned

"The illness lies in yet another area, dear friend. For since it resembles not this sadness that holds the heart in bitter thought, it remains to tell you of the height of my woes.

"The ministers of perdition were not satisfied with the disgraces offered the root of the ancient family tree, but dishonored me further. Alas, where is the princess equal to me who might willingly witness her ladies in waiting—venerable and worthy women of noble birth,

---

[30] The allegory is not all together clear at this point. In *Advision* 155–156, n. XIV/60–64, Reno and Dulac identify this passage as a reference to a struggle between the King's uncles—Louis d'Anjou and his younger brother Philip, Duke of Burgundy—for control of the regency of the young Charles VI.

appointed by ancient law to assist at her deliberations, carry the seals of her edicts, and support her long trains and the gold decorations of her head—unjustly taken, expelled, beaten, banished, imprisoned and replaced by soiled, dissolute, and debauched women? Alas, dear friend, I am this woman, I who speak to you; but so that you may the better believe me, I wish you may experience the truth of my words." Then, as she opened a small window, she said to me, "Behold the prisoners! Your discernment must judge whether the representation of their honor would be more appropriate in the royal palace than under hidden roofs. Consider those who once governed me in the time of my joy; now the persecutors of my glories have stolen them away from me."

Then as my eye directed itself to the prison's small window, I saw three ladies of surpassing beauty and honor but different demeanor. Oh God, what divine beauty I beheld in one! Her body was tall, straight, and well-formed; and from the loveliness of her face issued a most brilliant ray of light. In her hand, this lady was holding a large, very bright mirror, from which the reflection of the aforesaid ray was reverberating so that no small corner was so dark as not to be totally ablaze with the great beauty and light of its radiance.[31] Oh, what a pity to keep such loveliness concealed! She should have been seated in public assemblies so that all might rejoice in her splendor! She was incomparably lovely and even more noble. For she was said to be the daughter of God the Father and stronger than anything else as she boasted of triumphing over all things.

Lying pale and gloomy on a bed, I saw another lady of great authority with the countenance and appearance of a sick and infirm woman, a trampled and broken thing; and she was said to be the sister of the first. I saw a scale lying on her right side; on the other was a measuring cup and ruler.[32]

At a certain distance from this lady, I saw a large, robust lady who was fully armed, lying dishonorably asleep on the ground. Her shield, lance, and spurs were lying on the earth beside her. She was holding her head in the lap of a foolish and very fickle woman, who was singing and stroking her head, the better to put her asleep.[33]

---

[31] This is Dame Reason, who also appears in the *City of Ladies* and the *Long Road of Learning*.

[32] This is Dame Justice, identifiable by her scales, who also appears in the *City of Ladies*.

[33] Dame Chivalry (who also appears in the *Long Road of Learning*) is lulled to sleep by Dame Lust.

Then, while I was intently studying these amazing figures, I saw that several times enemies with many troops came from various places. Some would cry out in a loud voice to the sleeping lady to defend herself, and she would move her head a little and half open an eye. Then the foolish lady would exert herself to put her back to sleep. Another crowd would return to shout in her ear; and the lady, totally exhausted, would raise her head, and the foolish woman would once again put her to sleep with her song. Others would return who hammered heavy blows on her shield, and she would rise straight up to give chase; but the dishonorable one would take her by the neck and put her to sleep again. The strongest would come to overrun and beat her; then she, enraged, would arise and swear that she would kill them all with her force. So she would strike those she could hold with her lance and killed several, [she] would often pursue them and often was pursued; but repeatedly she would return to her refuge which she could not leave.

I.16. Wherein she speaks of the vices, which are everywhere rampant

As I was observing these things, the lady said to me, "Behold her, behold her, the indecent and licentious woman who dishonors my people! She lulls my defenders to sleep; several of my palace over whom she is mistress she puts to shame. Alas! at the time of the truthful renown of my pleasure, she would not have dared to be seen or found! Think not, however, if you see her resting here to hold the armed lady asleep and imprisoned, that she will always be there. For she has many daughters (her fellow creatures) in different guises; so she leaves a number of these around this sleeper and, hurrying along, moves through all my cities and towns, everywhere people assemble, in search of whomever she may be able to attract to her shameful following. If she encounters no great opposition, there is no place where her presumption does not seek to insinuate itself, even to the innermost chambers of my ladies, who are not prudent enough to know how to vigorously reject her.

"Now mark, sweet sister, what company is the lady in waiting prepared by such a demoiselle! But I still wish you to see how these two hellish ladies, may God confound them, have accompanied me. Look around this prison; behold the position of the traitorous woman who receives great wages for her sorry labor."

Then outside of the prison she shows me a dirty, ugly, terrible old woman who devotes herself continuously to such duties: around the prison night and day, she would wander with [her] robe filled with moss that she had tucked up. She would watch very attentively lest the forceful light of the shining mirror within should break through the wall; and as soon as she would see any of it emerge from any opening, she would immediately seal it up vigorously with moss, so as to let none of it escape.

And I, observing this false solicitude, could not hold my peace. I said to my mistress, "Lady, for God's sake, tell me the name of that enemy of virtue, for although I may have restrained myself from asking about the others since their roles make them obvious to me and well enough known, I ask to know of this one not that I may become acquainted with her but to avoid her. I beg you to tell me." And she told me, "Sweet friend, since you know the lady who holds the bright mirror, you should not overlook her opponent who wishes to extinguish it. But it would greatly please me for you to know her. So I tell you that she is Dame Fraud, may God confound her." I then cried out, "Oh who led you here, most treacherous enemy of truth? Did not Dante of Florence, wisest of poets, once see you as a horrible, long-tailed serpent in the swamp of hell when Virgil accompanied him there, as he relates in his book?[34] And came you here? Better, I advise you, to attend Persephone with Megra, Alecto, and Theisphone, the goddesses of infernal fury, than be established at this court!"

Then the lady told me, "Now be silent; you will see more." At this point, she led me high up in the palace to a large room filled with iron-banded boxes in which I saw an old woman—pale, thin, lean, sullen, and quite ugly. But I was amazed above all by the shape of her hands, which were so incredibly large and strong that no one might snatch away anything that she held except with great effort. She had long, sharp nails curved like the griffin's, but that all of them were bloody revolted me exceedingly.[35] She would thrust these claw-like nails everywhere she could plunge them—in refuse or the flesh of people, it mattered not to her—then she would drag them toward herself, and she would steal money from everywhere. So that I might know this by experience, when I entered, the lady accompanying me could not protect me from her so that those bloody claws might not extend as far as me so that they plucked me of all my feathers, right down to the quick, whence I suffered great pain. And she placed everything into coffers. "Friend," the lady said, "mark

---

[34] The long-tailed monster is Geryon who appears in Dante's *Inferno*, Cantos XVI and XVII. On this borrowing, see Richards, "Christine de Pizan and Dante: A Reexamination" 107.

[35] This figure is Avarice, traditionally depicted clutching a purse or sitting on a coffer.

what an occupation! Am I well accompanied? Know that this is the one who causes the invalid to lie bed-ridden and ill; and the most righteous daughter of God, whom you saw lying on the ground in that prison, dares not complain. And this one, against my wishes, replaces her in my company. And thus, as you can hear, my beloved ladies in waiting, come from heaven, have been stolen from me and replaced by these perversities from hell. So judge, friend, having seen the whole of my condition, if I should be joyful.

"There is yet another matter that greatly grieves and wounds me. For since I must love (as I naturally do) my children, my dear servants, and loyal subjects, I am suffering from a serious illness, incurable if the remedy comes not by the grace of God, which is widespread throughout my land, and especially more among the great than the small. I will tell you its cause and its nature. It is true that a subtle wind blows around and near here, more in the mountains than in the valleys, so poisonous that all attacked by it become swollen and distended. Now it happens that the most powerful dwell high up in tall towers and lofty dwellings; consequently, they receive the blast of this aforesaid wind openly and fully. And since they are also more sensitive than more common men as their life is more refined, they are more apt to receive this wind more penetratingly than others. Beware of this thing; you will see many infected by the cruel affliction. And few are saved from it unless they protect themselves by the wise provision of erecting an obstacle against it. Because of such prudence, there are some who are well, but they are in the minority; nevertheless among the well, some more than others, depending on how they are infected and disposed to it, there are the ill ones. So this plague is so widespread, which is worse than an epidemic throughout my land, that it is a great pity! And even the servants are not generally healthy; rather, many are more swollen since they take fewer precautions than their masters. Such a quality has this swelling that it changes the gaze, countenance, and speech and makes the person contemptuous, exceedingly irritable, and malicious; and for many it drives them to a cruel death without escape. This scourge is so common, no less than those of Egypt in my realm, that the great, middle, and low, all the way down to the earthworms, are commonly infected by it and so much so that foreign regions denounce and insult my subjects because of it."

I.17. Concerning the wind of perdition that ravages the land

"In regard to the swelling of this malady that ravages my land and the ensuing misfortune where it makes its way, the prophet Daniel recites in the third chapter the vision that the proud King

Nebuchadnezzar once saw.[36] It says he saw a tree so tall, large, and lofty, that it reached all the way to the sky; it had so many branches that they extended on every side of the world. All earthly creatures alike were filled by the great abundance of fruit of this tree; the birds of the air would make their nests in these branches, and the beasts of the earth would gather below them. And then when this had been seen, a loud voice was heard crying from heaven commanding that the tree be cut to the surface of the earth and all its branches lopped off, and the birds should fly away from it, the beasts depart, and the fruit be scattered and lost.

"That said tree signifies the swollen ones mentioned before, the powerful who live in the high towers of my land receiving the wind of perdition, who have such rank, force, and power that they believe they will easily reach heaven; and the swelling of this aforesaid wind so infects them that their spirits are not only contemptuous of creatures (which shows they are quite disdainful) but also of God and His Church. The extension of the branches throughout the world signifies that these swollen ones extend the power of their force through every region, because of which they are feared and dreaded by all. The birds who were nesting and the beasts who were shaded are the sacred and secular things they wish to subjugate, govern, and appropriate for themselves. The abundance of fruit from this tree is that detestable, contagious plague which is widespread to all.

"This prophecy signifies that aforesaid infirmity. But now listen to the explication of its sentence—the explanation of death and the ending of this affair. The voice cried from heaven that the tree must be cut down and uprooted from the earth: this means that by God's will, the force and power of these swollen individuals will end and be removed, and they will be thrown down from their high positions. The branches which will be lopped off and the birds and beasts who will depart means that after their force has failed, their subjects and those who feared and questioned them because of the contemptuous cruelties caused by their swellings would abandon them in their persecution. The fruit which will be scattered is their similarly small members, likewise swollen, which will be humiliated. And at that time will be affirmed the prophecy of the Virgin who said, '*Deposuit potentes de sede et exaltavit humiles*' "[37]

---

[36]   The story of Nebuchadnezzar's dream is found in Dan. 4.
[37]   This quotation from the Vulgate is found in Luke 1:52 and is spoken at the Annunciation by the Virgin.

I.18. Of the punishment of the vices

"Listen once more to the fair praise of the three disgraced demoiselles given me as companions in place of my beloved imprisoned friends whom you saw below, and consider whether I must rejoice in the company of such shameful women, and yet note to what end their qualities will lead.

"Above all, of that first one you saw who held the armed lady in her lap and who so greatly corrupts and diminishes my people, understand the vision, how in the spirit of prophecy the prophet Zechariah saw her as he relates in the fifth chapter of his book: 'A woman,' he said, 'I saw sitting in the middle of a vessel full of water, and she was holding a great mass of lead that she was forcing into her mouth.[38] Then I saw two other women who had wings like those of the vulture. They took this vessel in which the woman was seated and lifted it up between heaven and earth. At this moment,' he says, 'I asked the angel what this vision was showing me, in which these women were carrying the vessel with the woman seated in water, and he answered me: *Ut edificetur sibi domus in terra Sennaar*. They carry it,' he said, 'to build her a home in the land of Shinar.'

"The previous filthy hag is understood through this prophecy as are all the people she attracted to her company, who are determined to indulge freely and run unchecked in all pleasures and carnal delights, just as the waters are fluid and running. The mass of lead, a heavy and hard metal which she was throwing into her mouth, stands for the severe offence to God, the guilty shame that is so heavy and painful which this disgraceful woman forces the men and women she envelops in her snares to commit. The two winged women carrying this seated woman are two sinful excesses that carry and sustain her and her followers in their desire to indulge in every pleasure and carnal amusement. The first woman stands for excessive pleasure: hence she has two wings that carry her like a bird; one is Gluttony, which seeks nothing but to eat and drink, the other is Idleness, which wants only to rest and play. The second woman stands for excessive wealth: she consequently has two other wings: Larceny, which only wants to rob others, and Cruelty, which knows no compassion. These wings resembled those of the vulture because

---

[38] In *Advision* 157–58, n. XVIII/9–19, Reno and Dulac note that Christine alters this story from its version in Zech. 5:5–11 to allow the woman representing Wickedness to thrust the lead into her own mouth. In the original, the lead seals the bushel measure in which she is seated.

just as that bird lives only on stolen quarry, so one generally comes to this wicked excess of wealth through extortions and thefts.

"Now this perverse and indecent woman is described according to the prophet Zechariah. But what will be her end? What will they do with her, those who carry her as she floats on the waters? They will transport her to the land of Shinar, there to build her a house. Shinar—the equivalent of stench—is corruption which is the shame and trouble into which they will lead her. And in the end, they will build her house in the dwelling place of hell, or to experience stench and eternal torment."

I.19. More on the same topic and the lady's complaint

"Oh dear friend! Of the disloyal one hated by God, that perverse traitor envenomed with deceit who seals away the light of truth just as you beheld at the prison tower, what shall we say for from her malice, alas, I suffer! Do you not see—take care—how all is blackened by her breath? I rage with anger when I see her throw away the fees from my tolls, not haphazardly but with fixed guile, arranged for the riches of various purses in order to feed the insatiable fire; in my palaces the highest courts institute her orders, full of folly, and no one dares murmur against them. When I see that hideous figure, veiled by malice, feeding the evil ones and her followers and destroying the innocent, what can I say about it except to cry out to God? For the leaders of my institutions are her allies. Oh God, what a wound for me, so burdened by my other griefs! I am like the widow left by a good companion, whom everyone takes advantage of and no one pities. And what has become of the champions of right? Have they not fled? If there are any, this perverted traitor does not allow them to carry out their just work. Behold, behold, all my loyal friends, how I am governed since I lost the joy of my principal one! And this is done by that traitor, who takes no heed of rightful matters, so that I am left like a sheep without pasture, without the joy of a loving companion. Indeed, I should be perplexed when I see my line surrounded by that woman, who advises them in her perfidious ways. Is anything uglier than that which she supports? How is man so foolish that he considers not his end? O blind wasp, your vicious sting persecutes many! You work cleverly, Malice governs you, and Deceit holds the sword of your justice for these people. No man is now so wise that he sees you in all your affairs, for you disguise yourself in too many strange forms. You go wandering through the town, palaces, and rooms and all my places; nothing remains free of you, and everyone is poisoned, covered with your dust. Oh God, how long will this war last? But I take comfort, Sire, in the figure prophesied to me of Samson the strong."

Thus sighing, with the appearance of great sadness, that most noble princess made this plaint. And when she had said these things, she fell silent, like a woman exhausted and by grief overcome, covered by tears, so that she could not speak. And I, who looked on her behavior with compassion for her honor, the companion of her weeping, who would have cured her with a good heart if it were mine to do so, spoke to her as follows:

I.20. More about the same topic

"Ah, my most reverend and worthy lady, since it is unbecoming to the nobility of your authority to demonstrate the tenderness of womanly sentiment, leave aside these tears that are inappropriate to your constancy and tell me more about what you touched upon, that is, the remembered figure of Samson the strong, which, and it please you, explain to me." And she said to me, "Friend, since I desire the time for the destruction of the liar and her treacherous children, I will rejoice in this expectation, speaking of it with you.

"It is written in the fourteenth chapter of the book of the Judges of Israel, as prophecy and prefiguration of the ruin of my enemy and her accomplices, that when Samson (translated as *sol fortis* or strong sun)[39] had been pursued for a long time by the malice of the Philistines (over whom this perverted figure ruled), the time came when God opened the way for him to avenge his misfortunes through righteous revenge. This Samson then took several female foxes and coupled them together by the tails; one to the other, he bound them and carefully placed fire attached there; and as night had already arrived, at the first sleep, he threw these foxes, part of them, into the houses filled with grain of his enemies; the others he chased into their corn fields and vineyards and woods. In this way, just as God intended, the sons of the traitor died and she along with them—killed and burned in their sins.

"Oh dear friend, mark the prophecy of the hour of my glory! When this traitor will have punished me sufficiently, when God will wish her punishment to cease, when the cries of my complaints will

---

[39] See *Advision* 158, n. XX/12 which traces this etymology to Isidore of Seville's *Etymologiae* VII.6. In addition, the sun's rays were emblems of both Charles V and VI and were later taken over by Charles VI's son, Louis of Guyenne. They symbolized the monarch's obligation to uphold justice in his realm. Christine may be suggesting that the avenger will be someone of the royal house of France.

be compassionately carried before God just as once those of the children of Israel were when Holofernes laid siege to them with his great army, then Samson the strong, that is the strong sun, will become aware of the great malice against his enemies; this will be one of my sons, bright as a strong sun because the sun of justice will dwell within him. By a curious device this individual will destroy his enemies—that is, the children of that deceitful woman, the enemies of his virtue—who have persecuted me and my land for so long. He will take foxes, join them tail to tail, and place firebrands between them; then at night he will throw them on the traitors and in their fields, and he will burn all and they will die in their iniquities.

"The foxes represent the clever ideas of his own mind which he will use. Joining tail to tail, these are the various points by which he will take them in their malice. He will place firebrands between the two; this is the punishment for their misdeeds which he will allot them in righteous justice. He will throw them on his enemies when night comes and at the first sleep; this is when the time of their punishment will have come and they will have fallen asleep in their perseverance. He will throw part of these foxes into their grain and fields; this means that the possessions they have wrongfully acquired through his judgment will be dispersed into the hands of the rightful heirs."

I.21. More on the condemnation of vices in general

"But what shall I tell you about that one with the foul, curved nails in whose false government you see the little bees of my hive, who has perverted the honey of their wax into savage bitterness? Have you not already felt the experience of her services? Should, so help you God, such a monster be found in my house so my children may poison me and be perverted and so vilely diminished and by the false admonition of her flatteries dishonored by this wicked woman who defames all her acquaintances in heaven and earth? Is there anything more worthy of reproach than the being in whom she dwells, however consecrated the place may be by another virtue? Alas, you should not be seated here; for whoever she accompanies must not insinuate himself into my territories! Oh horrible and venomous beast, how did you make such a mortal leap from the pit of hell, which is your natural dwelling, all the way to the hearts of my children, where usually you do not dwell? Where have my ancient, virtuous gatekeepers—Pity and Charity—gone inasmuch as they did not impede your daring? My heart now swoons with anger, seeing your cruelty, which gives rise to no virtue but mercilessly snatches the unripe fruits from their stems. This does your perfidy establish in the highest reaches of my house;

and as the proverb says: 'According to the master, so goes the household.' The evil ministers follow the traces of their leaders through your lies, and you, perverse one, who despite me hold the keys over my coffers—which you open and lock as you wish—according to their great shame and they make their judgment. Oh brutalizer of the world, you infernal leech, who could fault you enough? Are you not that one who delivers my land to the torments of hell, who endlessly cries, 'To work, to work?' Great and insatiable fire, what could satisfy you? Has not your burning appetite, worse than the Greek,[40] already kindled my most cherished possessions? And now I see you so impudent and manifestly open that no shame contains you; nor are your companions ashamed, they have become so hardened.

"Ah, Solomon prophesied well the time which I see and the place where you are in the 30th chapter of his Proverbs, where he says, '*Generacio que pro dentibus gladios habet ut commedat inopes de terra, et pauperes ex hominibus.*' Ha, perverse generation, which uses swords in place of teeth, not to bite but to cut quite through. We plainly see this concerning the traitorous woman, who is unsatisfied with biting if all is not cut through."

I.22. The moving words of the crowned lady and the testimony of Holy Scripture

"Ah gentle friend and my dear servant, inasmuch as I know that God is just, must I not believe that He will not delay the peace of His righteousness forever? Does He not grant His grace when the tardy conversion awaits His mercy? But just as the mother naturally tender toward her children in spite of the sins she sees in them forgets not maternal love and fears to see the deserved ruin of her sons, so, sighing and tearful, fear and misgivings hold me in terror of sudden vengeance. Alas, have I not cause to think of the image of my ruin in what is written in the fifteenth chapter of the Book of Kings,[41] that God's divine law condemns this aforesaid vicious wasp as His enemy; because of her and her cause, he rejected Saul, the King, whom she seduced when God sent him into battle against the King of Amalek? The Lord had forbidden him to take the man for ransom but to put all to the sword without fail as horrible sinners,

---

[40] According to the glossary in *Advision*, Greek fire refers to a combination of sulphur, pepper, saltpeter, and resin that would stick to an object and could be extinguished only by sand or wet earth.

[41] This story is found not in Kings 15 but in I Sam. 15.

condemned by the Lord; He no longer wanted his life, nor was he to retain anything from the spoils. But as he preferred to obey this disloyal leech (who ordered him to do the opposite) more than obeying the commandment of God, he did none of these things. Rather, he preferred to fatten on the false pastures that God had forbidden and spared this accused king, for which God called the prophet Samuel saying, 'I repent having ordained Saul king over my people.' As the said prophet then rebuked Saul for the failure, he wished to excuse himself, saying that he had taken the spoils with the intention of sacrificing them to God. To this the prophet answered: 'Obedience is worth more than sacrifice. And since by believing the admonishments of that greedy woman you have disobeyed, you will be banished from your realm.' The prophet then deposed him and anointed David king.

"Dear friend, must I think God is sleeping? Do I not see the time when in opposition to His commandments, the wicked condemned to punishment by divine law are spared His justice? But provided they have fodder to thrust into the mouth of that traitor, then all is calm; but it is true that they are absolved by a false appearance of virtue as they practice their deceits. Do you see all the commandments of law set aside to feed and nourish her, sparing no one?

"What shall I say then if I fear not? That God is changeable, which cannot be? And if He is not, why does this story not pertain to me in such a case? Do I not see His preparations? For a fool indeed is the one who does evil and hopes for good—are not the foreigners also ready to receive new prey, as they were once wont to do?—and as he who feels himself guilty lives not without remorse of conscience, which makes him afraid and the fear of punishment never leaves him.

"Concerning this damnable woman's sins does Jesus Christ not also speak to me then in the parable of the vine, as he discusses in the Gospel the false cultivators, who, since they belonged to this distressing woman's household, did they not kill the loyal messengers, because they wanted the inheritance, the just petitioners for the harvest?[42] And since this crime grew, likewise their swords did not spare the rightful heir. As divine judgment, for these crimes, stripped them of all their possessions and gave them to foreign cultivators, my people having fallen into the same pit should I not fear

---

[42] This parable can be found in Matt. 21:33–46, Mark 12:1–9, and Luke 20:9–16; also cited in *Advision* 159, n. XXII/44–52.

the same verdict? For although the supreme master had established them as the cultivators of my vineyard in order to have a good return from it, have they not killed the messengers, the petitioners for its harvest (that is, the causes of my exaltation) and furthermore the rightful heir? That is, the gracious honor that has always been mine up until now. But just like the pregnant woman who fears the suffering of childbirth, even though she longs to see the fruit of her womb safely delivered, likewise, in spite of the joyful expectation of the coming beneficial reparation promised me by God, I am now frightened of the evil I must pass through before I arrive there."

I.23. More of her complaint

"Alas, still from the fear I have of my ruin have I not cause considering the deserts of my subjects? For perhaps before the expected restoration it will be very necessary for mine to die as it is true that things to come are hidden under God's secret, like the promise He made to Abraham to multiply and increase his line as rulers of earth. The word of God is certainly true. Nonetheless God often sent the people and the children of Israel long periods of merited punishment, as appears in the Bible, which mentions this; and then when God had punished them thoroughly, He recalled them. Today we still see them scattered and in flight for their sins. Their reparation, according to the interpretation of this aforesaid promise, will occur when they will be given the light of the true faith. This example makes me fear that there may be great hardships before the repair of my ruin, just as we generally see in storms great thunder and lightning and windstorms wreak harm before the weather clears. And if we wish not to believe the prophecies of the ancients about this such as Merlin, the Sibyls, Joachim, and many others,[43] who tell us in great detail about the arrival of our adversities and downfalls—and if you want to see these, in many places you will find them recorded fully and literally which said [texts] I omit since some might say they are apocryphal and should therefore not be cited as certain proof—then similar texts

---

[43] Here Christine refers to many of the non-Biblical prophets most often cited in sermons and tracts of the time. Merlin, of course, is King Arthur's legendary sage and prophet; the Sibyls are important prophets of antiquity. They also appear in both the *Long Road of Learning* (where a Sibyl functions as one of Christine's guide) and in the *City of Ladies* (II.1–3). Joachim of Fiore (ca. 1135–1202) was an Italian holy man popularly credited with prophetic powers; he predicted a coming reign of the Holy Spirit. For commentary on the use of these figures in Christine's time, see Millet; Reeves, "The Bible and Literary Authority in the Middle Ages;" and *Advision* 159–60, n. XXIII/19.

from the Holy Scriptures, which we cannot deny and in which there are no lies, should at least be for us the basis of fear and small assurance as well as the truths of accepted stories. What will keep me from trembling then when I know that nothing passes God's justice without punishment and when I see that all the instances of vice are all too common, especially the aforesaid daughters of perdition already described and whom you saw, and the penetrating wind that brings the brutal swelling which turns the mind of rational man to [that of] the mute beast?"

I.24. Concerning the punishment of the vices

"How frightened I am of the punishment that so incapacitates my neighbors from the examples of God's anger I find to read concerning far more minor things than those I see committed and currently rampant throughout my lands: as it is written in the last chapter of the second Book of Kings that King David, once attacked by this aforesaid wind, raised his heart swollen in the surging of ambition to know what power he possessed and how many armed men he might provide; in order to know this, he had his people counted, and only because of this swelling. God was so angry at him that through the prophet Gad, He ordered David to choose one of three punishments: he might have a seven-year famine throughout his realm or be in flight for three months in fear of his enemies or have three days of fatal pestilence among his people; then after he had chosen the third punishment, such a mortal illness arose that seventy thousand men died in his realm.[44]

"Oh gentle friend, now consider what a severe punishment for a matter that, in view of our great swellings, would seem a small swelling indeed! Furthermore, in regard to this swelling and the punishment sent by God (for He cannot suffer its progress for long), it is written in the fourth chapter of Daniel that as Nebuchadnezzar once paced through his room in his great Babylonian palace, glorifying himself and saying, 'Is this not Babylon the great, which I built for my royal house and the power of my authority and the glory of my beauty?'; then, as he said these words, there came a voice from Heaven which said to him, 'Hear, Nebuchadnezzar! Your kingdom has passed away from you, and you will be exiled from the company of men and will live with the savage beasts and eat grain with the cows.' That promise was no lie, for God did not delay long thereafter

---

[44]   This story is found in 2 Sam. 24:1–17 rather than II Kings.

before it was executed against his person, who was thrown out of human company and brought back in the form of a beast, eating in the fields in the rain and the wind.

"Why seek we other prophecies? Are these not enough for us? Do we not know that God is immutable, as I have said, that it is now as it was then? Are not the Scriptures full of the truths of His punishments? And the more he delays them, the more fearful we should be, just like the archer: the longer he delays in drawing the bow, so much the greater is the force of the shot when it strikes. What more might I tell you? There are many examples, an infinite number of them: let him who will not believe them read about them. Let this narration suffice concerning this aforesaid evil swelling."

I.25. More on the same topic

"More concerning that indecent woman who holds my defenders, my other officials, and even my closest relatives and nearest friends in her shackles, through the other aforesaid passions, as was said above. Alas, whoever happens to possess even one vice will have scant happiness! But bad indeed for those surrounded and filled by several or all of them! I cannot be silent concerning God's great condemnation of this sin and the evils wrought by it both today and in the earliest times; for several realms have been destroyed for this reason. I must be frightened then when I see the similar case, the same punishment. For example, Dinah, daughter of Jacob, was ravished by the son of the King of Shechem,[45] and this caused that realm's destruction. Amnon feigned illness to have his sister Tamar, for which he was killed by his brother Absalom.[46] Paris' rape of Helen in Greece caused the destruction of Troy. A king of France, as the chronicles relate, was driven out and exiled because of it.[47] The force used by the arrogant Tarquin against Lucretia, the chaste Roman lady who consequently killed herself, caused the disinheritance of King Tarquin and his son and because of this incident the Romans swore that Rome would never have a king.[48] Hannibal, the King of Carthage, as long as he was unacquainted with this shameful woman, was conqueror and victor in the battles with Rome and elsewhere; and his reputation for prowess was high, but as soon as

---

[45] See Gen. 34.
[46] See 2 Sam. 13–18 for the story of Absalom; the murder occurs in chapter 13.
[47] This king is Childeric, also mentioned in I.9 of the *Vision*.
[48] As noted in *Advision* 160, n. XXV/16–19, Christine has confused Tarquin with his son, Sextus. See also *Vision* II.8, where Christine gets the identification correct.

he rested and wrapped himself in pleasures, in which he became acquainted with this evil woman, he fell into the valley of misfortune, nor did good come to him thereafter.[49]

"I will tell you more, and mark that no matter who the man may be who is wrapped up with this shameful woman in general corruption, a marvel it is if he ever takes up arms and if Fortune does not oppose him in all of his exploits; for his spirit floats on the waters of these corruptions. And if it were permitted to speak ill of anyone publicly, I would give you the actual example of several men, living in the world without honor bound by such shackles. Moreover, I tell you that no country, region, or kingdom over whose leaders she is mistress prospers in honor or fame. Why would I cite more examples? Manifest experience declares it to us. But of her fall, whatever I have said before, there need be no other prophecy except the effects of divine justice; because of this lascivious woman lacking in the curb of shame which fills humankind, God said and declared that man would no longer live on earth. In consequence, He long ago sent the flood that spared no living creature save Noah and his household, whom God saved. So consider and mark how reassured I must sleep!"

I.26. More of the same

"More about that woman who seals the openings so that the truth may not emerge, this is Fraud the Perverse; and as Valere says in the ninth book, 'Her deceitful trickery is a hidden and spying evil whose most effective weapons are lying and deception, for she rejoices in falsehoods and duplicities, which are the corrupt tools of her devious art.'[50] Isidore speaks of this in his *Synonyms* which says that 'Fraud or deceit is to demonstrate one thing by appearance and put another into action.' A person who maintains her within himself is a liar and because of her wishes to counterfeit and feign the appearance of virtue. From this evil one come treason and false promises. Beware, then, if my land and all my courts are sown with such false pastures

---

[49] In *Advision* 160, n. XXV/20–25, Reno and Dulac trace this story to the fifth book of *Faits et dits mémorables* (see note 50).

[50] Valerius Maximus was a Roman historian whose *Facta et dicta memorabilia* (Memoral Deeds and Sayings) was translated in Christine's lifetime as *Faits et dits mémorables* by Nicolas Gonesse and Simon de Hesdin. In *Advision* 161, nn. XXVI/4–7 and XXVI/7–8, this quotation, and the ensuing one from Isidore of Seville's *Synonyms*, are traced to a collection of quotations, the *Manipulus florum* by Thomas Hibernicus, one of Christine's favorite sources.

now firmly rooted in the highest of places. Alas! How would the vice of false promises, lies, and treachery between brothers, families, friends, and their close acquaintances not displease God since He commands them to love one another and even wants men to keep faith with enemies? And that he is angered at the contrary is made clear enough for us by the example signifying the great punishment of my people, that is by what is written in the last chapter of the Book of Kings concerning Zedekiah, King of Jerusalem, who broke the faith he had pledged to Nebuchadnezzar, the King of Babylon, because of which Nebuchadnezzar came to lay siege to Jerusalem.[51] And God delivered the said King Zedekiah into his hands. So he told him, when he had him, 'The lord who hates all betrayals born of broken promises and lies wishes to punish you by my hand.' Then he had his children killed before him and his two eyes put out, and bound with chains, he made him his prisoner to lead into Babylon. Now behold! What must my people expect from the treacheries that they perpetrate against one another every day and which are so common and so much the rule that they cannot have confidence in one another, nor can loyalty scarcely be found from the greatest to the least of them? Who has ever seen before the art of sophistry so common, for it seems that everyone is a master of it; and this infernal and diabolical art has sunk so deeply into their spirit that hardly a word is said, an appearance formed, or a deed done that is not falsified in such a way as to appear better in true merit than it is revealed to be. Because of these things, I am like that woman who has the baton over her head and awaits the blow."

I.27. More about this topic

"Just as the virtues descend from one another and accompany and attract one another, these daughters of perdition likewise stumble from one to another and know each other and appear together. And that it must be true, for what reason is Fraud found if not to fill the coffers of Greed? She is the directress of her riches and agreements; it is she who finds the way to inveigle money for her and carry out her bargains. Ah! If she lost her, how distraught she would be! Never was there such a servant nor one who had such a good opinion of her mistress! God, what company and what a couple, Greed and Fraud! But from their foul hands *Libera nos domine*.

---

[51] See II Kings 25:1–7.

"God! Did this vile harpy with the curved claws not begin when only three men existed on earth, when Cain offered God the worst fruits of his land and the worst beasts of his fold? And since God, who knows intentions, did not think his sacrifices acceptable, He admonished him. Because of which Cain fell to the second iniquity, or envy, and then to the third, by the murder of his brother Abel. Who could recount the evils that have arisen because of her and still do not cease? Why would I tell you about empires, kingdoms, cities, and peoples destroyed by her in the past? No other example but of the present is necessary. Is she not the one who establishes division and schism in God's Church? Certainly, if she did not exist, two popes would not be necessary; rather, one would hardly wish it so. Is she not the principal one in my realm's debate? If she were not found here, the conduct of government would not be so contested. Do we say that long ago she was greater for the King of Babylon so that he robbed God's temple only once? Alas, let us consider how many thefts occur among things dearer to Him than His temple, that is, among His poor servants who are the indigent, of whom it is written that one might legally sell the chalices, jewels, and books and ornaments of the altar when needed to help with the necessities of life for these people. And everywhere they are persecuted and robbed of such wealth as they have, which is to say their sustenance. And God knows how they are employed! But in the cause of this said King, why does it not prefigure and prophesy for us a similar misfortune engendered by divine punishment? For as it is written in the fifth chapter of the Book of Daniel that Belshazzar once had a great dinner and sat at table with the nobles of his kingdom, he gave orders to fetch the gold and silver vessels, which his father had taken from the temple of Jerusalem, in which vessels they used to conduct the service of God. And that one, corrupted by vanity, presumptuously drank from them and made his concubines, who ornamented themselves from such spoils, drink from them; and they put the things of the Lord to vile use. But God, against whom no force can stand and who, even though He may wait, well knows how to avenge Himself, brought about the hour of this malefactor's punishment. By this example we can observe that the ruin of the arrogant often occurs when they think themselves most secure. For just as this Belshazzar, King of Babylon, was at the height of his joy, he raised his eyes and saw on the wall of the room a hand that wrote these three words: *mene*, *tekel*, *phares*. The first word *mene* means number and indicated that God had numbered the days of his life and their end had come. The second word *tekel* is weight, which signified that God had weighed his good and bad deeds and found him light in the good and heavy in the bad. The third word *phares* meant division, which signified that God had divided his kingdom and separated it from him. And so it came to pass. Because that very night Cyrus, King of Persia, and Darius, the King of Media, took the city of Babylon, and Belshazzar was killed, and his kingdom delivered into the hands of the Medes and Persians."

I.28. More of the same

"Dear, sweet friend, I might tell you such examples of different punishments for they are so numerous. Alas, and my subjects take no heed! Does the rural and common proverb not say that he who beats himself indeed chastises himself for another, and that he who sees another's house burn should fear for his own? There is no punishment so fair as that which comes unconstrained from oneself. It was more honorable for them to forsake their sins from pure desire than to be forced to abandon them. Is it not written that God rejoices more in the sinner returned to Him than in the righteous one who never failed? A human thing it is to sin but hellish is the perseverance. Ha! It is a sweet thing to follow the path to virtue for the one who wishes to be led there! Is it not said that the virtuous man already has one foot in heaven? And why does man, who is dust and ashes, exalt himself? Does he not know that his life is brief? Does he not take pride in worldly pleasures that are neither genuine nor his? And what is it worth to be lord on earth, to have great wealth, lands, possessions, and powers over others for a short time, if, by employing them, one seeks his own perpetual damnation? Who is the person so ignorant that he feels not the worm of conscience, whether he will or no, when he feels himself a sinner? Does he not already possess one of Hell's torments, which does not let him endure? But what is greater security than a clear conscience? That is celestial joy! Ah! But why or to whom do I say these words when I know that I will not be believed? For these words cannot enter into hardened hearts just as they say that the fool believes not until he experiences. My great will forces me to speak, however, like a tender mother to her children. But it disconcerts me that some seem to have become obstinate, a very perverse thing. Alas, I fear greatly that I resemble Cassandra, the wise daughter of King Priam, who, seeing the ruin prepared for the Trojans, advised them to pluck up their spirits against the Greeks before worse might come to them. She argued in vain, however, for she was not believed. And so everything she prophesied to them came to them; too late, they then repented their disbelief. So, in order to correct them and make peace with their God, with whom I now see war, I would very much like for them to give credence to my words that they might believe me before worse things come upon them and so that His anger might never be poured in grievous vengeance upon them.

"Oh wise, well-advised King of Nineveh who believed the prophet Jonah when through him God ordered you that within forty days you have incurred the sentence of destruction for your sins and those of your city! But then repentant, taking out your guilt in fasting, tears, and afflictions, you and all your subjects even to the beasts, carried on for three days, crying to God for mercy, clothed in sack cloth, ashes on your heads, you so humbled yourself that God took pity on your contrition and your humility spared His vengeance through beneficial appeasement.[52]

"Have not my people sufficient examples to make them repent? Do they not know that evil must come from evil? For although the literal sense of the Gospels may say that scandalous deeds must occur, it does not say afterwards that they want evil for the one through whom the scandal arises. Do they wish to resemble the thief who does not believe that wrongdoers are punished—whatever example he may see—until he has the rope around his neck? Alas! But this is too late! For it is much better for man to avoid the evil path from which he hardly ever or never leaves if he entered it."

I.29. The end of the crowned lady's complaint

"Good, sweet friend, what shall I say to you? Have I not held you long enough in the narration and development of my adventures? The good and bad, I have told you of them, in general and in detail, from the birth of my name until the present. And making the state of my troubles known to you has greatly comforted me, so compassionate of my afflictions I found you! Nonetheless, it is time that I do not allow myself to say more for it would be too long. Oh what pleasure and relief it is to speak and reveal the heaviness of one's thoughts to one's loyal friend, man or woman! For meat given to the hungry is no longer tasty! So, say no more what you said before, that no matter how I appear, I may be glorious. For I assure you unless God by His grace cures all this, I have not been more perplexed in quite some time. Alas! And even more it certainly grieves me, the

---

[52] See Jon. 3.

danger of worse, when I see the trouble I suffer, even though thoroughly beaten, just as one [who] sees the person he has injured fears that he has given the final blow. So my dear friend, at the end of my speech, I thank you for your loyal love and company, which, I beseech you, may never fail me to the end even though you may be requested elsewhere and have few rewards from me and mine, but may your good heart be unwilling to abandon the nurture of your childhood. So stay, steadfast, with me in the gracious labor of your writings, with which you will yet bring many pleasures to me and my children, whom I pray you will save for me and make the lamentations of my cries known to, and who, like loyal and true children, may willingly take pity on their tender mother, whose milk is still necessary and sweet nourishment to them, but they must wish to spare her sweet breasts lest they suck her to the blood."

At this point, the crowned lady's words ceased. Thereafter, I comforted her, to the best of my ability, as well as I knew how, telling her that her great danger notwithstanding, if God pleases, the prayers and appeals of many good creatures and the good deeds that are celebrated throughout her land, notwithstanding the great sins which are rampant here, would save her and draw her back from danger as God is merciful. I thanked her for the honor that she had done me and for the responsibility with which she had charged me, promising her true execution of it. And at that point, I left her to rest.

Here ends the first part of the *Vision*

Book Two

II.1. Here begins the second part of the book of Christine's *Vision*, which speaks of Dame Opinion and of her shadows

After these things, it seemed to me that, eager to search further, I went traveling through the city of Athens until I came upon the schools. Delighted to have arrived at such a noble university, eager for my mind to imbibe their erudition to my profit, I was pausing among scholars of the various learned faculties disputing together, about many questions forming numerous arguments. Then just as I pricked up my ears to listen, the sense of my sight went before that of my hearing. For lifting my eyes, I saw flying among them a great, feminine, bodiless shadow as if a spiritual thing quite strange in nature.[1] And experience proved that she was preternatural, for this substance I saw as a single shadow, yet more than a hundred thousand million (indeed innumerable) parts—some large, others small, others smaller still—was she creating from herself; then these parts of the shadow assembled as if by great crowds such as clouds make in the sky or birds flying in flocks together. But there were more of them than all the birds who ever flew. So the groups were differentiated each from the other by their colors; for by all the colors that have ever existed and more were they differentiated one from the other. There was one great mass all white, others all red, others blue, others the color of fire, others of water, and so on with all the hues. And those of one color would hold together just like birds of one species. Although sometimes they happened to intermingle, each would always return to its color. Yet even though each color would stay together, nevertheless some were tinted more deeply than others: so with vermilion, one was brighter, another paler, another more intense, and thus with all the hues, so that there was hardly one which did not differ somewhat from the other. And just as the colors of these shadows were set apart in groups, so were their forms. For there was no body, be it of human, strange beast, bird, sea monster, serpent, nor anything that God might have ever formed, indeed of the

---

[1] *Advision* 162–63, n. I–II points to Macrobius' *Commentary on the Dream of Scipio* (I.12.9) as one of Christine's important sources for Opinion. For a translation of this passage see Macrobius 135.

highest celestial substances or of anything whatsoever that thought can present to the imagination,[2] whose form was not present. There were so many strange things that no heart could conceive it. But forms of giants, horrible beasts or serpents nor any mortal thing did not terrify me as much as did the horrible, black, disfigured, and hellish monsters, whose memory still fills me with total horror.

II.2. Wherein she is told what use the shadows served

I saw [that] these groups of shadows flying through the air surrounded all the clerks disputing in the said schools. And before the one who wished to propose his question might speak, one of these shadows would come to whisper in his ear, as if to advise him what to say. Afterwards, when another would wish to respond or reply, another shadow would also come to whisper in his ear. And thus there was no disputant who did not have around his head one, two, three, four, or even more, who were all advising him. But each branch of knowledge separately had its own color of shadows, such as grammar, the greens; dialectic the deep browns; arithmetic rich and variegated shades; music, whites; geometry reds; astrology the azures; theology golds; philosophy brilliant whites, and so on with the other liberal and forbidden sciences. And those who were arguing were surrounded as long as their disputation lasted only by the shadows of the color pertinent to the science of their disputations; but even though all inclined toward one color, those who were proposing were more or less strongly tinted than those who were responding, so never were they without difference. And if similar ones happened to come to the parties who were disputing, then the two disputants agreed. The matter was so arranged that it seemed that these shadows were the cause of their discords and debates, which would sometimes grow so greatly among them that they made the hot-natured ones come *de verbis a verbera*.[3] And since it might seem a strange thing to those who hear or will hear the description of this vision in this part— which the eyes of my understanding saw more clearly than I know how to explain or describe—that I call these things shadows and so say they had various colors, for it seems contradictory to be shadow

---

[2]   Modern readers should be alive to the difficulties of this word, which cannot be simply equated to the modern "imagination." The French "yimaginer" has many different meanings. *Advision* 163, n. II/37 refers readers to Lucien Foulet, "Étude sur le vocabulaire abstrait de Froissart; deuxième article: imaginer," *Romania* 68 (1944–45): 257–72 for a discussion of the term.

[3]   The phrase means "from words to blows."

and color at once, I say that the shadows were this. For outside causes gave them their forms; they had them not of themselves. They had to be colored—they were not otherwise—yet all of them, great and small, were so transparent that one saw right through them, except for a few so opaque that one saw nothing at all. Moreover, just as they were separated by colors, so they were by form. For as I said before, these shadows were imprinted with all imaginable forms and things. Those belonging to philosophy were like flowers of various shapes and colors. But they were so perfumed and lovely that all the schools were made resplendent by them so that it was most lovely to be there. The other forms of the shadows—as of humans, beasts, or other things—extended far beyond the colleges and were flying throughout the world. For they pertained more to manual labor and actions than to abstract thought and would be attributed more to the military and the order of chivalry, and the other mechanical and practical arts. Of all this it seemed to me that I had a clear understanding. But above all else I was perplexed and it was hard for me to understand that what I saw, notwithstanding these various parts of shadows which were expanding throughout the world, were but the image of one whole shadow in which all the others were violently churning.

II.3. What the shadow said to Christine

Then, as I was intently watching this wondrous, shadowy creature, she turned her attention to me and addressed me as follows: "School girl, what brings you here?" And I said to her, "Lady, chance, but your wonders have detained me here. And if I might, I would very much like to know you better." And she said to me, "What! Do you not know me then?" [And I replied,] "Lady I do not have any memory of it." And she said to me, "Oh! indeed I see that ignorance deprives humans of the knowledge of the objects of their work! But to grant your wish, I consent that you may know me; therefore by strong signs I will be revealed to you.

"Know that as soon as Adam was formed, I was created, and I am the daughter of Ignorance: Desire for Knowledge engendered me. I made the first man and woman bite into the apple through my deceitful advice. And after God condemned him for this misdeed to earn his living by the sweat of his brow, I caused him to seek out and research the properties of grasses and plants, and I made him learn how to work the land and made him seek out the nature of created things until he learned it all. Thereafter, I ruled humans and made them accept the law, which was at first that of nature. From these earliest times, there were a few clever men whom I incited to such inquiry that they discovered philosophy. And consequently all the sciences and arts by me were first investigated and the way to attain them was found, nor would the name of Philosophy ever have been invented if I had not existed, as I will explain to you more fully hereafter. And notwithstanding that Philosophy with her daughters existed before me and that she should be the daughter of God, I was also created as soon as human understanding was. And she and I opened the way to men of clear wit to find her, to human understanding first and me second. So I am her chambermaid in this mortal world, for neither in heaven nor hell do I dwell. I will endure until the Last Day, and then I will finish. I convey messages from clear-witted men to Philosophy, and I cause those who wish to apply themselves there to reach her by means of diligent study unless a flaw in their intelligence deprives them of reaching her through investigation. And therefore even though I may exist throughout the world, you see me principally here in these schools in which through me with the labor of study the students learn all the sciences; and without me, these could not be learned. Even though grace comes from God on high, I am the one who puts it to work in the person's heart; and without me nothing would prosper. I tell you most emphatically that if I existed not with Faith, Hope, and Charity, it would not exist within human beings."

II.4. What the shadow told Christine

"I say further to you that all the ancient prophets who have existed, even though that they might have spoken though divine revelation of the advent of Christ and the future, and even St. John the Evangelist in the *Apocalypse* and all the men and women who have prophesied, if I would not have spoken truthfully, they would not have spoken sensibly of divine secrets. But so that you may not be at fault in me and may the better understand me, I tell you that in spite of what I said, many prophesied truth in whom I was unreasonable. But I told them the opposite of their prophecy just as Caiaphas said of Jesus Christ that it was expedient for a man to die to save his people. He spoke the truth, but it was not at all in the sense that he took it. And so I was false in him, for I made him believe foolishly.

"I will tell you more of my nature.[4] As soon as a human being is born, so soon understanding begins to open a little within him, then I and my most cunning daughters enter within him. And as the child grows with his understanding, we likewise grow inside of him. And

---

[4]   In *Advision* 164, n. IV, Reno and Dulac trace this definition of Opinion to St. Thomas Aquinas' *Commentary on the Metaphysics of Aristotle* VII.15.1610.

in this growth, according to his tendencies, I place my daughters to dwell within him. If he is clever in abstract thought, I give him the things he lacks, and these make him probe further the areas to which he is inclined. If he is inclined toward arms, I give him the things he is missing, and these make him develop skill with weapons, and so in like manner with handicrafts, commerce, agriculture, painting or writing or discourse, depending on the works.

"Through me with inclination and the continual habit of instruction, everyone acquires his values, good or bad, wise or foolish, depending on how he applies himself. I thus cause all men to work, speak, come and go; and without me, they would not be moved to work. I am often changed within them by various accidents and frequently I make the good bad and the bad good, and the learned to err and tell lies in various instances and the simple to tread the straight path and speak the truth. And depending on what I am within them, I devote myself to understanding through their deeds and words. It is not so in those who conceal themselves through hypocrisy, yet they could not do this without some of my daughters. Often I deceive those in whom I dwell by making them believe lies. No one is so wise that I do not deceive him, nor might it naturally be otherwise.

"I am built on what the imagination tells man—good or bad. So I often produce an erroneous judgment and say that a thing is good or that it is bad, and thus its antithesis. Consequently, I incite hatred or love without cause—it often happens—defamation without desert and also often praise without merit.

"In wise men I am more definite and reliable and in the old with great experience; consequently with good cause they are summoned to the councils of government. I am naturally more lively and trustworthy in one man than another, depending on the powers of his comprehension which bring me into his thoughts. And in the man who often changes me, it is a sign of little constancy and frivolous spirit.

"I am never certain; for if certainty exists, I will not exist. I often speak the truth, but I say it under the appearance and nature of something else. And sound judgment lies in the man if the appearance is seemingly truthful and worthy of belief which makes me speak. I have the nature of inciting research and inquiry, and I was created for this. But as soon as that which I caused to be sought is clearly found concerning the matter, then my daughter—who was the reason for this truth's acquisition—leaves the person. I remain there, however, with several other of my other daughters, who likewise depart according to the truths acquired. For where it is we cannot remain; and thus we bring about its acquisition through the labor of inquiry.

"But judgments in any case are never worthwhile if they are not founded on reason. And he who works or speaks through me without invoking good sense errs and abounds in folly. I have, as is said, daughters good and bad, truthful and fraudulent. But whether they lie or speak the truth, the thought that holds them within itself is uncertain, no matter how great the faith invested there. Because I am not certainly known, you can see that I and hope in the future through genuine faith are the cause of merit among true, staunch Catholics. So you can note that because I change and alter in this way, you see my daughters here in different shapes and colors. For no man is so wise that he does not possess me in different forms. The reason is that my mother Ignorance does not allow the soul to work in the vessel of the body according to its subtlety because of the body's coarseness. And therefore it is necessary that I who am composed of the nature of the soul, inasmuch as I am contemplative, and of the nature of the body, inasmuch as I am ignorant, must be and exist within the heart of the human creature. But within intelligences that nobly see the truth and understand the nature of all things, I do not dwell nor anywhere ignorance and understanding are not together. And as it is said, no man is so wise that he is unaware of the causes of most things; and therefore, there is no one who does not vary in me. But because I am weaker in the less perfect, their reasons are feeble and deserving of censure."

II.5. More concerning these matters

"And listen carefully further concerning my power. I tell you that all the laws and sects which have existed in the world since its beginning—except for the written law given Moses by God and then that of Jesus Christ, which came from heaven where I have no dwelling place—all the others were found by me. The law of nature in which only one God would be worshiped which was the first and has been good to those who have held to it firmly was found by me. That of the pagans (the worship of many gods) I bestowed on foolish men and made them persevere for a very long time; and I still hold several areas of the world in this error.

I made Belus discover the first idols, and his son King Ninus worship the image of his father;[5] and although I did not discover the written law, for I knew not how to obtain it, I made several Jews

---

[5]   Belus and his son Ninus are kings of Assyria whose stories could be found in many different sources; however, see *Advision* 164, n. V/12–13 where Reno and Dulac report finding no source that credits Belus with the invention of idols. Several do credit his son Ninus.

frequently err in it who because of me committed many transgressions and evil deeds as when I even counseled the people of Israel to make a golden calf and worship it like God.[6] And in the time of Ahijah nd Abiah the Prophet I made King Jeroboam sow disbelief in God and His law;[7] and so on with many others. But also I continued the good in their meritorious work.

"I may only gaze into the law of grace, for it is absolutely true. But I made him who was its author suffer greatly through Envy, and I also caused many to convert to his law through divine grace. But even though I caused his death, yet he was wrongly judged out of fear in opposition to me. And this Envy and Evil have I likewise planted in earlier times within the hearts of those who persecuted the holy prophets and also in those who martyred the holy saints.

"I made Mohammed discover the false law that now exists, has been, and will continue for the punishment of Christians, so I hold the Saracens in this false belief. In times past I planted in several baptized in the Christian name various errors in the law and foolish beliefs that were hard to uproot: as it appears with Mani, the false heretic who founded the sect of those they call the Manichaeans; Arius, who created the Aryan heresy; in parts of Brittany Pelagius, who corrupted many Christians with his false doctrine; another toward Spain called Priscillian and several others in whom I was false and in their disciples, whom I made err; and even in several popes, patriarchs, and men of various ranks in the Church.[8] And I am still not so completely uprooted in many of the false that notwithstanding the true admonitions of Holy Theology, I may not occur within them with hidden and concealed Error. Fear of the fire, however, makes us keep silent and quiet."

II.6. Wherein the shadow speaks of the philosophers' opinions concerning the origins of the world

"In response to that which was said before, in order to prove that there is no one so wise that I do not lead him to error, let us discuss

---

[6]   See Exod. 32.

[7]   See 1 Kings 12:26–31; see 14:5–16 for Ahijah's condemnation of this act.

[8]   Mani was the founder of Manichaeism, a heresy proposing a universe in which good (light) and evil (dark) eternally war. Arius (ca. 250–336) ostensibly originated the Aryan heresy that denies the divinity of Christ. Pelagius denied free will and the necessity of grace. Bishop Priscillian of Avila (fl. 370–385) was an alleged advocate of Gnosticism. *Advision* xxxvii notes that this discussion of heresies follows Honoré Bouvet's discussion in I.6 of Honoré Bonet, *The Tree of Battles of Honoré Bouvet*, trans. George Coopland (Liverpool: Liverpool University Press, 1949).

the ancient philosophers, and what I was within them. And since the treatment of this material, even though it be subtle, can be useful to the understanding, I will tell you about it at greater length in more abstruse language, as the matter requires. I will tell you of the most ancient investigators of natural phenomena.[9]

"To those who first philosophized I said that those are only the principles of the nature of things which call to mind the material cause.[10] And this was quite clear to them; such reasons I made them investigate that four similar conditions pertained to the ideas of principles.

"First, they would say, since what a thing is made of seems to be the principle of that thing; because what a thing is made of is a true sign of the principle, and such is matter, for everything is made of matter. Similarly, because just as what things are made of we call the principle of their generation and consequently their cause, inasmuch as generation comes before everything is what it is, for before it is nothing. And yet everything is made first from matter as from its principle because matter precedes formation of things. And also matter is principally (not accidentally) the support of forms, by which it still appears that it must be the true principle. It follows that matter must be the principle of things.

"Thirdly, because as of all things this seems to be the principle to which finally all things return, for just as the principles are first in composition so they must also be the last in the resolution, and it is equally so with the matter. Fourthly, since the principles must endure, that seems especially to be the true principle which in every generation and after all corruption remains. Then as matter, which they

---

[9]   The next seven chapters introduce segments drawn from Thomas Aquinas' commentary on Aristotle's *Metaphysics*, primarily sections I.L.4, I.L.7, I.L.8, I.L.11, and I.L.12. Christine had used this commentary in her *Book of the Deeds and Good Customs of Wise King Charles V*, written shortly before the *Vision*. The precise analogs between Aquinas' commentary and Christine's text and a detailed discussion of Christine's changes and adaptations are given in the notes on pages 166–70 of *Advision*. An English translation of Aquinas' commentary is available, listed in the Selected Bibliography under Thomas Aquinas and cited in these notes as *CMA* to indicate passages Christine either directly borrowed or adapted for her text. For an analysis of Christine's use of Aquinas' commentary, see Dulac and Reno, "L'humanisme vers 1400" and "Traduction et adaptation dans l' *Advision Cristine* de Christine de Pizan."

[10]   Aristotle's system of causation included four types of causes: efficient, material, formal, and final. The search for first principles is the search for the original and basic substance of creation.

affirm [as] the substance of things, is such that it remains in all changes, although some accidental properties may vary in it, and to it equally all the other conditions said before apply, by these four premises, they concluded that matter is the element and first principle of the nature of things.[11]

"Therefore they said that nothing can be simply corrupted or created, for they said that just as when any change is made in any passion, the principal essence yet remains, [so] we do not say that this thing is simply created or destroyed but only in one respect, that is to say accidentally. If a white man becomes black, we do not say that this man is created when he takes on such an exterior or corrupted when he loses the first because his principal substance remains—that is his being which is his form. Equally so, matter, they said, is the substance of things and that endures forever, just as they concluded that nothing is simply corrupted or created except by accident. Rather, they said, all changes which happen in things are made in regard to some accidental qualities arising from matter, such as passions or different characteristics.

"Yet however much all these might have come together in positing matter as the first cause, I still made them differ in their position in two ways: that is, in regard to number (for some posited a single matter and others several material causes) and in regard also to nature (for some posited water, others air, others fire).[12]

"Thales, the ancient philosopher who was the founder of this philosophy, said it was water and asserted that the earth rests on water. He thus proposed it as the principle of things and said that thus was the earth established above as the effect is based on the cause. Now one should know that this Thales was the prince of this philosophy because while he was one of the Seven Sages,[13] more properly called the theological poets, he alone brought himself to consider the causes and principles of things, [and] the others remained occupied with only the moral sciences. The names of these Seven Sages are, first, Thales the Milesian, who was of the time of Romulus, the one who founded Rome in the time of Achaz, King of Israel, as one reads in the chronicles, around 687 years before the incarnation of Jesus Christ and 352 years before Aristotle.[14] For Aristotle was of the time

---

[11] See *CMA* I.L.4:C, 74–75.
[12] See *CMA* I.L.4:C, 75–76.
[13] The Seven Sages were fifth- and sixth-century BC Greek philosophers and thinkers, representatives of different aspects of practical wisdom.
[14] Adapted from *CMA* I.L.4:C, 77.

of Alexander the Great who came 335 years before Jesus Christ. This Thales was an astrologer, for he even, as we read, predicted an eclipse of the sun at the time of Uzziah and the founding of Rome a good one hundred years before it occurred. He was also the one who, one reads in the *History of the Philosophers*, fell into the ditch when he went out to observe the movement of the stars, for which an old woman admonished him: 'How,' she said, 'do you believe you will see what happens in the heavens when you do not see [what is] at your feet?'

"The second wise man was Pittacus of Mytilene in the time when Zedekiah ruled over the Hebrews and Tarquin the First over the Romans; which Pittacus killed Frenodaches, who went to war against him.

"The other five were Solon of Athens, who was the architect of the rights and laws of the people; Chilon of Lacedaemon; Periander of Corinth; Cleobulus of Lindos; and Bias of Priene. All lived during the period of the Babylonian Captivity. At this time in Brittany the Great there reigned Cordelia, daughter of King Lear of Brittany and wife of Aganipus, King of Gaul; which Aganipus at her prompting subjugated and conquered Brittany, occupied by her in-laws who had chased her father away. So he expelled them and restored the kingdom to the father, whom this Cordelia then succeeded, as it appears more completely in the records of their deeds."[15]

II.7. More about these matters

"Now among these Seven Sages, only Thales investigated the nature of things, and these disputations and theories that he made he sent by letters into various countries, a thing that none of the others did. For this he was called among them the prince of their philosophy. The reasons that led Thales to say what he said were that he saw the nourishment of all things to be moisture. And through three signs he proved his proposition.

"The first is said, that is to say, that all living things are nourished by moisture. But, he said, because that from which things have their existence must be the same as that from which they arise, thus moisture seems to be the principle of the nature of things. The second sign is that as the essence of all living things seems greatly conserved and maintained by their proper and natural heat, yet heat seems made and fed by humidity—humidity is also the nourishment

---

[15] This version of the Lear story was available in *Historia Regum Britannie of Geoffrey of Monmouth, I, Bern, Burgerbibliothek MS 568*, Ed. Neil Wright (Cambridge: D. S. Brewer, 1985) V: 41–49: *A History of the British*, trans. Judith Weiss (Exeter: University of Exeter, 1999) 42–52 and *Wace's Roman de Brut*.

for and the matter of heat—it appears and follows that humidity must be the principle of things. The third sign: as all animal life seems protected by humidity—because in the lack of natural moisture, every living thing dies and, as a result of its conservation, every living thing lives; therefore since 'to live' is 'to be' in things which have life, as was said before—it appears that it follows that humidity is the principle of things. These three points are interrelated.

"He also takes a point from the generation of substances. For, he said, since all generations, especially of living things, which are the noblest and most perfect of all other things, must be made through seeds, which seeds or spermata are naturally moist as everyone knows, it appears, he said, that humidity is the principle of generation of things. This Thales was led to this opinion by the authority of the ancients. For as some theological poets were still more ancient than he and these had held such an opinion about nature—that is that water must be the principle of these things—Thales possibly followed them because of their antiquity.[16]

"Now, you should know that the first men in Greece famed for science were called theological poets—poets because they composed songs and spoke devoutly about what they discussed and also theologians because they spoke of the gods and divine matters—the first and most famous of these were three, that is to say, Orpheus and his disciple Musaeus, and Linus of Thebes, the master of Hercules. These three were of the time of the Judges who ruled over the people of Israel, around 527 years before Thales; around forty-three years before King Theseus of Athens ravished Helen, the daughter of the King of Thebes; and around eighty-seven years before Troy was destroyed. Of all these three, Orpheus was the most important. And it was he who the poets say went to hell to seek his wife Eurydice, whom the serpent had bitten as she fled through the meadow when Eurystus, the brother of Orpheus, wished to rape her. This fable can be interpreted with a good moral meaning as Fulgentius in his book *On the Nature of the Gods* most clearly explains.[17] Of this Orpheus, Boethius also speaks at the end of the third book of his *Consolation* and Ovid in the tenth book of the *Metamorphoses*. Also Orpheus— to speak literally and without myths—as Boethius relates in his

[16] For Thales' arguments, see *CMA* I.L.4:C, 80–82.
[17] In *Advision* 167, n. VII/35–63, Reno and Dulac, following Cropp, specify that the reference to the Metamorphosis refers to the *Ovide moralisé*. They also note that Christine has mistaken the name of Eurydice's attacker. It is Aristaeus not Eurystus.

Music, was an excellent player of the cithara; that is, he made such melodious sounds with his harp that by the proportion of his well-ordered harmonies he cured many of the sick and made the sad happy.[18]

"These three said poets, speaking of the things of nature after the manner of fiction and metaphors, said that the Ocean, or the sea or the abyss wherein exists a great flood of waters, and Thetis, whom they called the goddess of liquids, were the parents of generation. By this, he said, as by a particular metaphor, they made it understood that water was the principle of generation for things. Moreover, this meaning they hid by another fabulous story, saying that the gods' sacrament or oath was by the water that they called the Styx, which is a river of hell. And because of this they said the gods made their oaths and sacraments on water; since a sacrament is always made with what is most worthy—because the perfect comes before the imperfect in nature and in time—they gave themselves to understand that water was the most honorable and worthy of the gods. And so, as it appears that they must have believed water the first and most ancient of the gods,[19] which gods they perhaps understood to be heavenly bodies or other palpable bodies, for they did not yet know about separated substances—he says there was no known opinion about natural bodies more ancient than this. Yet this notion was even recently renewed by some, not that they said that water was more noble nor as noble as God as these first ones said but they did say and affirm without any fiction that it was the first and also the last of the things of this world. They even propose it is older than the sky. For the first sphere—that is to say the one they imagine comprises the ninth—they consider water, as Brother Roger Bacon more clearly relates in his *Book On the Heavens* in the twelfth chapter.[20] And perhaps they were moved to this believing that the ancient poets agreed with them or perhaps because the books of the philosophers mention in several places that the waters are above the heavens. Yet these philosophers as much as these poets, inasmuch as they might have been led by good sense to at least most of these things, spoke covertly and obscurely: not the new ones but these ancient ones, inasmuch as they opened the gates of knowledge for you, you must excuse, love and support."

[18] Adapted with several additions by Christine from *CMA* I.L.4:C, 83.
[19] See *CMA* I.L.4:C, 83–84.
[20] Roger Bacon was an English Franciscan who studied and taught at the University of Paris.

II.8. Aristotle's refutation of the ancient philosophers

"Aristotle, who lived a long time thereafter, in whom I was quite true and certain because of his noble intelligence and understanding, which attracted me and my daughters, attacked Thales and the other poets; he did not attack them as poets but because they seem philosophers and are beyond truth. Also he speaks of Hippo, who, as he even relates in his *Book On the Soul*, had a very unsophisticated mind, for he proposed that the soul of animals and men is water. Aristotle says he entirely imitated Thales without contributing anything to him, and for this, he says, no praise or honor should he receive.[21]

"To other philosophers such as Diogenes and Anaximenes I said and made believe that air was the principle of all things. And they said that air was prior to water and the principle of all simple things, that is to say the elements.[22]

"So one should know that there were two Anaximenes, and both philosophers, that is to say one of the time of Aristotle, and nothing said here concerns him. But this Anaximenes whom he mentions was the disciple of Anaximander, who had been the disciple of the aforementioned Thales. This Anaximenes and Anaximander were of the time when Cyrus conquered the kingdom of Media and carried away the Persians, at the time of the destruction of the temple at Jerusalem. At this time also, that is to say, the time of Anaximenes, reigned Tarquin the Proud, the seventh and the last King of Rome, who was driven out because of his son Tarquin who raped Lucretia. This man was also Anaximenes's disciple.[23] Yet the two differed inasmuch as Anaximenes proposed air as the absolute principle only if it were made with divine reason. From this came a notion that is given in the first of *The Soul*. And possibly reason was the thing that moved them, for they saw that by breathing air the life of many animals, at least most of the beasts, is preserved and without air it is annihilated because they say that by mutation and as a result of air vary the creation and rotting of plants and various other things.

"Two other philosophers—that is, Hippasus and Heraclitus—proposed fire as the principle and matter of things. And possibly

---

[21] See *CMA* I.L.4:C, 85.

[22] See *CMA* I.L.4:C, 86 for this and the next paragraph.

[23] It is unclear whom Christine is trying to identify as Anaximenes' disciple: Tarquin, Anaximenes, or Diogenes. Aristotle's original text and Aquinas' commentary (*CMA* I.L.4:C, 86) specify Diogenes. See *Advision* 168, n. VIII/12–33, where Reno and Dulac note that Christine has abridged the passage from Aquinas' commentary.

they were moved to this because of its subtlety and nobility, for, because they saw this very thing shining and ascending, they believed that the heavens were made of fire. This Heraclitus, Pythagoras, Democritus, Anaxagoras, and several others lived at the same time, that is when Haggai, Zechariah, and Malachi prophesied in Judea, in the era of the aforementioned King Cyrus.[24]

"This Heraclitus, just as he believed in fire in respect to the principles and causes of things, was, as one reads, the very first of all the ancients who found the art of divination by fire. This art is called pyromancy; and as one reads in several treatises about it, he predicted the city of Babylon's destruction long before it occurred.

"Thus these men defined the material cause as being many things, that is, as water, air, and fire, adding to these the fourth element, earth. They said all things were caused by them and said they were incorruptible and ingenerable just like those who proposed one principle. But they proposed that the assembling of these, in greater or lesser amounts, accounted for the diversity of creation.[25] Thus, although Anaxagoras was older than Empedocles, he was still the greater novice in knowledge. For as everyone should limit the principles of things as much as he can, so he should have proposed fewer of them than Empedocles, who proposed too many of them as it is clearly evident in the first book of the *Physics*.[26] Moreover, in increasing them, he made them infinite, for he said that the elements and all substances are composed of an infinite number of small particles, which he claimed were the true principles. And he proposed that things are created and destroyed by the joining and separating—that is, by the assembling and disassembling—of these particles; otherwise they do not decay apart from this but endure forever.[27] From the matters already discussed, then, Aristotle concludes that through Anaxagoras, and in the opinion of the older philosophers, one can know only the material cause."[28]

II.9. More about these opinions

"Pythagoras said there were ten spheres which moved through the heavens although only nine of them are apparent: that is to say the

---

[24] See *CMA* I.L.4:C, 87.
[25] As noted in *Advision* 168, n. VIII/34–68, Christine attributes this theory to several philosophers, but Aquinas attributes it only to Empedocles in his commentary. See *CMA* I.L.4:C, 88.
[26] That is, Aristotle's *Physics*.
[27] Summarizes material in *CMA* I.L.4:C, 90.
[28] See *CMA* I.6.4:C, 92.

seventh comprised of the movement of the planets, the eighth by the movements of the stars, and the ninth by the daily movement which is the prime movement. But Pythagoras added the tenth sphere, the 'Anthixtonan'—that is to say moving contrary to the [other] movements and consequently producing a sound at variance to the others. For, as he proposed, and also led several others to say, that the movements of the heavenly spheres produce harmonies, as they pondered that naturally our thoughts, which they proposed were celestial in nature, must delight in the sounds, which are ordered by measure, and as they also considered that all sounds are caused by movements—for without movement no sound would be made—seeing in the sky the spheres and circles of various sizes, proportioned one to the other, it seemed to them, by most noble measures and moved also by movements appropriate to them, they imagined by these things that in the heavens great melodies were produced that they affirmed to be perfect music, and that from below to be derived from that above. Thus according to their law, the daily movement that travels from east to west in opposition to the others would be in the tenth; and the ninth would be that one that moved all the lower spheres in the opposite direction to the prime movement.[29]

"Pythagoras and those of his sect instructed by him proposed that the origin of things fell among these aforementioned causes. They consequently posited numbers just as matter and the principles of things and the attributes of numbers as the attributes or states of things—if by attributes we mean transitory accidentals and by states permanent accidentals—as they proposed that the attribute by which a number is even is also the principle of justice, because of the equality of its division. For all numbers divisible into equal parts—such as eight which divides into two fours and four into two twos, and two ones, and several others by like manner—they said to be principles of justice. And similarly, other accidental attributes of things they likened to accidental attributes of numbers and proposed that even and odd were the principles of numbers because these are their basic differences. But the even number they proposed as the principle of infinity and the odd number as the principle of finite things, as is more plainly discussed in the third book of the *Physics*, that is to say, the even number seems suitable to division. And for this reason, infinity seems to result chiefly from the division of the continuous. And the odd number includes the even and unity within itself, which is the cause of its indivisibility. They also held that odd

[29] See *CMA* I.L.7:C, 123.

numbers, added one to the other in succession, retain the figure of square numbers. But the evens vary their figures,[30] just as, three added to one (the principle of numbers) results in the number four, the first of all square numbers because two times two is four. And likewise five, the first odd number after four, added to four makes nine, which is the second square number, because three times three is nine. Again, seven added to nine makes sixteen, which is the third square because four times four is sixteen. And afterwards, nine added to sixteen makes twenty-five, which is the fourth square, and so on with the others. But if the number two, which is the first even number, is added to one, it forms the triangular number which is three. And if four, which is the second even number, is added to it, it makes seven, which has no such figure. Thus even numbers added to squares do not keep the same figure; and for this reason they attributed infinity to them and finitude to the odds. And because finitude signified form, which pertains to active power, and infinity referred to matter, which pertains to passivity, for this reason they called the even numbers feminine and the odd masculine.[31] And from these two differences—even and odd, finitude and infinity—they formed not only numbers but also unity. Because unity, they said, is virtually even *and* odd since all the differences of numbers meet virtually in unity. All return into it, and it into none. Even though it is not actually a number, they still said it is every number virtually. And for this, they held that it is composed of even and odd, and that all numbers are constituted of it. They proposed that the sky and all substances apprehended by the senses are made of numbers. And such was the order of principles they proposed."[32]

II.10. Still more of the same topics

"There were several other ancient natural philosophers who proposed motion, that is, inasmuch as they proposed a principle, which by rarification and condensation, they described as mobile, from which they believed the diversity of things was created. In this way, they said, the world was created with respect to all the differences of its parts. Yet because they posited change only in accordance with

---

[30] Pythagoras arranged pebbles in the sand to represent numbers: four, represented by two rows of two, was a square number; three, represented by two pebbles crowned by a third, was a triangular number.

[31] See *CMA* I.L.8:C, 124–25.

[32] See *CMA* I.L.8:C, 126.

the world's accidental characteristics, they concluded that in regard to substance, all earth was one.

"There were several other opinions it would take long to recount. But briefly these ancient philosophers more or less agreed in saying that in things there was one material principle such as Thales, Diogenes, and their fellows. Some proposed several of them, like Empedocles; several others noncorporeal things, such as those who believed in a dyad, that is to say Plato, who proposed the great and small which, he said, were noncorporeal. The Italians also, which is to say Pythagoras, set up infinity again, which they claimed to be noncorporeal. Empedocles also held four corporeal elements were the principles. Also Anaxagoras proposed an infinite number of like particles, that is, an infinity of similar, indivisible parts, as the principle of all things. All of these touched upon such a kind of cause as the material cause. And so did those who claimed air or water or fire for the principles or another one midway between these elements such as denser than fire or rarer than air, all these proposed that body as the first principle and element of things. And so it appears by what has already been said that everyone previously discussed proposed only the material cause. Several other ancients followed, whom I exclude for the sake of brevity.[33]

"Nevertheless it should be noted that as much as we have from their writing, we have no causes or principles beyond those proposed in the *Physics*, for none of them defined very precisely but only rather obscurely. Yet some seem to approach it, that is, those who said this matter is the principle, be it one or many, corporeal or noncorporeal; and Plato, who posited the great and small; and the Italians, who posited infinity; and Empedocles, water, fire, air, and earth; and Anaxagoras, the infinite number of similar particles. For truly, all these men also touched upon this cause, and also all those who mentioned air and water or something denser than fire or rarer than air, which they assigned as the first element. These all touched only upon matter.[34]

"But others seized upon the principle of movement, that is all those who proposed friendship or hate or understanding as the principle. Yet what 'being' or 'substance' must be in things no one plainly said. They believed, however, that these things caused immobility and rest. And therefore in respect to the substance of things,

---

[33] See *CMA* I.L.11:C, 173.

[34] As noted in *Advison* 169, n. X/29–39 this passage appears to be a summary by Christine.

they proposed that elements are the causes and infinity is responsible for the elements."[35]

II.11. More about this topic

"Since these matters are obscure for uneducated people to experience and crude when expressed in the common language, and even to your understanding strange because of its coarseness, I will move beyond these opinions of the ancient philosophers, whom I caused to err in various ways concerning the principle of things. But about these matters I was clear to my beloved son Aristotle, the prince of philosophy, who disproved these ancients with lively arguments just as I will briefly touch upon here for you without defining every particularity. For long would be the account, displeasing to those who do not understand it. Aristotle, then, criticizes the opinions of these ancient philosophers on the principles of things and, to do so, divides it into two parts. First, he criticizes individual opinions, and then he summarizes the things said and links them to those that follow.

"The first part is divided into two others. First he criticizes the opinions of those who wrote as natural philosophers, secondly those of Pythagorians and the others. Again in the first part, he does two things. First, he disapproves of the opinions of those who proposed one material cause and secondly of those who proposed several of them. Again, in regard to the first, he does two things. First, he criticizes the aforementioned opinions in general and secondly in detail. He criticizes them in general by means of three arguments, the first of which follows: for as some things are not only corporeal but are also non-corporeal—as it appears in his *Book On the Soul*—that these ancient thinkers proposed only corporeal principles, which thing appears in that they posited unity, that is the world, is only one substance and one nature—corporeal matter—which corporality they proposed admitted measure which is to say dimension, and yet a body may not be the cause of a noncorporeal substance, it appears that they have erred in this, that they defined the principle of things inadequately. And they failed not only here but in several other things, as he says more plainly thereafter.[36]

"The second argument is as follows: that whoever must determine movement must propose a cause for movement. Now these said philosophers should have necessarily treated of motion for two reasons: that is, because they tried to devise the cause of generation and

---

[35] See *CMA* I.L.11:C, 174.
[36] See *CMA* I.L.12:C, 181.

decay, which do not exist without motion; and also because they wished to deal with everything naturally—yet all examinations of nature inquire after motion since nature is the principle of movement and rest, as it appears in the second book of the *Physics*—it follows they should have treated of the principle of movement. And since they omitted or forgot this, they apparently failed.[37]

"The third reason: because everything natural must have substance and essence (which is to say form) because form is the principle of being and what it is, then because that from which all things have their being is the principle of them and of understanding them, since the aforementioned philosophers did not posit the being of things as a cause and they left off form, it appears that they failed.[38]

"Here he criticizes their opinion more in detail, and he does so in two ways—first in reference to those who proposed that fire was the only principle (although fire was sufficient); secondly in reference to those who omitted earth, for it at times appeared to be first. First, he summarizes their position: because as they proposed that each of the simple bodies change from one to the other so that some are created from the others by separation or combination, that is, by attenuation or augmentation, as coarse material from the fine-grained, and for this they proposed that one of these three was the first principle.[39] Because the others were created from it either by combination or separation, which differ, however, in respect to priority or posteriority, that is to say according to one way, that seems to be first by which the other is created by combination, and this method he proposes in two different ways. But, he says, that this may be the first from which the other is produced by separation or attenuation, it appears, he said, by those who proposed the simplest bodies as the principles, that is the bodies having the smallest parts from which, by combination, they said, things are made, just as some proposed fire because it is very subtle. Also each of the other elements also had a philosopher who judged it primary. But why, he asked, did they not propose earth as the principle? It could not be said that it would have been contrary to common opinion, for the accepted notion was that earth was the material of everything. Even Exodus, one of the theological poets, maintained it saying that the earth was made first. By which since it appears according to these poet theologians who came before the natural philosophers that the earth was

---

[37] See *CMA* I.L.12:C, 182.
[38] See *CMA* I.L.12:C, 183.
[39] See *CMA* I.L.12:C, 184.

the principle, only the naturalists avoided proposing it because of the coarseness of its parts. And therefore, since they saw that air had bigger particles than fire, and water than air, and they saw nothing as fine-grained as fire, it follows, he said, that according to this principle of condensation, no one spoke as well as those who thought fire was the first principle. For if a thing should be called the principle because of its subtlety, then the principle must be more subtle than anything else. Yet if what they said were true, great difficulties would follow, which is to say if it were nothing but fire, it would follow that if anyone said air was denser than fire or more fluid than water, they would be mistaken."[40]

II.12. More about this topic

"To be sure, however, he gives here another argument by which it appears that the earth must be very appropriately the principle. For it is quite obvious that whatever is last in generation is first in nature since nature at the end of generation holds to that which is first in her intention, but the denser, thicker, and also more composite the substance, the more it tends to be the last in generation, for, in the course of generation, one proceeds from the simplest things to the most complex—as from elements to mixtures, and mixtures to humors, and humors to parts until finally one comes to man who is the most composite—likewise since that which is densest seems to be last in generation, and consequently the principle of nature, this conclusion appears to contradict the previous one. For thus earth, which is densest and thickest, will be prior to water and water to air and air to fire.[41] And thus one should know that there is a difference between looking for that which is first [in a being] and that which is first in an absolute way. For if one seeks to know what is first in an absolute way, it is certain that that which is perfect is prior to that which is imperfect and that that which is actual is prior to that which is potential.[42] For nothing is led from imperfection to perfection or potency to actuality if not by some perfect being, that is to say by some being of perfect actuality. Here one should know that I define potency (to the extent that I distinguish it from actuality) as the possibility of any

---

[40] See *CMA* I.L.12:C, 185–86.
[41] See *CMA* I.L.12:C, 187.
[42] In the translation of this sentence, we are following suggestions made in *Advision* 170, n. XII/17–52. See Richards, "Somewhere between Destructive Glosses and Chaos" 51–52 for a link between this passage and Christine's refutation of the Thomist position on the conception of women.

non-extant effect whatsoever, that is, of anything that can be produced and led to some state of being—good or bad—that does not yet exist but is capable of doing so. And for this it is called an empowerment with being or non-being. But when it exists, it is called actuality, with the difference of being able to exist. Thus, it appears that actuality is the noblest. For which if we speak of the perfection of God, God is most perfect and consequently the most primary because in His essence there was no potency before actuality. But in individual things, which go in their being from potency to actuality, potency in these precedes actuality in respect to time and thus imperfection comes before perfection, even though actuality must be prior in nature, that is with respect to her intention and method of knowing how to produce. So it appears as a messenger traveling to a place. Although he is brought to come to the place where he is going in respect to labor and his intentions, yet he was first in respect to his intention because otherwise he might not have moved. And since in the place when he attains it, one might say that he was there in actuality, also before he is brought, his intention could be called power. And thus it appears that actuality if not in time, yet in regard to nature or intention, comes before potency. It is thus obvious that the first principle of everything must be very simple because everything is composed of simple elements and not *e converso*. Then, it was necessary for the ancient natural philosophers that one and the other should attribute to the first principle, that is to say, to the principle of the world, what they had to attribute with supreme simplicity, sovereign perfection. But as these two cannot be attributed to any corporeal principle because in generations and dissolutions, the simplest things are the most imperfect, for this reason, it seemed to them that they were obligated to posit separation in principles."[43]

II.13. How the shadow begins to speak of other matters

"Much more I would tell you about my nature within the ancient philosophers in various cases, both even in this matter discussed at length above and also the explanations of Aristotle, the true dialectician and wise master. Whoever wishes to know more of this should seek out the philosopher in his *Metaphysics*. But as this material is quite obscure, let this much suffice. Just as in a rich shop or treasure chest there are with the pearls various precious stones of particular virtues, colors, and prices, which at the pleasure and taste of sundry

[43] See *CMA* I.L.12:C, 188.

bargaining clients are sought, so these things in the treasure trove of your volume must be reserved for learned men of subtle understanding, and let the less expert proceed to lighter and more commonplace matters. Henceforth let our rhetorical method be changed into more commonplace and elegant speech in returning to our first discourse. Let the proofs of the aforementioned matters satisfy you, holding me free of the promise I made you, that is to say, to tell you the limits of my power, manifest even in the wisest men of the subtlest understanding."

II.14. The shadow speaks of the power that she possesses

"Now I have sufficiently proved to you by what was said before that I am the first cause of human undertakings and that if I were not the origin, no work in humans would have effect: I wish you, then, to retract some of your statements in your book entitled *Mutation of Fortune*,[44] which you compiled with great labor and study. For even though the discovery might have come to you through me, you were quite mistaken—may God preserve you—when you authorized the power of Dame Fortune so much that you said there that she was the sole directress of the deeds prevalent among men, and my sovereign power over all mutual influences in common deeds, which excels all others, you forgot. So be not ashamed to offer amends to me, the absolute mistress, injured by you in this respect, making yourself repentant, as guilty of being badly advised, recognizing that I am supreme over all the related powers ordained here below by God. So that this thing may be obvious to you, I wish you to untangle this argument for me: I ask you, which is nobler, the author who is the principle of the thing first formed or the work which depends upon it and comes from the power of the author, the first principle?" I told her, "Certainly Lady, I hold that as God must be the principle of all things—and also as Aristotle says, understanding is the supreme blessing, for all the others must obey it—the first principle of things I confess to be more perfect in the actuality of the work, as was sufficiently proved before." And she told me, "You have answered well. Now I have conquered you by your own judgment! For notwithstanding that understanding may be prior to me in regard to the concept, yet I am still the first cause of everything good or bad,

---

[44] *The Mutation of Fortune* (1404), a long text that examines the role of Fortune in Christine's life and the history of mankind, is available in Suzanne Solente's edition. The historical review that Opinion now begins draws on material that is also treated in Parts IV, V, and VI of this book.

done or pursued through thoughts or human works. And then, as said before, if it is so—that I am the principle of speculations and all things that can be done as it appears—I conclude that my proposition is true: I am superior to the things done, and Fortune, to whom you attribute so much power, is only my paid servant, the directress of actions for whose accomplishment I have already arranged.

"But so it does not seem that from the prodding of envy I may wish to diminish the authority of her reputation, know yourself to be right that in arranging work, Fortune has the power to guide individual acts, good or bad, according to the force of her influence. But remember that our operations are different. For I tell you again that I work in the spirit and Fortune can operate only in matters already designated by me as ready to receive her influences, in matters exterior and external; but in the bastions of thought where I am hidden, she has no power. You can understand then that she is servile and submissive to my authority since she is in the world as superfluous as the nets of the adversary; and I must be the one without whom nothing is accomplished and without whom no work's fruit could guide any man to everlasting glory."

II.15. Of the lordships that the shadow says she has interchanged

"What should I tell you about my powers? Doubt not that they surpass and excel all earthly things; and be assured that from the world's beginning, the whole universe has been, is, and will be governed by me alone in the works of man. Notwithstanding that noble sciences, written laws, princely ordinances, and earthly customs may be in general use, I tell you that I am superior to all their powers and stronger than all of them together. And [to show] that this must be true, it appears that notwithstanding these customs or establishments, often I make even those who are the wisest and most expert err and enter into such arguments that their conclusions are erroneous and damnable, as the discussion of the ancient philosophers has already proved.

"And since you claimed in your aforesaid *Book of the Mutation of Fortune* that she is the directress of the vicissitudes of realms, I tell you that of all these changes I am the principal cause. Was it not I who, as early as the second age, made Nimrod the giant build out of arrogance the fortified city and tower of Babylon that never had an equal as will be said hereafter? So I led him to such error that he lost control of reason.

"Later, as I was firmly planted in the heart of the King of Nineveh, put up to it by me, did he not seize that fortified city of Babylon which his wife Semiramis through me and my industry by means of her chivalrous spirit had re-enforced with good trenches and fortifications?

"Similarly, long thereafter, did I not give Cyrus the heart to fight Astyagas, his overlord, who had ordered him killed? I so eagerly pursued him that his intention was realized concerning this and all of the Orient, which he conquered. And as the story of it is a fine one, I will speak more of his conquest. Since I gave the spirit and bravery to Cyrus to undertake these difficult things—these very things which Habakkuk discusses in his prophecy—he captured the said city of Babylon, which seizure was so astounding that, as Orosius and St. Augustine relate, it could hardly be believed it had been conquered by human strength or built in this mortal life and then taken.[45] For, as they say, the city was well situated on all sides, very sturdily constructed, shaped in a square. Its walls were fifty cubits high and four times as thick. The walls were all made of baked rock interlaced with cement and had 100 bronze doors and covered 480 stades, which is equal to fifty-one miles or twenty-five and a half French leagues. For as Orosius recounts, as Cyrus had conquered the whole East and wished to subjugate Babylon, which remained to him, and since at one of his attacks there, he lost in the river Euphrates, which circled the city, the one of his knights whom he loved the most, who also excelled all the others in valor and skill, he swore this river that had drowned so valiant a knight he would divide into so many parts that none would be deep enough to reach a small woman's knees. And so it was, for he divided the river into 460 streams through the force of men in the field, so that the very noble flood which passed within the city was diminished and taken away from her, was subjugated and taken."

II.16. More about these topics and other domains

"For the sake of brevity, I leave aside countless other matters that I brought about during this period, and even those you impute to Fortune. Did there not come from me the invention of deeds of all the past conquerors that I saw in thoughts before their realization, notwithstanding that often I saw them differently than they occurred?

"After many other adventures passed, did I not make King Xerxes believe that he would conquer all of Greece by leading his

---

[45] The reference to Orosius probably indicates not *Historiarum Libri Septem* but the *Histoire ancienne jusqu'à César*, a source for Christine in *Mutation of Fortune*. Orosius was popularly believed to have written the book. See *Advision* 171, n. XV/33.

great force there? Thus to do so, he assembled so many men that the mountains and valleys were covered by them. So I appeared to judge the victory for him. But since Fortune may often be hostile to me, especially in feats of war and things to come, I admit that she freely gave the victory to the Greeks, felling that powerful man in the snares of adversity, as you yourself, at other times following other authors, have recorded in your books. Yet even though I might have been a cheater and deceiver to him, I was the first birth of this undertaking.

"Afterwards, because of me and my admonishments were begun and continued the great Trojan wars. Did I not make Laomedon, King of the first Troy, believe that the Greeks, who descended on his harbor when they went to seek the Golden Fleece, were coming to spy on his land and seek his harm? Because of me and without cause, he sent to have Jason, Hercules, and the other barons basely exiled from his land, because of which vexation I placed myself firmly in the aforementioned barons' hearts and promised that they would be well avenged, as later they were. For I was simple and foolish in this King Laomedon, who foolishly believed me and was badly frightened of these Greeks, in whom I was so wise and true that they sagely managed their campaign with the aid and arrangement of Fortune, the directress of their prosperity, so that they destroyed and burned the city and killed the King and all his people.

"Afterwards did I not make Priam, son of Laomedon, rebuild the second Troy, which was so beautiful, strong, and powerful that it was astonishing to behold? Because of me, he later undertook vengeance against the Greeks; hence I made Paris go into Greece and ravish Helen and do everything done in this affair. Because of my advice, with the aid or opposition of Fortune, the Trojans would win and lose. I was responsible for the death of Hector, for I made him believe that he need not be wary of Achilles, who was so ceaselessly on watch for him that he killed him in the end. Afterwards, I likewise deceived Achilles until he fell into the traps of Queen Hecuba, who with good cause hated him. All because of me and through my pursuit, Troy was finally taken and destroyed, from which city I hereafter caused several barons of royal blood to depart with a great number of people, who spread by sea into different countries, of which Aeneas and his company arrived in Italy. So I made him covet the daughter of the Latin king and for this reason undertake war against Turnus, who was challenging him. Thus from this Aeneas, his intention realized, were later descended the founders of Rome."

II.17. The shadow speaks further about these marvels

"Hereafter, was I not the one who advised the successors of these men to undertake great and astonishing things, which by the aid of Fortune, propitious for them, they did so successfully through their work, assistance, and good sense for such a long time that they conquered the world, as the histories of their deeds recount and as you yourself, following others, record in your aforementioned book, the *Book of the Mutation of Fortune*? So there is no need to narrate it at length.

"Also, was I not the one who gave to Alexander the Great from his earliest youth the idea of undertaking great and fierce battle, promising him Fortune in his aid, that he might govern the whole world as it later came finally to pass? Likewise, before and after, of all conquests and sovereignties and all strange things put into effect by chance or by deliberate proposition, I was the means and principle. This you cannot deny me. So, do you still not know me because of stupidity; what say you? Am I sufficiently revealed to you? Do you know me?" "Lady," I told her, "say more." "What do you wish me to say further? Do you not see the experience revealed by me every day in the country where you live through debates I incite throughout the city and in all other places? Behold and consider what discords I bring about even among the princes who are of one blood and naturally friends: through my diversities that are at odds in them, I often find them at odds and in each I am so antithetically strengthened in what seems good to him that I cannot be renounced. For each says he is right and intends to maintain it; and in order to discuss their reasons, do you not see the assemblies that are made from a number that are called wise men. And by each for himself from his adherents who differ one from the other, which things cause great misfortunes, for in the country, kingdom, empire, or city where I may exist or generally have existed in various opposing and antagonistic forms there is only rebellion and great discord, disturbance and battle: it neither was nor could be otherwise, for assuredly the place where I am not in general agreement will not have peace. But concerning the right or wrong among the said pre-eminent princes, I hold my tongue, for to determine this is not my duty, [I] who am always in doubt and uncertain. But it would be appropriate to ask it of the bright, resplendent, powerful goddess, whom you saw cloistered and imprisoned, concerning whom Fraud strives to block and seal the paths of her light, just as was apparent to you yourself and of whom, the ministers, even though it displeases them, dare not say a word or raise their eyes to under pain of torture. But from their arguments, I everywhere cause new quarrels to arise among their ministers and followers; throughout the town each

speaks negatively against the other. And even [among] those who do
not know them in foreign parts, in whom I am diversely established,
so that I make them often fight each other and question even things
that do not concern them at all, one saying against another: that such
a lord is right for such a reason, and the other replying no for another
such reason. And so by 'he has not, yes he has—he was not, yet he
was' I make people often kill one another, even in taverns it often happens. I am strong when there is wine, and I abound there. I make men
fight over the archbishop's cape[46] or the wars in Antioch—who was
right or wrong, who is wiser and not at all; hence I reveal the ignorance in humans who argue among themselves about things of no use
or relevance to them. Oh! What folly in man, in whom the sense
should govern reason, to base his sense on me and decide with surety
through me about uncertain matters of which they are ignorant! What
should I tell you about it? I make people live by me, that is, arrange
their actions according to my advice. And when they can achieve the
order of living that I make them want, then they are content with their
wishes. But I am different within them. For I make one person think
and believe that one manner of living and certain desires which please
him are good, but to another these same things would not be pleasing
at all; indeed, he would be pleased by their complete opposites. These
differences arise in accordance with men's conditions and ages, as I
am different in the young from what I am in the old and even differ
within the two ages between them. Because I differ in this way, I am
the cause of conflicts in the world, and everyone believes that I am
better within him. To one man I make it seem no joy is greater than
having florins. I make it seem to another that no good fortune is
greater than having beautiful women; some conclude that learning is
the supreme thing, others that chivalry is better and nobler, and so on
with other things. For this reason, Jesus Christ, like the man who is
able to live virtuously, was never so perfect as to be pleasing in everyone's opinion. Yet I tell you with good cause that living virtuously and
doing good wins most of the popular voice."

II.18. What the shadow said about those she deceived by false beliefs

"How do you think I might be, as I said, strongly connected to the
speculative students and among others to the alchemists, who believe
they have discovered the science of making gold by understanding

---

[46] Randle Cotgrave's *A Dictionairie of the French and English Tongues* (1611 edition) indicates this expression means "to contend or brabble about trifles or
things that belong to others."

the language of some obscure books? It is astonishing! For if it is true that some philosophers might have actually found such an art by investigating the secrets of nature—which seems hard to believe— yet so cryptic are their authors' texts that human intelligence does not know them readily, nor comprehend them but haphazardly, or understand them but indifferently. Here, however, is what deceives those who practice this art; that they say and declare that since it must be unsuitable for so noble a secret to be discovered by ignorant ordinary folks, for the benefit of the clever they wished to so hide it so that it might not be stolen or taken away by nobodies. And here is the deception, for everyone involved believes he is among the clever- est and deceives himself in his understanding as he studies these books, which give out the sense of their terms in such double mean- ings that the most clear-sighted see nothing at all there. I then estab- lish myself within them, however, and make them believe that by assembling the sublime metals in various ways—how and to what end they should be mixed from various materials and fed into the fire—they will obtain the art of nature; and after a time [the mixture] will be converted into gold or silver. And yet one understands the manner of composition in one way, and another in another; and the workers keep it secret, not conferring together, for fear that their ideas and methods of working may tell another how to discover the road to success; few if any ever work as the others do. Thus they waste time and lose and foolishly spend much money in the vain hope that perchance in their error comforts them by a meager show- ing or suggestion of some unusual congealment made from different mixtures and fire, some hard material to replace into powder or water or otherwise; they think by this to arrive at the level to which they aspire, things which are perfectly frivolous and turn into madness and misfortune, and all day and night they tend the fire, contemplat- ing a furnace. Ill nourished and ill clothed, they feed on the wind and build castles in Spain,[47] thinking how comfortable they will be when they know how to make gold and how much money they will man- age. And what do you think that from such alchemists sometimes arise great charlatans, who deceive the lords and make them believe that if they had had a little money, they undoubtedly would have already acquired a great secret, so they would draw a great profit from it? And so by some show of subtle truth in this art, they reveal a token of some substance that appears genuine. And in the end everything comes to nothing as you yourself have seen happen in

---

[47]   An expression roughly equivalent to "building castles in the air."

your own lifetime to several who had a considerable reputation. And many believed in them such as the one in Germany named Master Bernard who made himself so famous by the position that he held— and even sent your father letters—and did so many things that too many people believed in him.[48] And clerks would go to him from everywhere, and yet in the end it was discovered that all was trifles and trickery. And several others whom you have seen who were finally killed as their reward for the lies they told the lords. Sometimes it happens that I am so rooted within them that through their reflections, which are too intense, I make them all become completely fanatical and so convinced that they become impossible.

"It is a good joke when some uneducated fools are so engaged, believing that they understand and interpret the texts of the authorities better than the wisest men, and they read and ponder over them. And God knows the fine fantasies they have! Just like the goldsmith who wished to become an alchemist but was the antithesis of his aspiration, for he thought to make gold and he unmade it since he was a rich man and became poor. Studying a chapter, this one understood that mercury, which is to say a metal that they name there, was the working material of the science, and as he passed on, always reading, he once again understood that the source of the work's perfection was a material reputed to be base and that one found on the garbage heap like a despised thing. Then since he was strongly intent on fully considering this thing, what it could be, he finally determined that truly by what was said, that is to say 'mercury,' since the authorities had given out their terms obscurely, one must reverse the word: that is *cure ton marc*, by which he understood that one should purify the dung of man.[49] He further certified that what he found on the garbage heap was found like a vile thing. So he stopped on these points and began to work in his excrement, drying it in the fire and making powder. And the result was that he would stink like carrion, and everyone would flee from him and mock him, who thought to make gold from dung.

"There was another who believed in making gold from worn-out old shoes and he went on the garbage heaps with great diligence,

---

[48] Bernard of Trier was an alchemist of some repute. On the correspondence between Bernard and Christine's father, see Willard, *Christine de Pizan: Her Life and Works* 38 and Solente's edition of *Le Livre des faits et bonnes mœurs du sage roi Charles V*, Vol. I: xi–xiv.

[49] "*Cure ton marc*" means "use your dung." This seems to be a humorous example of antiphrastic reading gone wrong. See, for example, Brown-Grant, "*L'Avision-Christine*: Autobiographical Narrative or Mirror for the Prince?" 102.

seeking for them; then he would burn them and work until his neighbors, who were invaded by the stench, chased him away.

"Of such fools there are a good many workers in this science from which nothing remains but loss of time and poverty. And does the common proverb not say that the sciences have no greater enemies than those who are ignorant of them; whether it be true or not, I will not ascertain for you. Yet I tell you without bias that its difficulty for emphatic reasons—Nature's works being impossible to obtain sophistically—would give several of the wisest cause not to lose time and money in a foolish occupation, believing strongly in a vain hope."

II.19. Concerning the nobles whom the shadow says she was deceiving

"In regard to the nobles following the profession of arms, are they not, as you believe, deceived by me? Certainly they are; often there are many of them. For I cause them to misuse chivalric deeds because they do not know or want to know the proper limits, which are such: it is not permissible for anyone to arm himself to go into battle or fight except for certain reasons, that is, for God's law against miscreants or heretics contrary to the faith. Similarly, for the defense of the Church, his prince, his country, his land, the public good, the rights of the innocent, and his own possessions. Otherwise there is no other law that permits it, nor is the battle just and without damnation. Now take heed that all of these who are armed hold to these points righteously and so no one goes to [war] over evil quarrels.[50]

"As you must know, lawfully waged battle is permitted by divine law and the laws of men, which is no other thing, the law says, but the intention of putting in order by force of arms the thing wrongfully disputed by another. So consider its nature only as lawfully restoring law by law and changing war to peace; nor are the evils committed therein at all natural to battle, rather by bad practices customary in war they are committed. That battles in just causes are permitted by God appears in several passages of Holy Writ as when He commanded a man named Joshua as to how he should draw up his battle and that he should make an ambush to surprise his enemies. On this,

---

[50] *Advision* 173–74, n. XIX/5–13 suggest Christine may have used the Decretum of Gratian for her source here. They also suggest the timeliness of this concern: in the autumn of 1405, as Christine was writing this text, the forces of the Dukes of Orleans and Burgundy were assembled outside Paris awaiting open hostilities. On this passage, see also Forhan 149.

our Doctors say that God is the conqueror and arranger of battles, as several times is apparent.

"But those whom I incite to wage dangerous and senseless warfare and give to believe that great honor will be theirs if for the love of their ladies without visors or [with] one arm uncovered, or unprotected by some of their weapons or in some other peril they undertake a deed against another with whom they have no quarrel, them I deceive and likewise those who accept such arms and join with them."

II.20. What the shadow said about those who fight in single combat

"And those who give wager to fight to the finish in single combat over some quarrel—be it right or wrong—I promise you are in such a case deceived by me; for they are committing a crime against God and sinning greatly.[51] And I will tell you how single combat is against the divine law, which comes from God and the Holy Scriptures, against the law of man, the civil law, the *Decretals*, and against canon law; and the one who accepts the challenge likewise sins. The reason is that one should not ask God for miracles or anything unnatural since doing so is a way of tempting God in the hope that He will aid the law. So one should not question by experience God's will. And [to show] that such a test is false, one has often seen the innocent defeated: just as a decretal tells of two brothers arrested for a crime, and since they were vanquished on the field of battle in this cause, although both were not culpable; afterwards the truth was known by the confession of the very ones by whom the crime had been committed. Such has similarly been proved by several. The law forbade the further use of such unjust tests.

"Likewise, judges are established to understand these causes and do justice. And it is established law that no one may judge his own case. And he wants to be it who wants to prove his deeds through himself and his victory, which is under the dispensation of Fortune and chance.

"Likewise, canon law commands that one must obey the pope, who under the pain of excommunication forbids as a condemned and illegal act that such a test be made. You will ask me then, "How will secret malefactors be punished?" I reply to you that God has reserved

---

[51] Christine is objecting to duels. For the discussion in this chapter as well as II.19, *Advision* xxxvii suggests consulting Honoré Bouvet's *L'Arbre des batailles*. See also *Le Livre des fais d'armes et de chevalerie* IV.7 in the recent translation and edition by Charity and Sumner Willard 197–99.

the punishment for Himself. And a decretal says that if in this world all the evil were punished, there would be no place for God's judgment. And he presumptuously wants to give it to himself who wants to be given the victory of vengeance.

"And how is man so foolish that he feels himself full of vice and sin, supposing that he has a good suit in a case, that he thinks that for him, a sinner, God will perform a miracle concerning the hidden matter that he seeks? But if he were wise, he should fear God's punishment in his just cause, for it often happens and has happened that God has pretended to take vengeance on the sinner when he deserved it and then punished him in something of which he was innocent."

II.21. The shadow speaks again

"What do you say? Does this suffice? Have I told you enough about the fact of my powers, concerning which you might not hear all the examples in your lifetime, as I already said to you, there are so many and so varied? Do you know who I am yet?" And I said to her, "Lady, I might have thought I knew you, but the contradictory arguments that you have told me make me hesitate about knowing you. For if I have completely understood it, from the very first you told me that where truth is attained you cannot stay; yet I well know and am certain that in many matters you have clarified the absolute truth here for me. So I do not understand how this can be: that a doubtful thing may bear witness to the unadulterated truth." And she said to me, "Daughter, open the sense of your understanding and hear and take note. For I promise you that although at other times in various matters I may have been untruthful, in this one I have told you the truth if you listen well to it, and do not contradict me if I remind you of what I said, that is, that I am the cause through the means of study and understanding of making the truth obtained. But it is indeed true that as soon as it is obtained, I depart from that case, nor do I stay there any longer. And that this must be true, you have proved; for despite these things that I told you, I myself have not confirmed them for you, but intelligence by means of study has brought it to your understanding which by reason is certain that this must be so. Therefore, in this case, I will leave you, and instead, leave you certainty.

"And through weightier example do you not remember me and my knowledge by the various accounts that I had you write down and make commentaries about? Was I not the one who brought about the debate among the clerks—disciples of Jean de Meun as they call themselves—and you concerning the compilation of the *Romance of the Rose,* about which you wrote each other from opposite positions, each party maintaining his or her arguments, just as it appears in the small book written about it?"[52]

II.22. Christine's reply to the shadow

Then, as my mind discerned with clear understanding who was the one who had conversed with me for so long, I spoke thusly:

"Oh! strong and powerful Dame Opinion, truly, I should know you quite well, for I have been acquainted with you since childhood! And certainly I know and acknowledge that your authority is quite vigorous and strong. Although you are often blamed, he who uses you well cannot err; and it is bad for those in whom you are unsound. But since it pleased you by your grace to honor me so much that you are so clearly revealed to me, telling me of your great properties, I still ask [you], if it does not weary you, to answer some questions for me." And she said to me: "Daughter, say what you please."

"Lady, since it is that from you comes the first invention of human deeds—good or bad, crude or subtle, according to the disposition of the understanding, as said—please certify for me if in the matters engendered in me by you—which, in so far as I was able, I acquired through the means of study and such learning and understanding as I possess—which are expressed in my compilations and volumes, if I have erred in any matter; for there is no sage that sometimes does not make mistakes. For if it was so, I should prefer to correct them later than never."

And she told me, "Dear friend, be at peace. For I tell you no, even if I accused you of wanting to bestow the preeminent honor on Fortune, as I said before, of forgetting about me, as I am the principal one, there is no fault there, even though because of me many people argue about them in various ways; for some say that clerks or monks forged them for you and that they could not come from the intelligence of a woman. But those who say this are ignorant, for they do not know the Scriptures which mention so many valiant women—wiser than you and literate—and even the prophets who lived in the times past, and since Nature is not diminished in her power, this can even yet be so. Others say that your style is too obscure and that they cannot understand it, so it is not very enjoyable. Thus variously I cause some to praise and others to repress praise as anything that pleases everyone is impossible. But I tell you

---

[52] For a record of this debate, see the translation of Eric Hicks' edition by Baird and Kane.

this much: truth, by the testimony of experience, does not let censure affect reputation. I advise you then to continue your work, as it is valid, and do not suspect yourself of failing because of me. For inasmuch as I will be founded in you on law, reason, and true judgment, you will not err in the foundations of your work in the matters which seem most truthful, in spite of the many and various judgments some from me alone, others from Envy. For I assure you that when she and I are found together then very false judgments are made, nor is there any so good that it is spared. And thus I am dangerous when Envy directs me. We make the person blind in other things and in his own action in whom we are. So we gnaw at his heart, leave him no rest, and make him long to do many evil things, which sometimes come to pass. Ill-governed is the one who falls in our hands, however good he may be or however powerful.

"Did we not refuse the gates of Rome once to mighty Julius Caesar, who returned there flushed with triumph, and pursue [him] until he was finally killed? We are responsible for many such deeds, nor is anyone wise enough to know how to protect himself from us. I have told you enough then about my adventures; and at this point, let it suffice. For since I make one person believe that one thing is good and well done or that it is true and another believe the opposite—from which arise many controversies and many conflicts—the prolixity of my stories, if recounted here, might bore the readers. And so I prophesy to you that several people will bear witness to this commentary in different ways. Some will give verdicts on your language in different ways; they will say it is not very elegant, others that the composition of the material is strange. And those who will understand it will speak well of it. In times to come, more will be said of it than in your lifetime. For this much I tell you again: you have come at a bad time. For the sciences are not highly esteemed at present but are like things out of season. And that this is true, you see few who because of this are raised to Fortune's house. But after your death, there will come a prince, full of valor and wisdom, who—because of the content of your books—will wish you had lived in his time and will greatly long to have known you. So I have described myself to you. Now explain clearly what you think I am." I told her, "Lady, since your own description teaches me the definitive response, I say, since I now know you perfectly, that you are truly the daughter of Ignorance—attached to one side in perpetual mistrust of the other. And in this, I am counseled by what Aristotle says about you in the first book of the *Prior Analytics*, that he who has you fears always that it may be otherwise than he thinks as you are uncertain.

And St. Bernard also says in the fifth chapter of the *Considerations* that you are ambiguous and can be deceived.[53] Consequently I say and conclude that you are an attachment to one party, which attachment is caused by the appearance of some provable argument, whether or not the one holding the opinion questions the other side. And concerning your power I say that because of the ignorance which is in man, the world is governed more by you than by great learning."

Here ends the second part of the book of the *Vision*

---

[53] See *Advision* 174–75, n. XXII/75–80 which suggests that the source for these two definitions of opinion, drawn from the fifth book of St. Bernard's *De consideratione*, may be the article "Opinio" in the dictionary *Catholicon* by Jean de Galles.

Book Three

III.1. Here begins the third and last part of Christine's *Vision*

In the aforementioned schools, after these remarks, as I was wandering from place to place seeking out the various colleges, I was escorted through numerous rooms and levels; and the passages and defiles of these levels were laborious and difficult for those who wished to acquire and possess them—who were not permitted to do so if they were found inadequate—to me, who was wandering through these in passing, the way was rather easy. Just as the treasures of the princes are often shown and opened with pleasure to the foreign traveler wherever they go, so that they may see their magnificence and wealth so that they may report them in their own country, I was, peacefully and without great danger, led everywhere throughout the said colleges. And of the beauty and treasures that I saw there I refrain from speaking for the sake of brevity. But this much I do say about them, that with the inestimable loveliness that appeared to me there, the subtlety of these different works—how they were made, worked, and woven, and of what kinds of materials—my understanding was not worthy of conceiving nor understanding nor sharing. To mount higher to see various beautiful things was sufficient only my great desire and longing to obtain a place and permission to learn more. Thus escorted by the sacristine of Philosophy, the abbess and mother superior of this convent, I was led through all the floors filled and amply furnished with every good and lovely thing. And as still more grace I received from this noble conductress, from her generosity and bounty, she gave me leave to boldly thrust my hand in and take as much as I might carry from the said treasures of her coffers. And I, not refusing this, eager for enrichment, thanking her, knelt to fill my lap with treasure. But as they were too heavy for my feminine and feeble body, I carried away very little by the measure of my great desire, but not so little that I might exchange them for any other treasure or wealth.

Thus escorted, I was led to the highest tower where was located a very beautiful room—bright, shining and very richly painted in choice colors, in which all the sciences and their subordinate branches were portrayed around their walls. And throughout the said room, places had been arranged to seat the students listening to the lessons of the masters reading in that place from a lectern that was high and very finely decorated. Delighted to have been led to such a lovely spot, I amused myself with the rich portraits vividly made and by clever artists.

Then since I wished to explore everything, I noticed a small, very beautifully carved ivory door that was firmly closed and barred. As my gaze was very attentive and I was rather close to this area, presuming by conjecture from what I saw that a great treasure must be enclosed therein, accounting fortunate the understanding of one given knowledge of it, and I was longing for such a worthy thing to be revealed to me when, while in this thought, I heard within a great deal of movement and various women's voices in sweet and gentle conversation. Soon thereafter, I heard the bars pull back, the key turn, and the said door roll forward. Then, as I was in this area so I might be ready without fear of presumption or error to enter at once, I stayed as close at hand as possible. But as happy as I had been hoping for this opening, I was just as amazed and terror-struck as it opened. For as soon as it was opened, such a brilliant light struck me in the face and eyes that I believed myself completely blinded. Because of this, out of fear and amazement, I fell on the threshold of the door, faint and repentant for having risen so high. Then as I was still lying on the ground, a woman's voice from this high enclosure issued forth, sounding neither horrifying nor terrible, rather, sweet, beautiful, and very gracious. But as if from afar, I heard it calling me by my name, saying, "My most loyal servant, arise and be not afraid. Because of the love you bear me, the desire which leads you here, in compensation for your ignorance, will be of use to you." Then I rejoiced doubly: that is, that the venerable lady's voice, it seemed, was calling me and, secondly, that I would know part of what I desired; she reinvigorated me, and I was greatly cheered.

Then, again eager to see the astonishing beauty, which, it appeared to me, was located whence such brightness arose, I addressed my view directly through the aforesaid door. But just as when one looks up along the ray of sunlight into the heavens, one seems to see in the shining sphere a face so bright that the human eye cannot endure it, likewise, there I saw such a luminous sphere that the whole room was filled with a great brightness. And around this sphere were nine ladies, radiant as stars, who I knew were appointed to serve her, and seemed to me were of great reverence. So I quickly lowered my now perfectly dazzled gaze; placing my hand before, I spoke as follows: "Highest and noblest creature, the knowledge of whom is obscure to me, since it pleases you to honor me so that you deign to call me your handmaiden and servant, please assure me, then, of your qualities, my honored mistress." And she said to me, "My young servant, know that, even though your feeble eyes may not see me clearly due to their coarseness, I am she who nakedly and visibly appeared in the time of his exile and misfortune to my dearly beloved son Boethius, the venerable philosopher, whom with my consolations I kept from death and the numbness of despair."[1]

III.2. What Christine says to Philosophy

When I heard the venerable goddess speak thus, through which words and signs she was known to me, then I threw myself on both knees, saying, "Oh, most glorious Wisdom, on whom all understandings depend: with great good heart I thank God and you, who have so kindly made me worthy of your acquaintance and have not despised me, an ignorant woman, unworthy to undo the laces of your shoes.[2] Rather, like a most loving mistress you summoned me to you, which courtesy assures me that you will not refuse me, your servant, the small scraps of your comfort sufficient for her nourishment. For since you fed with the milk of your breasts and your own precious foods your aforesaid beloved son, who so loved and honored you, nor did you forget him in the time of his great need and also other of your children, likewise, I believe that you will not forget me, your humble servant, whom you have fed from the scraps of the great repasts of your tables; rather, you will bestow a comforting remedy on the wounds of her unfortunate woes. Because for that cause, I believe that God the Holy Spirit, the father of the poor and their true administrator, led me to the end of knowing you, just as He knows the weight of my troubles for which comfort is not given me by humans anywhere. And as the weight of my troubles is kept hidden and secret by me, not revealed to the worldly, rather quite concealed, since possibly the uncharitable might turn the laments of my tribulations to scorn and derision without any fruit of consolation ensuing from them to me, and therefore, to you, celestial knowledge, separated from the baseness of here below, the just and true physician, I

---

[1]   The principal source and model of the third book of the *Vision* is Boethius' *Consolation of Philosophy*; Glynnis Cropp demonstrated that Christine used not the Latin text but a popular French translation, *La Consolacion*. For commentary on how Christine adapts her source, see Semple, "The Consolation of a Woman Writer;" *Advision* xxviii–xxxi, and Paupert, "Christine et Boèce."

[2]   Semple, "The Consolation of a Woman Writer" 46 points out that this statement echoes John the Baptist's description of Christ. See Mark 1:7.

will release the complaints of my meditations, confident that your kindness will not scorn the humble voice of your servant, and that you will oversee the reparation of my ruined hopes, laid low by the blasts of Fortune, in whose disfavor I have been since my earliest childhood in various ways, notwithstanding that often she may have shown me her bright face; but when I would think to rejoice in it, she would immediately cover it with her dark cloud."

III.3. Christine's complaint to Philosophy

"Reverend lady, obeisance in the fashion prescribed to your Serenity.[3] May the recitation of my adventures not weary you by their prolixity and may it please you to deign to extend the assistance of your counsel to aid the feebleness of my thoughts. Oh lady, dear mistress, please mark how inconstant Fortune has always been to me, as is said, the bitterest and cruelest mother, especially considering the condition of my childhood. For I was born of noble parents in the country of Italy in the city of Venice, where my father, born in Bologna-la-Grasse[4] (where I was later raised), went to marry my mother, who was born there, because of the acquaintance my said father had long had with my grandfather, a scholar and doctor, a native of the town of Forlé and a graduate of the University of Bologna-la-Grasse, who was a salaried counselor of the aforesaid city of my birth; because of this relationship, my father was known by the Venetians and for the importance and authority of his learning was likewise retained as a salaried counselor of this said city of Venice, where he resided for a time with great honor, wealth, and profit.[5]

"Now tell me, was it not Fortune who at that time soon after my birth led my father to go to the said city of Bologna-la-Grasse to handle certain business affairs and visit his properties, where there soon came to him news and unexpected messages and tidings from two excellent kings at once, who, for the great prestige of his scholarly authority, summoned him, beseeching and promising him generous

---

[3] As noted by Reno and Dulac, the word "predite," a neologism for *praedictus*, is difficult to translate. It is translated here as "prescribed." Their suggested translation into modern French is given in *Advision* 176, n. III/2.

[4] See *Advision* 176, n. III/9–10, where Reno and Dulac note that this name (Bologne the Fat) was frequently used in the late Middle Ages and derived from the richness of the soil around the city.

[5] See Willard, *Christine de Pizan: Her Life and Works* 18 for a discussion of Thomas' work in the civil health services of Venice.

wages and rewards, each to his court, so that he might willingly come to him; one of these was the sovereign of Christian kings, the King of France, Charles the Wise, fifth of that name and the other was the King of Hungary, the one who because of his virtues and merit left such a reputation after him that he was called the Good King of Hungary.[6]

"Then since the satisfaction of these ambassadors might not be deferred, out of respect for the honor of the said princes, my father decided to obey one of these parties, that is to say the worthiest—and also from the desire to see the colleges of Paris and the nobility of the French court—to proceed to the King of France, hoping to see the king briefly, obey his commands, visit these aforementioned colleges for a year and then return to his wife and family, whom he had ordered to stay on his inherited property in Bologna-la-Grasse. And all these things having been done and arranged with the permission of the said government of Venice, he left and came to France, in which place he was, by the said King Charles the Wise, most graciously received and honored. And soon thereafter, having seen his erudition and knowledge, he appointed him his special, privy, beloved counselor, which he found so agreeable that at the end of the year, he could not have leave to depart; rather the said King generously wished that at his own costs and expense, he should send for his wife, children and family so that they might always live near him in France, promising properties, rents, and pensions to maintain their standing honorably. Nevertheless my said father, always hoping to return, delayed this matter for nearly three years, but in the end decided it had to be done. And so, as said, our removal from Italy to France was accomplished.

"The wife and children of your beloved philosopher, Master Thomas, my said father, having arrived in Paris, were grandly received; the most kind, good, wise king wished to see and joyfully receive them into his presence, which matter was accomplished soon after their arrival still wearing their richly ornamented Lombard clothing and headdresses customary for wives and children of rank. It was in the palace of the Louvre in Paris in the month of December when the aforementioned household was presented to him, with the fair and honorable company of relatives, which wife and family he received with great joy and promises."

---

6   This is King Louis I of Hungary (1326–1382).

III.4. Christine speaks of her good fortunes

"Fortune was most favorable to us during the lifetime of this good, wise King Charles, and with the other glorious successes received in the joyous, full, and peaceful married life, since every loyal servant is naturally delighted to see the prosperity of his good master, God be thanked, since the time of the arrival of my said father into the service of the King, governed partly, even in warfare, by the assistance of his wise counsel according to the science of astrology, the value of his good luck grew and steadily improved, achieving several victories and triumphs over his enemies. And that these things are true, I refer to the princes who are alive and others of this time who know about this, that the said merit of the Prince was the height of his loyal servant's joy. Despite the fact that as customary with philosophers, there was no saving of my father's money and possessions—which (may he rest in peace) I do not hold to be a laudable custom of husbands who must manage the care of their household, which may be impoverished after them by their prodigality—yet despite the liberality of his habits, the good king's provision would not let his favorite's household lack for any necessity.[7]

"To come to the point of my fortune, the time arrived when I was approaching the age when young girls are customarily assigned husbands, although I was still rather young.[8] Notwithstanding that several men—knights, other gentlemen, and wealthy scholars asked for me—and this truth should not be interpreted as vanity, for the authority of the honor and affection that the King showed my father was its cause not my own worth—since my father considered the most worthy the one who possessed the greatest learning and a good character, he looked to a young scholar and graduate, well-born, of a noble Picardian family, whose virtues surpassed his wealth; I was given to him, whom he accounted a proper son. In this matter, I make no complaint against Fortune; for truly, to choose in all the proper graces, as I have said elsewhere, I did not wish for better by my own wishes. Because of his ability, soon thereafter our aforementioned good prince, who liked him well, gave him the office, since it was vacant, of notary and his

---

7 Details on the bequest of the King can be found in Willard, *Christine de Pizan: Her Life and Works* 23. Willard draws her details from Christine's *Book of the Deeds and Good Customs of Wise King Charles V* and the *Book of Peace*.

8 Christine would have been 15; see *Vision* III.6

secretary of purse and wages and retained this most beloved servant at his court."[9]

III.5. Christine begins to speak about her misfortunes

"Thus this happiness lasted for several years. But as Fortune obviously envied our honors, she wished to block the source whence they came. And was it not truly through her, dear mistress, that in this realm was procured the grievous harm that Master Thomas' household sorely felt? It was then that the good, wise prince, not grown old in the course of nature, but at the fairly young age of forty-four, fell into a rather brief illness from which he died.[10]

"Alas, truly it often happens that good things last but a short time. For still today if God had pleased to spare his life, so necessary to this kingdom—whose government and fortunes now differ so disastrously from those of the past—he would not be very old. Now was opened the door to our misfortunes; and I, still very young, entered. And as is the general custom when powerful men die, great is the upheaval and change in the state of affairs at their courts and household, which is caused by many opposing wills; and hardly can it be otherwise unless great wisdom remedies it, as it appears of the great Alexander, as it is written, the various discords which arose soon after his death among his barons notwithstanding the divisions of regions that he had selected for them. So my father's large pensions disappeared. He no longer had 100 francs a month well paid with his rents and gifts, which were less than before as he learned. And as for the hope that the good king had given him of settling on him and his heirs 500 livres of land and other assorted benefits, the failure of the good king's memory and the untimely death prevented the realization of this promise, even though he was retained by the governing princes at wages sorely reduced and infrequently paid. Also the time of his old age had already arrived which soon thereafter brought a long period of incapacity and illness from which came many deprivations for which he would have needed the resources spent. For this reason, in my opinion, it is just, prudent frugality in youth that helps man in his old age.

---

[9] For details on Etienne's career, see Willard, *Christine de Pizan: Her Life and Works* 34–35.

[10] See *Advision* 177, n. V/7–9 which notes Christine is incorrect about Charles' age at death: he was 42.

"His understanding remaining sound to the end, recognizing his Creator like a true Catholic, my father died at the very hour he had predicted in advance, for which among the clerks his fame endured; not in his lifetime nor for more than a hundred years previously had there lived a man of such imposing intellect in the mathematical sciences and astrological judgments. Additionally, among the princes and other familiars, his genuine reputation for probity, his good deeds, loyalty, honesty, and other virtues, and lack of vices made his death mourned and his life regretted, in which nothing reprehensible was to be found if one does not fault him for the excessive liberality of refusing nothing he had to the poor, even though he had a wife and children. And that I do not say this simply out of love, still today many of his acquaintances, princes and others, know of this truth by experience. He was such a man that his own colleagues wept and mourned for him with good cause."[11]

III.6. More of the same

"Now my husband remained head of the household, a young gentleman wise, and worthy and highly-esteemed by the princes and all those who frequented his office, by which through his wise prudence was maintained the position of the aforementioned family. But since Fortune had already placed me on the downward swing of her wheel, set toward the misfortunes she wished to give me to throw me as low as possible, she did not intend to let this good man continue with me for long. Because of said Fortune, Death when he was in his flower, fit and ready and on the point of rising to a high rank, as much through scholarship as wise and prudent government and acquisition of properties, she deprived me of him in the flower of his youth, at age thirty-four; and I, at twenty-five, was left behind, burdened with three small children and a large household. So I was justifiably filled with bitterness, regretting his sweet company and the past joy that had lasted but ten years for me. Seeing the approaching flood of troubles rushing upon me, I longed more for death than life, and mindful of my vow and the good love pledged him, I decided in a sound determination never to take another.

[11] As cited in *Advision* 177, nn. III/41–44 and V/35–40, scholars have suggested Christine sometimes exaggerated her father's accomplishments, depicting his elevation to the status of counselor as occurring more rapidly than it did, obscuring evidence about his work as an alchemist, and ignoring the criticisms his errant predictions excited.

"Now I had fallen into the valley of tribulation. For, as said Fortune, when she desires anything's utter ruin—be it kingdom, city, empire, or individual—goes searching far and wide for her most adverse provisions to drive the thing that she has struck in anger to the point of wretchedness, so it happened to me. For since I was not present at the death of my said husband, who was overtaken by a sudden epidemic—yet, by the grace of God, he died as a good Catholic—in the town of Beauvais where he had gone with the King, accompanied only by some of his servants and a supplementary escort, so I could not precisely know the condition of his finances. For as it is the general custom of married men not to tell or declare all their business affairs to their wives, from which there often comes misfortune, as experience has shown me, and it is not reasonable when wives are not foolish but prudent and wise managers, so I well know that all he possessed did not come to light for me.

"Now I had to set to work—which I, being raised on rich fare and indulgently had not learned to do—and to be the pilotess of the ship remaining on the sea in the storm and without a master, that is, the desolate household misplaced and in a foreign land.[12] Then I was beset by troubles of all sorts, as this is the fare of widows, lawsuits and legal actions surrounded me on all sides. And those who owed me attacked me so I might not come forward to demand anything from them. And God knows that it is true that one such demanded what the evidence of the financial papers of my husband, an honorable man, denied as the debt of the false one as paid and a liar in his demand; he was thwarted by this and dared no longer speak or sustain his lie.[13] Soon an obstacle was placed before me in the heritage purchased by my husband. And as it had reverted to the crown, I would have to pay rent on it and so could not profit from it. And in the *Chambre des Comptes*, I, involved in a long suit against the ruthless one who was and still is one of the lords and masters from whom

---

[12] This same metaphor for Christine's assumption of responsibility on her husband's death can be found in the *Mutation of Fortune* I:12, lines 1325–1408; there, however, she is also changed into a male, a transformation that has received a great deal of attention. For a discussion of this transformation's subsequent rewriting in later works, including the *Vision*, see Kelly.

[13] While this sentence is a bit awkward, the general sense seems to be that a creditor had asked that the accounts of Etienne, who was known for his honesty, be falsified to indicate that the creditor's debt had been paid, but this demand was found out and turned to the discredit of the creditor. See also *Advision* 178, n. VI/39–43.

I could not have justice, was most grievously and unjustly harmed by
him, as it is obviously to be seen. Many know this; and he, now
grown old in his sinfulness, still does not consider it nor have it on
his conscience.

"This was not the only plague. For since the monies of my little
orphans were placed by their guardians, with my consent, into the
hands of a merchant reputed to be an honorable man in order to
increase and augment their meager possessions, since in the space of
a year, this had yielded a suitable return and been reasonably increased
by half, that person, tempted by the Devil, pretended he had been
robbed and disappeared. And again it cost to sue, and it was lost.

"Other suits sprang up before me because of inherited properties
on which old revenues and large arrears were demanded, things not
mentioned in the bill of sale for our purchase. Advised by the wisest
lawyers that I should defend myself boldly in this matter and that I
should doubt not that, since I had a good case, the verdict would be
for me to call on the securers of the sale, [but since they] had died
poor and in a foreign land, there was no relief. So that I might arrive
at the point where Fortune was leading me, at this time at the height
of my misfortunes, I succumbed, like Job, to a long illness. Because
of this thing there followed the straying of the suit, as I maintain,
and, by the lack of a full arbitration, the failure of my cases; because
of the unfavorable verdicts, satisfying the costs was on all sides on
the head of my meager capital. And it is astonishing how fiercely and
relentlessly Fortune could pursue me. For in every way that losses
can be unfortunately created for a person arranging her affairs by
good advice and due ordering—as God knows I was doing to the
best of my ability—they came to me contrary to what reasonably
should have arrived in all my business needs and general affairs.

"Oh virtue of patience, I did not always have you at hand; rather
bitterness would often trample you underfoot in me. I saw the time
when at four Parisian courts I was a defendress in lawsuits and legal
actions. And on my soul I swear to you that I was wrongly injured
by wicked parties, wherefore, if I wanted to have peace—since I perceived the wrangling of those eager to draw me from the suit, like
one who perfectly hated it as a thing contrary to my peace-loving
nature—I finally had to give into them, thus forfeiting my rights at
great expense and cost. Do not think that this might have persisted
for one or two but for more than fourteen years: that when one would
end for me, another would appear in so many different ways and
fashions that long would be half the tale and tedious. And so that
leech Fortune did not finish sucking away my meager possessions

until she had finished them all, and I had nothing more to lose. And then my lawsuits ceased but not my misfortunes.

"Oh sweet mistress, how many tears, sighs, moans, laments, and sharp sorrows do you imagine I had and suffered in this situation when I was alone in my retreat or when at my hearth I would see around me my little children and my poor relatives and I would think about past times and the present misfortunes whose floods were sinking me so low and which I was powerless to remedy! Because of these miseries, I would weep more for my loved ones than myself: as I once replied to someone who told me I had nothing to do but grieve as I was without obligations as one who was single and alone. I said he had not observed me very well for I was three times doubled; and as he did not understand me, he said so. I explained to him, saying that I was six times myself.[14] And with this, do you not think, dear mistress, that my heart was troubled by the burdensome fear that someone might discern my position, and the worry that from the position there might be apparent to outsiders and to neighbors the decline of this unfortunate estate, come from my predecessors not from me, which my ignorance made so bitter for me that death would have been preferable to its decline? Ah what hardship and suffering for the heart which is unduly attached to the will to survive against Fortune's apparent wishes! There is no misery like it. And no one believes it if he has not experienced it. And God knows how many misfortunes happen because of this and have happened to many people! So I promise you that from my external appearance and clothing the burden of my troubles was scarcely discernible among people. Rather under the gray fur cloak and the scarlet surcoat that was infrequently refurbished but well preserved, I often shivered; and in the beautiful and well-appointed bed, I had many a bad night. But the fare was sober, as is suitable to a widow, and yet it was necessary to live. God knows how tortured my heart was when actions against me were taken by the sergeants and my little possessions were taken away from me! The injury to me was great, but I feared the shame more! But when it was necessary to borrow some money, no matter what the source, in order to avoid a greater misfortune, good Lord God, how shamefully, with such blushes, did I request it although the person was my friend! And today I am still not cured of that malady which I believe damaged me as profoundly as an attack of fever might have.

[14] Christine may be referring to family members in her charge: her three small children, a niece, and her mother. See Lefèvre 280.

"Ah, when I remember how many times I wasted the morning at that palace in winter, dying of cold, searching for my counselors to recall and solicit my need; or the many times I heard there on my days of appearance in court the varied conclusions which made my eyes ooze and the many strange responses! But above all else, the expenses troubled me.

"From the example of Jesus Christ, who was willing to be tortured in all parts of his body to teach us patience, Fortune meant my poor heart to be tormented with all sorts of cruel and bitter thoughts. What greater evil and unpleasantness can arise for an innocent person, what greater cause for impatience, than to hear herself unjustifiably maligned, as appears by Boethius' words in his *Book Of Consolation*?[15] Was it not said of me throughout town that I had lovers? True, but it is not true that Fortune did all this with her various blows. For such reputations generally come and go (and often unjustly) through the large acquaintance of a great many people who are frequently in each other's company, and from conjectures and apparently truthful subterfuges—but I swear to you on my soul, that this man knew me not, nor knew who I was, nor was there any man or creature born who might have ever seen me in public or in private in the place where he was, for my path did not lie in that direction, nor did I have reason to be there, and may God be my witness that I speak the truth, and since considering his rank and mine such a thing was not possible, nor was it reasonable for anyone to have imagined it, I often marveled whence such words sprang, which were carried from mouth to mouth reporting, 'I heard it said.' Then like one who knew I was innocent, at times when they said this about me, I would be troubled, and at times I would laugh about it to myself, saying 'God! And he and I know well enough that there is nothing to it!'

"Nor did my suffering end here. For since I always struggled as best I could against the battle and campaign of Fortune, seeing the drastic depletion of my funds, since I had legal notifications verified

---

[15] This complaint against unfounded slander is modeled on a similar complaint found in Boethius' *The Consolation of Philosophy* I.4, 8–15. In these notes, passages borrowed, summarized or adapted by Christine will be linked to the *Consolation*, an English translation cited in the select Bibliography. In *Advision*, Reno and Dulac link this and other passages to the French translation Christine used, cited in these notes as *La Consolacion*. For the passage on unwarranted slander, see *Advision* 178, n.VI/ 135–38 which connects the borrowing to I.3 and I.4 of *La Consolacion*.

and passed by the *Chambre des Comptes* for a sum of money still owed my deceased husband from the wages of his said office, I obtained the King's order to the counselor generals that I should be paid.[16] Now came the tedious pursuit that, constrained by necessity, I had to make in great pain, pursued by many responses yea and nay for many days. And that this can be a long and taxing business, I call to witness those who have experienced it. And it is more displeasing now than ever as the ancients say. Now you can understand that for me, a woman, weak in body and naturally timid, making a virtue of necessity was a dangerous and unseemly business according to my upbringing; I had to run after them according to procedure, then in their courts or antechambers sit and wait with my file and summons, most days without accomplishing anything, or after long delays having ambiguous replies and false hopes. But long was the wait. Oh God! What tedious speeches, what silly looks, what jokes I often heard from some, those sated with wines and plump with pleasures, at which things in fear of imperiling my action, like one in need, I hid my feelings, without answering anything, turning away or pretending that I did not understand, that I took it for a joke. And may God please to mend all guilty consciences, for I found some very bad ones!

"Because of this pursuit, since I met nowhere any charitable person, great or small, even though from several nobles and important men I requested the assistance of their word, hoping that the law of justice obliged them to help widows and orphans, and I found in fact nothing good for myself, one day, disconsolate over these matters, I composed this ballad, weeping:

> Alas, where shall they find comfort,
> Poor widows, despoiled of their goods,
> Since in France, once their haven
> Of safety, where the exiled
> And uncounseled once fled,
> They now no longer have friends?
> The nobles take no pity on them,

---

[16] Willard, *Christine de Pizan: Her Life and Works* 39 suggests that Christine was suing for payment of her husband's bonus, which would not have been paid him while he was in Beauvais, where he died. See *Advision* 178, n. VI/158–61, which notes that there is no record of this legal action, but that the accounts from this period are incomplete.

Nor do the clerks, great and small.
And the princes do not deign to hear them.

From the knights they have not safe refuge;
By the prelates they are not well advised;
The judges do not ward off injustice;
The magistrates do not award them two pence;
In most cases the strong ones harass them;
Before the great they would never
Win half, elsewhere they must understand,
And the princes do not deign to hear them.

Where to flee, since in France
There's no refuge, where they're given
Vain hopes and deadly advice?
For them, the road to Hell is made ready,
If they willingly trust the false counsel:
Jumbled methods that win not their suit.
There are none so versed in their business
As to help them without causing harm,
And the princes do not deign to hear them.

Now good, brave men awaken
Your virtues, or to much ill fortune
Widows are willingly condemned.
Help them and believe in my song,
For I see no one tender toward them
And the princes do not deign to hear them.[17]

"The cause that moved me to make such a pursuit in person, against my own wishes, was that when I would send my messenger there, he would have no audience in their presence. But at least when I would come there, to remind them of my widowhood, kneeling before them, asking for their help in the name of pity, at least some appearance of compassion would I find within them. This problem and the others did not continue for me a short time; rather, I was constantly for more than six years in the pursuit of a not very large sum which by lawyers in such labor and petitions to the lords saved the remainder which is still owed. I have not been paid."

---

[17] This poem is from *Autres Ballades*, one of Christine's earliest works. See Roy, Vol I, 213–14.

III.7. Christine still continues her complaint

"Sweet mistress, do you understand in what sad pleasures I passed the early days of my widowhood! Had I cause for excessive flirtatiousness to incline me to foolish love affairs? But even though this should have satisfied that one for such a long time—she through whom all this came upon me—the traitor was not appeased toward me, about whom at other times I have complained with cause. The pain in the tooth draws the tongue there; rather, I will tell you, pursuing this matter all the way to the present, how her currents have guided me and still have not ceased.

"It is true that in the time of the aforementioned woes, in order to show others, as I've explained, these adversities and misfortunes are not reasonable (why? because charity is rare and can lead only to servitude and little merit) but since it is a grievous burden to keep all this inside oneself without speaking it, Fortune had not yet wounded me as much as she might have, if I had not been accompanied by the little muses of the poets. Notwithstanding that you drove them back and chased them away from Boethius' company during the time of his afflictions to nourish him with nobler fare, these led me to compose tearful rhymes lamenting my dead love and the good times past, just as it appears in the beginning of my first poems, at the start of my first *One Hundred Ballads*. And likewise to pass the time and attract some gaiety to my sad heart I began to compose amorous and gay poems of other sentiments, as I say in one of my virelais."[18]

III.8. Christine tells of how she changed her way of life

"Thereafter, since my youth and most of my outside occupations were behind me, I returned to the life that naturally pleased me the most: that is to say, solitary and tranquil. Then, because of this solitude, there returned to me from the earlier days memorized passages of Latin and the languages of the noble sciences and various learned sayings and polished bits of rhetoric that I had heard in the past when my dear, dead husband and father had been alive, notwithstanding that because of my folly, I retained little of it. For although naturally and from my birth I was inclined to this, my occupation with the tasks common to married women and the burden of frequent childbearing had deprived me of it. Also too great youth, the intemperate

---

[18] See *Advision* 179, n. VII/24 where this poem is identified as the fifteenth virelai located in Roy, Vol. I, 116–17.

enemy of good sense, which often does not allow children, whatever intelligence they may have, because of the desire to play, to pursue their studies unless fear of whippings holds them. Since I did not have this fear, the desire to play so mastered intelligence and spirit that I could not be steadfast in the labor of learning."

III.9. Christine complains of youth

"Ah! Foolish youth, blind and capricious, ignorant of the advantageous and good things, who delights in nothing but idle and vain things nor seeks to do anything else! And in truth, whoever governs himself by you follows the road to perdition and blinds himself in his own understanding! I should hate you, for in the time when I was at the two beautiful fonts of Philosophy themselves—beside those noble fountains so clear and pure—I, like a young, over-indulged fool, notwithstanding that the beautiful water was pleasing to me, would not take my fill of them. But just like the fool who sees the bright sun shining and not considering the rain thinks it will last for her forever, I neglected these things and in time thought to recover what I lost. Ah, Fortune, what treasure you stole from me! You grievously injured my understanding when you did not allow these things to last for me until the age of greatest comprehension! Indeed, you were so bold as to harm the very character of my soul. For if I had such clarity at my side now, with my present desires, wearied of all other occupations and pastimes, as of useless things, being devoted entirely to study, so great and thoroughly would I fill myself so that no woman born for a very long time would surpass me. Alas! when I had beside me masters of knowledge, I took no account of learning. And now the time has come when my mind and feeling are beggars, longing for that which they cannot have because of the failure to learn it—that is, your art, my mistress Philosophy, knowledge. Ah! sweet, savory, and honeyed thing, which excels all other treasures in value as the sovereign one! How happy are they who taste you fully! And although I can judge only haphazardly of this, as of something which I do not fully know, nonetheless the most delectable taste and savor that I find only in the minor branches and divisions of learning, this gives me an understanding of it (for higher I cannot reach) and makes me presume to her goodness from those who love and relish her and feel the supreme pleasure. Ah! children and youths, if you knew the goodness that exists in the taste for knowledge and the evil and foulness that lie in ignorance, how well advised you would be to complain little of the pain and labor of learning! Did Aristotle not say that the wise man naturally rules the ignorant just as we see that the soul rules the body?[19] And what is lovelier than knowledge? And what is uglier than ignorance, so unseemly to man? As I once replied to a man who reproved my desire for knowledge, saying that it ill suits a woman to be learned since there are so few, I said to him that it is less seemly for a man to be ignorant as there is so much of it.'"

III.10. Christine relates how she set herself to learning

"Thus at this time when my age had brought me in due course to a certain degree of understanding, pondering the adventures of the past behind me and before me the end of all things—just as a man who has passed along a perilous road turns back, regarding the road in wonder, and says that no more will he enter there but will try for something better—so considering the world so filled with dangerous illusions, and that for everything there is only one single good which is the way of truth, I turned to the path to which my own nature and the stars incline me, that is, the love of learning. Thus I closed my doors, that is, my senses, which no longer strayed to external matters, and snapped up from you those beautiful books and volumes saying I would recover something from my past losses. I did not arrogantly begin with the depths of obscure sciences, in terms I might not be able to understand: as Cato says, 'To read without understanding is not to read.'[20] Rather, like the child one first puts to his ABC's, I began with the ancient histories from the beginning of the world, the history of the Hebrews, the Assyrians, and the early kingdoms, proceeding from one to the other, descending from the Romans to the French to the Britons and several other histories; and thereafter to the deductions of the sciences, according to what I could understand in the time I studied them.

"Then I went to the books of the poets, and the good of my understanding was increasing, I was pleased when I had found the style natural to me, delighting in the veiled language and the beautiful material hidden beneath moral and pleasing tales, and the beautiful style of their meter and prose, agreeable because of the lovely and polished rhetoric adorned by clever language and

---

[19] In *Advision* 179, n. IX/35–37, Reno and Dulac identify the source as Aristotle's *Politics* but note the idea also appears in the prologue to Aquinas' commentary on Aristotle's *Metaphysics*.

[20] See *Advision* 179, n. X/15–16 which identifies this quotation as coming from the *Distiques Moraux*, a work erroneously attributed to Cato the Elder and often used to teach reading to children.

unusual proverbs; because of this science of poesy, Nature rejoiced in me. She told me, 'Daughter, be comforted inasmuch as you have attained in fact the desire I gave you, thus continuing and wandering every day through your studies, comprehending the precepts better and better.' This was not sufficient at this point to my sentiments and mind; rather she wanted that the engenderment of study and the things seen would inspire me to new readings. Then she told me, 'Take the tools and hammer out on the anvil the material that I will give you, so durable that neither iron nor fire nor anything else will be able to destroy it. So forge pleasant things. When you were carrying the children in your womb, you experienced great pain in order to give birth. Now I want you to bring forth new books which in the time to come and perpetually to the world will present your memory before the worldly princes and throughout the world in all places; these in joy and pleasure you will deliver from your memory. Notwithstanding the pain and labor, just as the woman who has given birth forgets her pain as soon as she hears her child cry, so you will forget the pain of labor on hearing the voice of your books.'[21]

"Then I began to devise pretty things, at my beginning rather light, and, just like the worker who grows more and more clever in his work as he does it, so, always studying different subjects, my mind drank in more and more new things, amending my style with greater subtlety and more noble subjects from the year 1399 when I began until this year of 1405, when I have not yet ceased. During this time fifteen principal volumes[22] were compiled, excluding other individual small poems, which all together are contained in around seventy large quires, as can be seen. And since great praise for this is not becoming as there is little cleverness in boasting, God knows I say it only to continue the narration of my good and bad adventures."

III.11. The pleasure that Christine took in study

"Now was my way of life greatly changed, but nevertheless my ill fortune did not improve; rather, like a sadness amid the prosperity and solace of my scholarly, solitary life, her malevolence persevered not only against my person but in spite of me against

---

[21] On this depiction of Christine's artistic mission and the role of Nature see Huot 366–7.

[22] In *Advision* 180, n. X/50–55, Reno and Dulac give a detailed list of the manuscripts Christine had prepared by 1405.

some of those closest to me, which I attribute to the development of my misfortunes.

"It is true that as word of the order and manner of my life, that is its studiousness, had already spread and even among the princes—for even though I would have preferred it hidden, it was revealed to them—I presented them as novelties, small and feeble though they were, from my books on various subjects, which by their grace, as kind and gentle princes, they willingly saw and joyfully received them and more, I think, for the novelty of a woman who could write (since that had not occurred for quite some time) than for any worth there might be therein. In this way my said books were in a short time discussed and carried into several places and various countries.

"Around this time as the daughter of the King of France was married to King Richard of England, there came from there for this reason a certain noble count of Salisbury.[23] And as this gracious knight loved poems and was himself a courteous poet, after what he had seen, some of my poems, he begged me through various important people so that I agreed—albeit unwillingly—that the older of my sons, a very clever and a good singer of thirteen years of age, might go with him to England to be a companion to one of his own sons of the same age. This said count conducted himself so nobly and generously toward my child and promised more for the future—in which matters I believe that he would not have failed since he was powerful—certainly, the promises he made me were not found to be lies. Now note, dear mistress, that what I say is true, how by taking my good friends from me, she was still adverse to my prosperity by not allowing them to live. This good she did not want to suffer for long, she who has done me much harm, that is to say that Misfortune who not long thereafter brought the harsh plague to the said country of England against the aforementioned King Richard, as everyone knows, because of which thereafter for his great loyalty to his rightful lord the aforesaid most gracious count was most unjustly beheaded. Now ended the good fortune of my said son's entrance into the world: still a child in a foreign land at the time of the great pestilence, he had good cause to be terrified. But what happened? King Henry, who still reigns and who had stolen the crown, saw these aforementioned books and poems—several of which I had already sent being eager to please the said

---

[23]   Sir John Montague, Earl of Salisbury, came to Paris in 1398 to arrange the marriage of King Richard II of England to Isabelle, six-year-old daughter of Charles VI. See Laidlaw "Christine de Pizan, the Earl of Salisbury, and Henry IV" on this episode from Christine's life.

count. All this came to his attention. Then he most joyfully brought my child to his court and held him in favor and a very high situation. In fact, by two of his heralds—distinguished men from there, named Lancaster and Hawk, king of arms—he actually asked me [to come], beseeching me and promising great benefits if I might go there.[24] And since I was not tempted by this in any way, seeing how things were, I concealed my feelings until I might have my son, expressing my thanks profusely and saying that I was fully at his command. To be brief, I did so much with great effort and by means of my books that I obtained leave for my said son to come and fetch me to take me to a place I have yet to see. And so I refused this bequest of Fortune for me and for him because I cannot believe a traitor might come to a good end. Now I was delighted to see this one whom I loved, for Death had left him my only son and I had been three years without him. But the financial burden increased and was not easy for me. Because I feared that the high rank he had held over there might make him wish to return (as children, whose powers of observation are not very great, are prone to be attracted to what seems better and more comfortable to them). So I sought for him a great and powerful master, who might graciously retain him. But as the small abilities of the young child were not very striking in the throng of important people at his court, I always had to maintain his position at my own expense without drawing any benefit from his service. In this way, Fortune cut me off from one of my good friends and one of my best hopes, but since then she has done still worse to me."

III.12. Christine complains of Fortune who deprived her of her good friends

"As previously noted, my said works had already given me a reputation, because of the presentations made to many princes of foreign lands; they were sent not only by me but by others as a novelty arising from the judgment of a woman. As the proverb says, 'New things please;' I say this not in any boastful manner as that is unsuitable here. The sovereign Duke of Milan in Lombardy,[25] who was informed of this thing (and perhaps more grandly than there was cause), wanting to attract me to his country, very generously had

---

[24] In *Advision* 181, n. XI/45–59, Reno and Dulac identify these heralds as Richard Bruges and John, named "Falcon, king of arms."

[25] The Duke of Milan was the father-in-law of the Duke of Orleans, who was brother to Charles VI and a patron of Christine.

arranged for perpetual annuities for my position should I want to go there. And several gentlemen of this same land appointed for that embassy know of this. But Fortune in accordance with her habits and customs did not want the ruin of my condition repaired, so she soon took from me through Death my well-wisher—not that I would have readily chosen to leave France for certain reasons, even though it was my native land. Still she wounded me when she deprived me of a good friend which is no small loss, and such a friend, as the report of distinguished people has told me, that even without my departure from France would have valued me for the merits of my books."

III.13. More about this topic

"It still remains to speak about my greatest loss, occasioned by the death of the high prince, since the time of the aforementioned wise King Charles. Was this not an obvious sign of the hateful envy of that perverse one against me when soon thereafter the most venerable, powerful, and noble Prince Philip, Duke of Burgundy, who was brother to the said wise king, who had taken me into his favor for his acquaintance with my said books and volumes which I had presented to him only recently[26] as I had not thought them worthy of being opened in the presence of his sagacity; but as his kind clemency—considering more, I believe, the expenditure of my labor than the great craft in my work (for there was not much)— liked them, as was apparent to me from his words of praise and even more from the results of his good and great assistance to my situation not only to me but to my aforementioned son, retained by him at wages as a well-liked servant—and to me likewise, along with other benefits, he deigned to esteem my knowledge to such extent that he charged me from his own mouth, which I considered a great favor, as he wished the fine life and distinguished deeds of the wise aforesaid king recorded in their own book so that a lasting memory would endure in the world as a good example of his noble name, I should compile a book about the said matters[27]—alas! and soon thereafter, when his good will toward me was steadily growing, the traitorous woman took him away from me through Death, which

[26] *Advision* 182, n. XIII/2–25 notes that in her biography of Charles V, Christine mentions giving only the *Mutation of Fortune* to the Duke of Burgundy; however, the library inventory made at the Duke's death lists two other books by Christine: *Epistle of Othea* and *The Long Road of Learning*.

[27] This book is *The Book of the Deeds and Good Customs of Wise King Charles V*; only the first part was completed at the time of the death of Philip, Duke of Burgundy, on April 27, 1404.

death renewed the wounds of my afflictions and was likewise a grievous loss to this realm, just as I record in piteous regrets in the said book he had commanded of me which was not yet finished at the time."

III.14. Christine concludes her complaint

"Now, I have told you, most honored mistress, the motives and causes of my past troubles—not all because God knows I have passed the time in so many other misfortunes and vicissitudes that a tedious and lengthy thing it would be to tell—and of the persistence of these which still continue, nor do I see the end!

"At present, concerning how things are for me, I tell you that, notwithstanding the supplications and requests that by force of various affairs and losses come in the manner described above by the waves of misfortune often running over me, that I many times brought before the French princes still living, requesting their help, not appealing to them by my merits but begging them because of the former love that drew my said father, their servant, from Italy and by his good deeds, that they might wish to help me and his small household abandoned and in a foreign land, but, although I neither lie nor am ungrateful, the help of some of them, since it was given me rather late, by assignation and not very generously, and the delay in payment and the wearisome pursuit of their treasurers also diminished the value of grace and the merit of the good deed. Oh dear lady, what do you think? How painful it is for a woman of my disposition, solitary and little interested in the allures of greed, to be forced against my nature, neither very eager nor very ardent in desires for wealth but by necessity constrained through great responsibilities, to pursue these men of finance vigorously and be led around day after day by their fine speeches! And so it goes now in the condition of my fellow widows, honored lady, from whom nothing is hidden. And you yourself, who know how little I care for the amassing and gathering of riches or the improvement in rank except to maintain what came to me from my predecessors, for I would be a fool to care for them, recognizing that all worldly things are as the wind nor are my thoughts desirous of superfluous ornaments or the luxuries of life, be my witness that only the love and welcome responsibility I feel for my good mother—in her old age dependent on her only daughter, who does not forget the great maternal benefits received from her—willingly and in recompense, as is right, perplexes and saddens me when Fortune does not allow the realization of my wishes and a woman of such perfect honor, noble life, and fair estate, as she is and always has been, is not maintained and supported as she deserves, with the other burdens of marrying off poor relatives and other friends, nor do I anywhere see Fortune inclined to help me.

"Again in regard to the pricks of my sad thoughts along with my other troubles, do you think that before the face of Fortune I consider myself very miserable when I see others, accompanied by their families, brothers, and well-placed relatives, contented and merry together, and I think that I am far away from mine in a foreign country? And even the two younger brothers that I have—wise men of a moral life, who because they were unprovided for here had to go live in Italy on the legacies that came from father? And I, who am affectionate and kind to my friends, complain to God when I see the mother without her sons whom she longs for and myself without my brothers. And thus you can see, dear mistress, that entirely against my wishes have I been used by Fortune, who still perseveres in her malefactions.

"And that I speak the truth in these matters, God, who is properly you, and you, who are properly God, know! So I return to my previous statement: although Fortune, my enemy, ceaselessly continues such torments, which are hardly trivial to a feminine and feeble spirit, the obstacles she erects to my studies through these occupations grieves me the most; many times they trouble my fantasy so that the understanding cannot wander to the good that pleases it—so troubled is it by the bitter stings—done by the sorrows I suffer."

III.15. Philosophy replies to Christine

When thus I finished all my explanations, I fell silent. Then the excellent goddess spoke in such a way that she seemed to be laughing to herself, just as a wise man does when the arguments of the simple are presented to him. But still my ignorance did not deprive me of the use of her valuable words, which she spoke to me as follows:

"Certainly friend, from your speech I perceive how foolish partiality deceives you in the judgment of your own condition. Oh blind creature, who attributes to misfortune God's gifts and His own chalice, from which He gives you drink! Why do you ungratefully complain of the blessings you have received? Certainly, most perverted is the stomach that receives proper food and digests it to the detriment of its nourishment! Where then is the good sense of your understanding that it knows not what is of use to it? That you are deceived I will prove through the application of a simple example. Just like the skillful doctor who considers the power of the nature and complexion of his patient and according to his strength or weakness gives him a medicine and purgative, so I will employ a light and restrained diet in you because of the weakness of the stomach of your understanding, to which heavy and weighty things, those like the ones I once gave my beloved Boethius (as you found in his book), would be hard to digest and convert to the sustenance you need. And as country examples make the ignorant more easily understand the form of things, by this way on the foundation of Holy Writ, the most sure, I will lead you back, if I can, to a genuine understanding of your error. Good friend, from what I can understand, in your case you complain a great deal about and think yourself discontent with Fortune who you say is and has long been the enemy of your prosperity and who, when she led your parents and you with them into France, was devising the snare of adversities into which she wished to lead you and then the other adversities that you say came thereafter to your great grief. To which things—not each one particularly, for that is unnecessary; my general response will serve for all—I will show you your rampant folly and ignorance which deceive you in this part and prevent you from seeing the truth of your affair.

"Reconsider for a moment even the great persecutions and deadly misfortunes that then existed and still exist, for there cannot be peace in the country of your birth; and think hard about whether God did you a great favor, despite your complaints about it, to remove you and your family from among the flames of those who are burning. Do you think that because of your faith, you might have escaped from it until now without your share of misfortune either on you yourself or seeing some of your own experience it? For even so have you wept for your family there who have experienced it. But after that, I smiled to myself at your simplicity, which ascribes to the power of Fortune the death and passing of a human being, as you say about King Charles and your other friends. And that which is written in the secret of God who disposes all things and governs at His good pleasure, it seems you wish to apply to chance when you say that Fortune took them from you, as if she had nothing to do but occupy herself with your annoyances. And do you know what leads you to such fancies? It is the excessive good opinion and affection you hold of yourself and your easeful pleasures, which makes you attribute to your imagined design everything that may have gone contrary to your wishes. Because as for the deaths of the King and also the others, God arranged them at that time for the best as with everything He does. And if it had been better to leave them, He would have done so. And the judgments of God, although they may seem astonishing to you, it is not for you to dispute in bold words; because as He is omniscient, He knows quite well what He is doing.

"In the other adversities you complain about, you resemble the spoiled child who suffers from the small blow of the birch given her by her father and does not understand the good it does her. Thus you most certainly complain without cause, for you do not rightly know what tribulations are, and in this reveal you are a weak, frail, and impatient woman who little knows herself. And this I will prove to you by the following reasoning."

III.16. The comfort of Philosophy

"You, who complain if a few troubles unexpectedly befall you, as if God were more beholden to you than another, consider what many good people and Christians like yourself can say, who by strange Fortune have lost not only their temporal goods but also their limbs, mangled by long illness and other chance adventures, and in various other cases are tormented in spirit and in their bodies and still with this in such poverty that they do not have their own place or anything with which to cover themselves nor are allowed to feed their life if they do not drag themselves laboriously among you, seeking your alms where they often find little compassion. What do we say about them and others who have various and grievous adversities in many forms? That they are unhappy, unfortunate, and despised by God? No, no! This is not in accordance with the moral principles of our laws, which are the Gospels. Rather let us say that they are blessed, just as God Himself says about them and those who are patient: *Beati pauperes spiritu quoniam ipsorum est regnum celorum. Beati pacifici quoniam ipsi filii Dei vocabuntur.*[28]

"So I tell you that you judge unwisely, for the unfortunate are not, in regard to God's just allotments, the most persecuted; rather they are the most blessed, inasmuch as they come closest to the life of Jesus Christ, tormented in this world in every adversity for your example. So I tell you that you are happy—and I show it to you unless you want to deny the Holy Scripture—when you approach to any extent those who have suffered sorrows, and you should have

---

[28] "Blessed are those who are poor in spirit, for theirs is the Kingdom of Heaven. Blessed are the peacemakers, for they shall be called the sons of God." See Matt. 5:3, 9.

been happier, if you had more patience than you had, for your merit would be so much the greater; even if you are firm in your belief that you were born to misfortune, it is not so, so doubt not what I tell you.

"And on this subject does Saint Augustine not speak in *On the Twenty-First Psalm*? 'Everyone should know,' he says, 'that God is a doctor who gives tribulation to the sick sinner as medicine for his salvation not as pain for his damnation. Oh sick sinner, when you receive God's medicine in tribulation, you grieve, you moan, and cry out to your doctor. He hears you not according to your desire, but He listens to you in regard to your salvation.' "[29]

III.17. More about this topic

"But let us move on, thanks be to God, to know why you can address yourself to Him and not fault Fortune. Certainly, as it seems to me, in you I perceive great ingratitude and ignorance when for the many benefits and graces that He has so often granted and grants you every day, not only do you not thank Him, but you think yourself the recipient of a grave injustice, as if you were worthy not only to have the best but everything as you desire. And that this must be true, think, think, how many great benefits and such notable gifts from God you, unworthy one, have received and every day receive. If you consider these matters well and wisely talk them over with yourself, you will find that the misadventures that have come your way in this world, which you attribute to ill Fortune, are advantageous to you, especially suitable to the usefulness of your earthly life, and in your best interests, as hereafter I will demonstrate to you; but your sensual nature deprives you of a true understanding.[30]

"I note that among other blessings, there are three things among you earthly creatures which you account your most important joys and glories. And without some or all of these three, I imagine that there is no treasure whatsoever that would gladden man's heart, nor any treasure among Fortune's favors so great that he who lacks these

---

[29] This quotation from St. Augustine comes from the section on *tribulacio* in Thomas Hibernicus' *Manipulus florum*; in *Advision*, Reno and Dulac give the exact Latin for this and other quotations from this source in their notes. In this case, see *Advision* 183, n. XVI/29–35. They also discuss Christine's use of *Manipulus florum* in *Advision* xxxiii–xxxv.

[30] *Advision* 183, n. XVII/8–82 links this whole chapter to *La Consolacion* II.3 and 4; see also *Consolation* 27–33.

would not willingly have given it (if he had it) to possess these. Two are outside one's self, and the other is within.

"The first is being born of noble parents, by which nobility I mean virtues. The second having a body free of deformity and rather pleasant, healthy and not diseased, but of good complexion and sound discretion and understanding. The third joy—not a small one—is having beautiful children, gracious to the world, intelligent, moral and God-fearing. Oh, woman, consider your ingratitude! Are you then deprived of these beautiful favors along with many others which God gave you? It seems that you must have forgotten how it is with you when you deem yourself so miserable. Do you know of a woman today more glorious in parentage than you? Do you not remember the eminence of your father, our noble philosopher, who was so close to us in our studies that we sat in the chair with him discussing our secrets and through acquaintance with our ingenuity was in his time reputed the supreme master of our speculative sciences, and with this he was a true Catholic as appeared always and at his end, and so virtuous that I tell you he was only the more esteemed? Meditation on his knowledge which remained in you is more advantageous than having anything he might have left you, despite your complaints. Think if I should hold you content of this blessing.

"What shall I say about your most noble mother? Do you know a woman more virtuous? Remember that on any day, from her youth to the present, she ever abandoned the contemplative life constantly in the service of God, no matter what task she might have? I think not! Oh what a noble woman! What a glorious life was hers, how it was never vanquished nor her noble courage ever broken by impatience! And what an example of living with all the virtues for you, if you but consider it well! Consider what a great favor God still does you to let so noble a mother live and accompany you in her old age, full of such virtue. How many times has she comforted you and led you back from your impatience to an understanding of your God! And if you complain that your heart is grief-stricken because it seems to you that you cannot do what is appropriate for her, I tell you this desire, with patience, is commendable to you and her, and without fail her worthy conversation and noble life make her outstanding among women, a noteworthy and most blessed thing.

"Similarly in regard to the second of your blessings, did God not bestow upon you, by your faith, a body strong enough and well formed in accordance with your humor? Can you ask anything of Him if you do not change? Take care, then, that you make good use of such understanding as you have lest it be better for you to have known less.

"Concerning the third joy, do you not have children, beautiful, gracious, and sound of mind? Your first offspring, who is a daughter given to God and His service, assigned by the divine inspiration of her perfectly pure desire and in spite of yourself to the Church and the noble religious community of ladies at Poissy where, in the flower of her youth and in great beauty, she carries herself so nobly in the contemplative life and devotion that the joy arising from the report of her fair life often gives you great comfort and when you receive from her the most sweet and devout letters, understanding and wise, that she sends for your consolation in which she, a young and innocent girl, persuades and admonishes you to hate the world and disdain worldly success.

"Have you not also a beautiful, gracious, and well-mannered son, and such a one who from his youth, while not more than twenty years old, has studied in our basic sciences? One would not find in grammar or rhetoric and poetic language, to which he is naturally inclined, a person more capable and subtle than he is with his fine comprehension and other good mental qualities. That I do not lie about these things enough has been revealed for everyone to see. Nor do I tell you this to lead you to vanity, but so that you may give thanks to Him from whom all blessings flow, who has given you these aforesaid benefits and many others and which He, not Fortune, bestows through His pure and unique grace on whomever He pleases.

"The other complaints you made about your dear younger relatives, whom you do not see and who are far away from you, I do not count. For as this world is only a death, I must hope through the prayers of your good mother and their worthiness, by God's mercy you will be led to the city of joy. It is there in heaven above, where you will be with each other forever."

III.18. Philosophy reprimands Christine for her complaints

"Concerning your complaint that Death deprived you of your husband at an early age, I tell you God did you no wrong when He wished to see his servant again to raise him to a higher level. It pleased Him for you to remain in the valley of tribulation in order to test your patience and purify yourself in virtue. As Saint Augustine says in *On the Sixtieth Psalm*, 'In the same furnace the straw burns and the gold is purified. The straw turns to ashes, and the gold cleanses itself of all scum and filth.'[31] And what is meant

---

[31] This quotation comes from the section on *tribulacio* in *Manipulus florum*. See *Advision* 184, n. XVIII/6–15.

by the furnace, sweet friend, do you know? That is the world where you live. The straw are those who come to a bad end, the gold are the just, the fire is tribulation, the goldsmith is God. Whatever the goldsmith wished to do with you must please you; wherever he wants to place you, you must wish it. You have the order to endure; he has the duty of cleansing. And however much the straw burns in this fire, that is the pain you feel; yet if you are wise, you will be purified like the gold.

"And yet with all that, I will show you that all this has been in your best interests and to the advantage of your understanding. There is no greater good in the world—and you yourself will not deny it to me—than that which comes from understanding and which perfects it in knowledge, which thing is done by study which teaches science and the experience of many things. These two causes make the person wise, unless a flaw in the mind deprives him of it.

"By your own words, there is no doubt that if your husband had survived until the present, you would have spent less time on your studies; for the household chores would not have allowed it, this benefit of scholarship you set yourself to as to the thing you deemed the noblest after the life that is in all respects for the perfect, the contemplative life, which is wisdom. This benefit of study I know you will admit that not for all of Fortune's favors would you have willingly missed being occupied there (however little you have done so) and without the pleasure that suits you so well. Then you should not consider yourself wretched when you have among other blessings one of the worldly things that it most delights and pleases you to have, namely, the sweet taste of knowledge.

"Similarly, if you had remained rich, powerful, and without cares, fed on rich fare (which things lead a creature to many improprieties), you would not have had the experience of knowing the world and cause to hate it so, (which God wants), and consequently, you would not have been so wise.[32] For surely you must know that the wealthy, as everyone agrees—not because of themselves but because of their possessions—do not have as much reason to know the world's fallacies or who their true friends are as those who essay them and pass through adversities. For it seems to them that since the world smiles on them, there must be no other paradise. And that this must be the

---

[32] *Advision* 184, n. XVIII/33–44 refers readers to *La Consolacion* II.2 and II.4 for Boethius' development of this argument against riches. See also *Consolation* 24–26 and 29–33.

truth, you yourself have heard it said many times of these wealthy ones that they would prefer that God keep His heaven and leave them in this world forever. Consider, then, with what damage earthly pleasures torment when they reduce the will, which should follow reason, to such bestiality that it serves only the dumb beast in base pastures and neither arises nor looks to its proper and natural place, which is heaven, whence the soul came formed in the image of God and should strive to return.[33] And to show that it is true that the experience of hardship must benefit you, I tell you that if God brought you back a little more from the comforts of ease and prosperity, you would not for any reason wish you had not experienced hardships. Draw your own conclusions then, and take heed since they are useful to the mind and for the good of your body; to the soul, if you use them well, they are more advantageous. For Saint Augustine says in *On the Gospel of Saint John*, 'The tribulations God wants you to suffer in this world is not the pain of damnation, but the lash of correction. And you, children of God, are called to the eternal heritage; so refuse not to be whipped!' "[34]

III.19. More about the same topic

"Afterwards, it seems to me, you complain and say that when you fell into the traps of cruel Fortune as soon as you were widowed, the wicked assailed you through various difficulties from lawsuits and many misfortunes they erected for you. Oh, my dear friend, it is nothing new for the wicked to persecute the innocent, who do not know how to defend themselves; but this is not to their damnation; these persecutors, if you knew well how to employ the attack of their arrows to your own benefit, would be the goldsmiths of your crown.[35] For as Saint Jerome says in his *Epistle to Cyprian*, 'The more a human creature is afflicted by the enemies' power and cruelty, the greater grows the crown of his reward.'[36] Oh fool, who reportedly wept from sadness at your hearth during the time of your troubles! Alas and you were thus fashioning from your benefit your

---

[33] *Advision* p. 184, n. XVIII/44–49 refers readers to *La Consolacion* II.5. See also *Consolation* 33–37.

[34] From the section on *tribulacio* in *Manipulus florum*. See *Advision* 184, n. XVIII/55–59.

[35] Dulac and Reno point out in *Advision* 184, n. XIX/5–9 that this argument can be found in *La Consolacion* I.3. See also *Consolation* 7–8.

[36] From the section on *tribulacio* in *Manipulus florum*. See *Advision* 185, n. XIX/9–12.

harm if it was because of impatience. For Saint Augustine says, 'Dear son, if you weep, take care that it is under the correction of God your father and not because of impatience. Because the rod with which He strikes you is not punishment; rather, it is a sign that you have a share in his testament, for God sent it to you in your best interests, and you knew not how to use it.'[37] Now consider the fair lessons of the Holy Doctors, for on such sustenance I intend to feed you as it may penetrate more deeply into your mind than would the force of subtle arguments, notwithstanding that at other times in such case I have used them to comfort human beings.

"Alas! does Saint Gregory not teach you from the tenth book of the *Moralia* what you should do when he says these words? 'The more patiently,' he says, 'we endure troubles for love of our Lord, the greater our hope in Him grows; for the joy of eternal reward cannot be reaped unless first it is sown in sorrow.'[38] Listen also to a beautiful excerpt from his writings:

> The ills that kill us here
> Force us to go to God.

"However much I told you before and it is true, that you had no cause for such distress according to the effect of things as you said you had them, nevertheless because you thought yourself unhappy, you were so, and this is what made you so.[39] For if you had not considered yourself so, you would not have been. As illness gave you your opinion, medicine was necessary whatever caused it. But so that my remedy may be of use to some of your friends who are similarly afflicted as well as other simple or ignorant people in the Christian community to whose understanding this will come, the remedy advantageous to the cure of such a disease will not be denied you by me; and still I see you have need of it.

"And apropos that you complain of little, listen to what Cassiodorus says in *On the Psalms*. 'We endure,' he says, 'small things. But if we remembered well what a draught for us was drunk on the cross by our Lord, who summons us to him, we have the reason for patience. Oh creature, if it is so that tribulations you may have received or shall

---

[37] From the section on *paciencia* in *Manipulus florum*. See *Advision* 185, n. XIX/14–18.

[38] From the section on *tribulacio* in *Manipulus florum*. See *Advision* 185, n. XIX/23–28.

[39] See *Advision* 185, n. XIX/31–37 and the *Consolation* II.4, 29.

receive, what a beautiful way of life God has given you if you know how to use them well! For trouble opens the ear of the heart many times when worldly prosperity closes it.' "[40]

III.20. More about this topic

"Concerning what you told me, that you became the subject of gossip when you were innocent, by which you were distressed, oh dear friend, what a gracious punishment God, who loves you—and whom you undoubtedly angered many times through numerous sins—He wished to give you by correcting you when you were innocent for sins perchance hidden in the conscience or in effect, in whatever manner you had committed them; and many times He does this to a creature. For in a way where there is no guilt, He punishes various sins. But it is a great purification for the person so punished in his innocence; and the lashes of the wicked are the instruments of His glory. And about this Saint Gregory speaks in the *Moralia*, the twentieth book. 'The Almighty,' he says, 'allows the wicked in this world to harm the virtuous so that by the excesses of the guilty may be cleansed the life of the chosen. One must not think that God ever allows the wicked thus to cruelly torment the innocent and virtuous unless he sees how much it will be to their benefit. For when the wicked rage against the innocent, then are the innocent shining and clean; and the perversity of the wicked rebounds to their greater loss.'[41] Oh God! And some among you who wish to pass from pleasure to pleasure, that is, from the comforts of this world, which you long for, to celestial joys, which cannot be done, listen to what Saint Gregory says in a homily. 'When I consider,' he says, 'Job lying on the dung heap like a leper, Saint John the Baptist dying of hunger in a desert, Saint Peter extended on the cross, Saint John beheaded by Herod, I think how God will cruelly torment those He condemns with His judgment since here at present He so cruelly afflicts those whom He loves and approves.'[42] And further: 'You worldly men, who think in your little trials that God must have forgotten you and that Fortune persecutes you, do you think He should be more beholden to you than to His other good friends, whom He

---

[40] Reno and Dulac note that this single quotation is actually comprised of several quotations from Cassiodorus and Gregory listed in the section on *tribulacio* in *Manipulus florum*. See *Advision* 185, nn. XIX/42–45 and XIX/48–49.

[41] This quotation and all quotations from the Church fathers in III.20 come from the section on *tribulacio* in *Manipulus florum*. See *Advision* 185, n. XX/11–20.

[42] See *Advision* 186, n. XX/22–28.

has allowed to suffer so?' But of this suffering what says Saint Bernard in his sermon? 'My brothers,' he says, 'we are in this world as if on a field of battle. And therefore whoever here does not appear wounded by sorrows will not receive in the other the crown of glorious victory.'[43]

"Oh dear friend how wise and what a true and good manager is that man or the woman who knows how to draw everything to profit and use it well, be it prosperity or adversity. But since worldly pleasures are harder to use for the good of the soul than tribulations, our Lord, for the good of the creature, generally sends them to those He loves the most; for it would not cost Him more to send prosperity than adversity. Rest assured, however, that He, who knows your frailty, does so in the best interests of the person to whom He sends them. For even though you often complain about them because of impatience, you are much more apt to go to heaven on the road of affliction than those fed on rich fare. And that this is true, if you do not want to disbelieve, like the heretics, the Holy Scriptures and the Blessed Doctors, you have sufficient proof. For if you tell me that the strong must pass through the tribulations of this world and suffer grievously alas! listen to the words that John Chrysostom speaks in *On the Gospel of Saint Matthew*: 'If anyone,' he says, 'considers the path of this life painful because of the afflictions which are here, he betrays his laziness. For if waves of the sea and the storms to the sailor, and the frosts of winter to the laborers, and wounds and horrible injuries to the knights, seem easy to bear because of the hope for profit or temporal honor which they expect from them, by what stronger reason should the tribulations of this world seem easy for us for which paradise is promised us in recompense!'[44]

"Ah God! And with all this do you think, among you sinners, that you have deserved still greater punishment for your many failings, that for the adversities you have that is not sufficient punishment? And when God, according to His mercy, moderates and softens His justice toward you a bit in regard to the troubles He gives you to suffer, are you not fully obligated to him? Of this Peter of Ravenna speaks in a letter. 'God,' he says, 'punishes you in this world so that the temporal pain ransoms your passion for death everlasting. For just as stones are not placed in an edifice unless they are first fashioned and squared by the hammer, nor grain stored in the granary until beaten by the flail, so you cannot be lodged in the edifice of paradise

---

[43] See *Advision* 186, n. XX/31–35.
[44] See *Advision* 186, n. XX/49–58.

nor placed in the granary of the elect unless you are sounded out by tribulations.' "[45]

III.21. Further consolation

"Dear friend, it seems to me that my recitation to you should suffice regarding my initial promise to show you your error in the great claims that you have made to me, that the hardships you say you underwent were not as great as you consider them, and that they are borne by you for your own benefit, if you do not make an obstacle of them; I think I have sufficiently proven this to you. But in regard to the present, in which you say your misfortunes still continue and in which you neither see nor discern the road to repose, I will respond, likewise confounding your opinions in that which you imagine.

"Later, in the time to come, if you want to believe me, just as the doctor after he has cured his patient gives him a diet to maintain his health and prevent a relapse, so I will give you the rule and way that lead to the true happiness that all human hearts must tend to, for there is no other. And first and foremost, because you do not know your condition, I will ask you a question[46] to make you know it. For from what I understand from you, you do not judge yourself content with that share you have of good fortune, and you think that many others abound in an excess of things you lack and have been deprived of. So I ask you if you know a man or woman—prince, princess, or other—more thoroughly filled with the favors of Fortune, whether in position, power, honors, or other noble things (I speak to you of worldly matters and omit from them the noble speculations of the mind) that you might have willingly changed your simple condition and way of life, the desire that you have and the love and pleasure of study you take and your solitary existence, to possess the care and burden of so many different affairs both of soul and of conscience, or the passion of greed, and all such emotions and even that your feminine and feeble body should be changed to a man's[47] in order to be transformed in conditions and everything else to that man or woman whom you account more blessed in Fortune's favors?"

Then I replied to the reverend lady. "Lady, why do you ask me this? Do you not know that greed holds so little sway over me that

---

[45] See *Advision* 186, n. XX/64–71.

[46] Reno and Dulac in *Advision* 186, n. XXI/14–27 suggest that this question was inspired by a line in II.4 of *La Consolacion*.

[47] This passage refers to the allegorical transformation of Christine into a man in *Mutacion de Fortune*; see I:12, lines 1325–08.

for all of Fortune's favors I would not have willingly exchanged my life for another's for all this wealth?"

"Oh fool! And how can it be that after such a judgment you think yourself unfortunate? For since your condition satisfies you better—that of a powerful and wealthy man would not make you abandon it—you thus consider yourself richer, which is to say happier, than the richest of men, in so far as his wealth is concerned. For since everything always inclines towards its perfection, if you thought the richest more perfect than you, you would have wanted your condition to be changed to his. And thus can you see that the bad or good that people experience comes to them through their beliefs and opinions and not through things.[48] For he is rich who covets nothing more, and he is poor who burns with desire. Dear friend, so have you not a bad case here? Now let the position God called you to suffice.

"And what you complain of, the burden of several relatives that you must bear, accept it in patience and do your duty; for it is all for your merit. And rejoice that it is good. And, as the psalmist says: 'Hope in God and do good, for He will never fail you.' Nature is sustained with little; he who lives by the necessities of nature is saved and he who lives by the excess of pleasures is lost and damned and shortens his days."[49]

III.22. Philosophy's consolation citing the Holy Scriptures as evidence

"But as you have not yet entirely traversed the sea of your pilgrimage, I will offer you the promised truth on the lesson of your life. You who long for happiness, if you wish to achieve it, come to me; I will open the way for you; notwithstanding that it may be fraught with trials, you can go there by no other road.

"Because of this among the other cruel pains to be borne it seems among you worldly creatures that unjustified injury and persecution received from your neighbors may be the hardest thing to bear patiently, I will base the beginning of our oration on what Saint Gregory says about our topic in *On Ezekiel*. 'All the good we do is nothing,' he says, 'if we do not bear patiently the injuries we receive from our neighbors.'[50] Of this Jesus Christ, who suffered more

---

[48] Reno and Dulac in *Advision* 187, n. XXI/42–43 trace this idea to *La Consolacion*.

[49] See *Advision* 187, n. XXI/50–52 for the corresponding passage (II.5) from *La Consolacion*.

[50] From the section on *paciencia* in *Manipulus florum*. All of the quotations from the Church fathers in III.22 come from this section. See *Advision* 187, n. XXII/10–13.

because of His own people than any other man would be able to suffer, gives us the example. But indeed Chrysostom speaks truth when
in *On Saint Paul's Epistle to the Hebrews* he says, 'There is nothing
which must create greater confusion to the persecutor who torments
another than to endure patiently and steadfastly his injuries and take
no vengeance against him in word or deed.'[51] Of this speaks also
Hugh of Saint Victor in the third book *Of the Soul.* 'Great virtue,' he
says, 'is his who is wounded if he spares him whom he might harm.
For the noblest victory a man might have is to spare a man he could
injure.'[52] And that the evil may often be the persecutors of the good
was not adverse to that which was said before when I told my
beloved Boethius that those of our profession wish to be hated by the
wicked, for since everything hates its opposite, will not the wicked
be participants in their wickedness?[53]

" 'Oh mortal man,' said Boethius, 'why seek beyond yourself for
the happiness that is seated within you? Ignorance deceives you. For
pure true happiness is having sovereignty over oneself. For man has
nothing as dear as himself, and Fortune cannot deprive him of that.
And so that you may know that in the things of Fortune one cannot
be happy, I tell you that happiness and well-being are the supreme
benefits of nature, and this is reason and understanding; and the sovereign good cannot be lost!'[54] These very words that I say to you I
likewise told my dear Boethius.

"Thus among yourselves use God's gifts and let these of Fortune
go, and learn how to master yourselves, and then it will not be so
burdensome for you to bear tribulations out of love of Him for whom
you shall do it.[55] For on this subject Gregory spoke in the fifth book
of his *Moralia*: 'If man's thought is directed attentively to God,
whatever is bitter in this life seems sweet and everything that afflicts
he considers repose.'[56]

"Again the blessed Gregory says, in *On Ezekiel*, 'God mixes His
punishments to us with His gifts so that whatever worldly things
were tempting us may seem bitter, so that in our spirits a fire of

---

[51] See *Advision* 187, n. XXII/14–18.
[52] See *Advision* 187, n. XXII/18–22.
[53] See *Advision* 187, n. XXII/24–27 for the possible inspiration of this passage in
La Consolacion I.4.
[54] See *Consolation*, II.4, 31. See Cropp 400 for a discussion of the corresponding
passage in *La Consolacion*.
[55] See *Advision* 187–88, n. XXII/37–40 for the passage (II.4) from *La
Consolacion*.
[56] See *Advision* 188, n. XXII/40–43.

loving patience may take flame which always encourages us to long for heaven, and thus He bites us delightfully, torments us sweetly, and afflicts us joyfully.'[57]

" 'Ah,' he says in the beginning of the *Moralia*, 'the blessed Job, when God allowed him to be stricken by the Enemy, the greater the voice of patience that he raised in his torments, the greater the arrows he threw back against his adversary; and even greater blows did he give him than he sustained.'[58]

" 'And in this,' he himself says 'the just thought is distinguished from the unjust, for the just in all conditions and all adversities bears witness to the praise of the Almighty and the unjust only grumble.'[59] And of this Saint Ambrose speaks in *On the Psalm, Beati immaculati*, 'In this you have the great virtue of patience if suffering from trials, you praise God's judgments, if you suffer illness, you give thanks. And in whatever state you are sorely afflicted, all the greater is your benefit.'[60]

"What might I still tell you about the noble virtue of patience? It is this above all which is the chief doorkeeper of paradise and without it there are no other virtues. Cassiodorus confirms this in *On the Psalms*. 'Patience,' he says, 'is the virtue that conquers all things, not only in combat but in suffering, not in grumbling but in giving thanks. It is the virtue that cleanses away all the filth of sensual pleasure and restores souls radiant to God.' "[61]

III.23. Philosophy teaches the disdain of worldly goods

"Concerning how much those among you so love the amassing of riches and how hard you work for these things, should I be silent? I will not be. For although my words might possibly penetrate your stubborn spirits very little, nevertheless do they not forestall the worthy ones concerning the evil, which our said friend Boethius speaks of in his book *On the Consolation*? And let us confirm them by the Holy Scriptures in the manner already begun. And consider the entry into these matters. 'Do you want,' he says, 'to amass wealth? You must take it away from someone. Do you desire honors? You will be scorned by the envious. Do you wish to climb above others? You will be in danger from those filled with hatred. If you rise in power, the fear of falling will never leave you. Do you

---

[57] See *Advision* 188, n. XXII/44–49.
[58] See *Advision* 188, n. XXII/50–54.
[59] See *Advision* 188, n. XXII/55–57.
[60] See *Advision* 188, n. XXII/57–62.
[61] See *Advision* 188, n. XXII/65–69.

long for fame? You must suffer greatly. You want pleasures? All who see you, the slave of your pleasures, will despise you; and thus you can see that your methods do not make man wealthy, which is to say satisfied.'[62]

"Hear more of his own words: 'Undoubtedly,' he says, 'riches do not satiate greed, which is insatiable, nor does power render the individual secure who by chains is imprisoned. And when power comes to the wicked, it does not make them good but reveals and demonstrates their wickedness. In view of which, you rejoice in desiring things that are not what you call them and that cannot be sufficiently condemned, for they are not true powers nor are they truly worthwhile, I can conclude then from all Fortune there is nothing that I should want or which naturally may be good since she never joins with the good and is not good to those she joins with.'[63]

"Aristotle quite agrees with this judgment in the book *Of Good and Bad Fortune* where he says that where the best mind and understanding is, is not always the best Fortune, and it often happens that where Fortune is propitious, there is not the greatest understanding.[64] That contradicts the arrogant who think well of themselves and believe that when Fortune favors them, it must be because of their great merit, knowledge, and value. But since experience of the opposite is often revealed to us, we see most of the virtuous and intelligent unfortunate in regard to worldly riches. For this reason, true is the Lombardian proverb which says: 'In the adventurous fool, there is no good sense.' Boethius claims, however, that 'ill fortune is more profitable than good because the good seems beneficial and so lies as in its favors there is no benefit. And the bad is true in that it shows by changing that it has no sure state. The good thus deceives, and the bad enlightens through the habit of sorrows.[65] And certainly, as he says, wealth has given many people a reputation for evil and malice.[66] These consequently believe there can be no other good fortune nor anything more worthy than having treasure, jewels, and great power. Oh base worldly honors and powers that you exalt among yourself to the heavens; you know not what power and true worth

[62] See *Consolation* III.8, 60 and 62 as noted in Cropp 401–03.
[63] See *Consolation* II.6, 39–40 as noted in Cropp 402–03.
[64] This book was wrongly attributed to Aristotle. *Advision* 188–89, n. XXIII/27–30 suggests that the reference may in fact come from *Faits et dits mémorables* (see note 50 for Book One).
[65] See *Consolation* II.8, 44 as noted in Cropp 403–04.
[66] See *Consolation* II.5, 33.

are! And that if wicked men ever had power over you, neither flood nor flames would be more disastrous.'[67]

" 'Alas, man, and if you look at your own body, you would find nothing more feeble; for the bite of a dog or a fly if it enters you, it sometimes kills you. And how can you, who are so proud, have power over another if it is not over the body or the affairs of Fortune?' But the heart which is free and strong through the guidance of reason, it is not possible for you to move by force." [68]

III.24. Wherein is said how, according to passages from the Holy Scripture, earthly prosperity is not to be valued

"And again concerning that God disapproves of the evil rich and that the simple should not be astonished if He allows the wealthy to have temporal possessions and agrees to the persecution of the virtuous, let us return to the Holy Scriptures. For concerning this, Bede speaks in *On the Epistle of Saint John*. 'Be not indignant,' he says, 'if the evil flourish in this world and if you, the servants of God, have to suffer. For it is not for the Christian religion to be exalted in this world but abased and oppressed. The wicked have nothing in heaven, nor have you anything in this world. And for this reason, in hope of the good you are striving to attain, whatever may happen to you in the course of this life you must rejoice in.'[69]

"And this Saint Gregory bears witness to in the fortieth homily on the Gospels, which says, 'The one whom God hates, He allows to have prosperity in this world; He also keeps the one He loves under the curb of sorrow.'[70] And of this my lord Saint Ambrose fully shows an example: when once he went through the country, and wished to take up lodging for the night at a hostel, so he called the host and, as was his custom, inquired after his fortunes; he told him that all his life he had flourished in honors and abounded in riches and had never fallen into hardship, disease, or any other trouble; rather things always came exactly as he wished. Then, having heard these things, Saint Ambrose departed and did not wish to stay even though it was night, and he said a continual succession of temporal good fortunes

---

[67] See *Consolation* II.6, 38 as noted in Cropp 404–05.

[68] See *Consolation* II.6, 38 as noted in Cropp 404–05.

[69] From the section on *tribulacio* in *Manipulus florum*. See *Advision* 189, n. XXIV/6–13.

[70] From the section on *tribulacio* in *Manipulus florum*. See *Advision* 189, n. XXIV/14–17.

is not a sign of being loved or chosen by God; rather, it is a sign of perpetual damnation.[71]

"Let Seneca come forward and speak his piece on our subject here in the eighty-seventh of his epistles. 'If you want,' he says, 'to have the true estimate of the man and know in what way or to what extent he is great, consider him perfectly naked. Take away his patrimony, take away his honors, and the other lies of Fortune and see him, if you can, not in the body but in the spirit; and there will you see how and in what way he is great, there will you know if he is great because of himself or another.' "[72]

III.25. The conclusion of matters previously discussed and more on this

"Have we not sufficiently proved that happiness lies not in riches and worldly honors? Then we must strive to find it; but since in this world it cannot be found, continuing still, we must talk about it. So it appears to be true enough what Boethius says. 'Things are not honors in and of themselves but because of the esteem and opinion of the people, who may give and take them away as they please. And since such honors can be unjustly bestowed, I conclude they are base.' 'Oh vanity,' he says, 'cast abroad on so many, you are nothing but a swelling of the ears! For we often see praised because of people's false opinion those who do not possess the good that is said to be there, and this cannot be without their great shame when they know they lack that for which they are praised. And if it is so, that the honorable man should be praised for his virtue, what does it matter to him inasmuch as he seeks not people's good opinion but the good of his own conscience? And if one thinks it is a fine thing to have fame, one considers ugly the one who has it not.' [73]

" 'What shall I say,' he says, 'about the pleasures of the body? When one seeks them, they give great pain; when one has them, they tax one with worry; when one has had them, they engender infirmities; and such are the wages of those who place their purpose there.'[74]

---

[71] This story about St. Ambrose is found in the Golden Legend. See Jacobius de Voragine 19–20. In the story, the innkeeper's hostel is destroyed soon after St. Ambrose leaves.

[72] From the section on *honor* in the *Manipulus florum*. See *Advision* 189, n. XXIV/28–34.

[73] See *Advision* 190, n. XXV/9–17 for the passage from *La Consolacion* that may have inspired Christine, as suggested by Cropp 406–07. See also *Consolation* III.6, 58.

[74] See *Consolation* III.7, 59 as noted in Cropp 407.

" 'So it is, then,' he says, 'that riches, honors, kingdoms, lordships, strength, beauty, and power do not bestow happiness.' For nothing is worthy of the name of happiness, as said before, if it is not eternal. And since such things are not, he who has them is not happy.'[75]

"But here is what he says later. 'Do you wish to know,' he says, 'the true happiness that feeds the soul and gives glory, renown, delight, and satisfaction? This is God and nothing else.'[76] As with the said book of Boethius I will prove it by his own mouth and the flowers that I have gathered from him and applied here to your purpose to make a sort of gracious chaplet with the sayings of the Holy Doctors to crown your book victorious at the end. Now put the roses from Holy Writ with our violets and let us strike out again against the arrogant ones of the world.

" 'You,' says St. Augustine, 'who so love the world, for what praise do you struggle? Is it not your greatest hope that you may be the world's friend? Alas and what good is that to which no one can come except through great improprieties? Mankind! Mankind! Let all these vanities perish, and turn to the only search that is glorious and perpetual.'[77] And what is this? This is the one God. 'Alas!' he says again in a letter, 'This world is more perilous when it appears sweet than when it appears harmful, most to be avoided when it most induces self-love.'[78]

"About this same subject he speaks again in *On the Epistle of Saint John*. 'The world,' he says, 'is full of sorrows, and see how everyone loves it! What would it be if it were peaceful? If it were beautiful, how you would depend upon it since when it is ugly and troubled you embrace it so strongly! And as you cannot withdraw your hand from the thorns, you would indeed gather flowers if they were there.'[79]

"Concerning this St. Gregory says in a homily. 'Here is the world,' he says, 'which is perfectly barren in itself. And yet it flowers

---

[75] *Advision* 190, n. XXV/22–26 suggests this section refers to arguments in *La Consolacion* III.8. See also *Consolation* III.8, 61–62.

[76] Cropp 408 suggests this passage refers to arguments in III.9. See also *Consolation* III.9, 63–67.

[77] This and the next two quotations from St. Augustine come from the section entitled *mundus* in *Manipulus florum*. For this quotation, see *Advision* 190, n. XXV/36–41.

[78] See *Advision* 190, n. XXV/41–44 for the original from the *Manipulus florum*.

[79] From the section entitled *mundus* in *Manipulus florum*. Thomas identifies the source as *Super Psalmos*, not, as Christine has it, *Super Iohannem*. See *Advision* 190, n. XXV/45–50.

in our hearts, everywhere dead, everywhere full of tears, everywhere in utter ruin. We are attacked on all sides; we are full of bitterness. And yet in our blind carnal thoughts and desires, we love this bitterness, we follow what is slipping away, we support ourselves on a thing that is falling, and yet when it falls we cannot hold to it without falling.'[80]

" 'But,' Saint Bernard says in his sermon, 'to whomever takes Jesus Christ to seem sweet, the world must necessarily seem bitter.' Again he says in *On the Canticles*, 'This world is full of thorns, they are in the earth, they are in your skin, and to live among these thorns and not be wounded, that is divine strength and not of our frailty.'[81]

"But of this Saint Gregory says in the twenty-third chapter of the *Moralia*, 'To the elect who are going to him, Our Lord has made the road harsh so that the ease of this life in the form of the sweetness of the road may not please them so much that they delight in traveling at length but quickly proceed to their day of rest, and that the road may not please them so that they may forget their own country, which is heaven.'[82]

"But here is what he says later: 'The spirits of the elect,' he says, 'who await the joys of paradise take heart and strength from adversities. For the greater the battle grows, the more they expect glorious victory. The desires of the elect profit so much that they are thus strengthened in trials just like the burning fire whose flame the wind beats down and yet causes to grow. And although it seems it should extinguish it, it strengthens it.' "[83]

III.26. More about this same topic

"Now we draw toward the end of our work, in which I wish to guide you to the good use of your senses, which is to say, to the end of the true happiness that you must hold to, as we have sufficiently demonstrated with many worthy proofs what the false felicities are. Although the desire for earthly things is enticing, it is not this; rather it is that which has in itself perfection and can desire nothing more:

---

[80] From the section entitled *mundus* in *Manipulus florum*. See *Advision* 190, n. XXV/51–58.

[81] These two quotations come from the section entitled *mundus* in *Manipulus florum*. See *Advision* 190, n. XXV/59–60 and 191, n. XV/61–64.

[82] From the section entitled *tribulacio* in *Manipulus florum*. See *Advision* 191, n. XXV/65–70.

[83] From the section entitled *tribulacio* in *Manipulus florum*. See *Advision* 191, n. XXV/71–77.

this is God, as is said, for one can think of nothing better than He. His goodness, then, must be perfect, for otherwise (Boethius says this, and it is true) He would not be supreme among the other blessings.[84] 'Thus we have said,' Boethius says, and we also concur with him, 'that happiness is the true sovereign good. And you see that man is blessed when he has happiness, and if happiness is God: then man is God when he has happiness. For in the same way that those who have righteousness are righteous and those who have wisdom are wise, so those who have divinity are gods, and he who has happiness is God. Thus all the blessed are God, but there is only one God by nature, and He is many by participation.'[85] These words are the very text of the said book of Boethius in *Consolation*.

"Now we have found this blessed felicity which we should desire. But what shall we make of this blessed happiness? Does it promise us anything? Let Saint Gregory come in his homily and tell us. See it here. 'If we consider well the nature and greatness of the things we are promised in heaven, we will consider small price everything we might have on earth, for all earthly substance compared with the supreme happiness is to us more a burden than a help. The temporal life compared with the eternal life is more death than life because the defect of our daily corruption is only a long drawn-out death. But who this is, who might be able to tell, or understanding comprehend, how mighty are the joys of that supreme city: to be eternally present in the company of angels with the blessed souls, to be present in the glory of Our Creator, to see the face of God and the Blessed Trinity face to face, to gaze upon His incomprehensible light, never to fear death, to enjoy the gift of perpetuity?'[86]

"Of this Blessed Trinity let us speak a little for the sake of greater efficacy following the sayings of the Holy Doctors. And in it I want your work to be finished which may grant you the grace that so it may be at the end of your life. But how will you dare to begin to meditate upon it, you poor miserable creature? For Saint Augustine says in the *Book of the Trinity* that, 'all the host of human thought is not strong enough to fix itself in this excellent undying light, if not well purified by the justice of faith.'[87] But to

---

[84] See *Consolation* III.10, 68–71 for the arguments in this section. For the passage in *La Consolacion*, identified by Cropp 408, see *Advision* 191, n. XXVI/8–10.

[85] See *Consolation* III.10, 70–71; Cropp 408–09.

[86] From the section entitled *gloria eterna* in *Manipulus florum*. See *Advision* 191, n. XXVI/20–34.

[87] From the section entitled *fides sive fidelitas* in *Manipulus florum*. *Advision* 192, n. XXVI/39–42.

declare it to you more subtly is unnecessary. For Saint Augustine says in this aforementioned book that 'one cannot stray more perilously elsewhere, nor can one search more laboriously for anything, nor can one find anything more advantageous than the Blessed Trinity of Father, Son, and Holy Spirit in the union of divine being.'[88]

"But of this he says even in the *The Book of Our Savior's Words* speaking against Arius. 'We see,' he said, 'the sun in the sky moving, shining, and radiating heat; fire also possesses these three things: movement, light, and heat. If you can then,' he said, 'false Arius, divide one quality from another, either in the fire or in the sun, and then so divide the Trinity.'[89]

"And therefore, as St. Bernard says in a sermon, 'Too much inquiry into the Holy Trinity is untoward curiosity, to firmly uphold and believe in the Trinity just as the Church and the Catholic faith repute it to be, that is surety.'[90]

" 'There are,' Saint Augustine says in a sermon, 'several trinities, that is, the trinity that made us, the trinity that unmakes us, and the trinity that remakes us. The trinity that made us is the eternal Trinity—Father, Son, and Holy Spirit. The trinity that unmakes us, this is a miserable trinity. What is it? It is impotence, ignorance, and concupiscence. Through this miserable trinity is unmade our reasonable trinity—memory, understanding, and will. For when our soul falls away from the eternal Trinity, the memory falls into impotence, the understanding into ignorance, and will into concupiscence. The trinity that remakes us is a beneficial trinity: Faith, Hope, and Charity—faith in the articles, in the commandments, and in the sacraments; hope of pardon, of grace, and of glory; charity from the pure heart, from the good conscience, and from the firm faith.'[91]

"But in truth, the Blessed Trinity, just as it is, is true happiness, alone and supreme, and nothing else is rightfully the end and goal of

---

[88] From the section entitled *trinitas* in *Manipulus florum*. See *Advision* 192, n. XXVI/43–47.

[89] From the section entitled *trinitas* in *Manipulus florum*. See *Advision* 192, n. XXVI/48–53.

[90] From the section entitled *trinitas* in *Manipulus florum*. See *Advision* 192, n. XXVI/54–57.

[91] From the section entitled *trinitas* in *Manipulus florum*. See *Advision* 192, n. XXVI/58–71. Reno and Dulac note that the *Manipulus florum* attributes this quotation to St. Bernard not Augustine.

every human being, to which happiness wishes to lead you—this Blessed Trinity, one God alone, reigning forever and ever."[92]

III.27. Christine replies to Philosophy and thanks her in the person of Theology

Then the reverend lady fell silent, and I began to speak as follows: "Oh most sovereign administratress of nourishment and medicinal restorative, who not only heals the invalid wounded by sorrow but gives her life, strength, and vigor by the sweet ointment and liquor of your comfort, you, Philosophy, the repository and substance of all the other sciences, which are your appendages, I see that what they say about you is true just as Saint Augustine relates. For you are all sciences, and to those you love you show yourself as it pleases you, depending on how they wish to search for you. To me, a simple person, by your noble grace, you reveal yourself in the form of Holy Theology to nourish my ignorant spirit most wholesomely for my salvation. Have you not treated me as your handmaiden, but better than you promised, that is, have you not served me with your most advantageous and worthy dishes which come from the table of God the Father, for which I thank God who is you and you in Him more than I would know how to express? Truly you are all sciences.[93] You are true physics, which is to say theology, inasmuch as you are from God, for all the causes of all of nature are in God the Creator. You are ethics because the good and honorable life that you lecture and teach is loving what should be loved, which is God and one's neighbor; and that, Theology, you reveal in the sciences of physics and ethics. You are logic because you reveal the light and truth of the just soul. You are politics because you teach the virtuous life, for no city is better protected than by the foundation and bond of the faith and by the firm agreement to love the common good, which is very true and supreme, it is God of whom you speak in the science in which you have revealed yourself to me, that is, theology. Oh Theology, how I long to praise in you, Lady, the sovereign philosophy, I know that when man learns apart from you, if it is harmful to him he knows the truth of it by you, if it is beneficial for him, you also show it to him and

---

[92] Reno and Dulac in *Advision* 192, n. XXVI/72–75 identify this conclusion as a summary of III.12 of *La Consolacion*.

[93] *Advision* 192–93, n. XXVII/17–27 notes this closing praise of Theology is taken, almost word for word, from a quotation from Augustine's *De doctrina cristiana* found under the rubric *Scriptura sacra* in the *Manipulus florum*.

so elsewhere he will have little to learn.[94] If in you he does not trust, all will be wasted time and ignorance, for you are true wisdom; no other is it than you, in whom is found what cannot be elsewhere—true happiness. And Saint Gregory bears witness to this in the prologue to the *Moralia*, that 'you make known that with which you can feed the humble (and of this my personal experience confirms it to me) and keep secret that with which you can seize the greatest minds in great admiration. For you are like a river that seems so shallow a lamb can step into it and is so deep an elephant can swim in it. Wondrous is your river, Holy Theology, which seems so shallow to a lamb—that means a good and simple person who depends on it—and so deep to a proud elephant—or the highest minds that hardly know you and do not fully understand you.'[95] And therefore the blessed Saint Jerome speaks well in the letter to his good, devoted virgin Demetrias. 'Use,' he says, 'Theology's lesson in place of a mirror to correct what is ugly in you, and preserve what is beautiful in you, and make yourself more beautiful. For you, Holy Theology, have a mirror that reveals impurities and teaches their purification.'[96]

"Of you and once again in your praise, says the blessed Doctor Saint Jerome, who loved you so dearly, that 'Just as the shadows of night do not darken the brilliance of the stars of heaven, so no worldly inequity can darken the souls which are supported in the firmament of you, Holy Theology.'[97] Oh Lady, Holy Theology, you affirmed for me what the Blessed Saint Gregory, your Doctor, said about you in the first book of the *Moralia*—that 'Your doctrine and the Holy Scripture sometimes are meat to us, sometimes drink. In the most obscure places, there it is meat to us, for when we explicate it, it is the meat that we chew, and when we understand it, it is like meat that we swallow. But in the places where it is most clear, it is drink to us because when there is no need of exposition, we drink it just as we find it.'[98]

"Lady, what can I say about you and the good that you have done me with the holy foods of your feast, which have satisfied me and

---

[94] In *Advision* 193, n. XXVII/29–34, Reno and Dulac note this quotation, from Augustine's *De doctrina cristiana*, is found under *Scriptura sacra* in the *Manipulus florum*.

[95] From the section entitled *Scriptura sacra* in the *Manipulus florum*. The remaining quotations from the Church fathers in III.27 also come from *Scriptura sacra*. For the original of this passage, see *Advision* 193, n. XXVII/34–45.

[96] See *Advision* 193, n. XXVII/45–50.

[97] See *Advision* 193, n. XXVII/51–55.

[98] See *Advision* 193, n. XXVII/57–64.

led me to know the ignorance of my misunderstanding, through which I know my error because you have determined it for me? So I say that you, Holy Theology and divinity, you are a most rich meat which contains in yourself all delights, just like the manna that rained for the Jews from heaven, which tasted in everyone's mouth as he or she wished it."[99]

Thus I take leave of my vision, which I have divided as if by the three different properties of three precious stones. The first is in the form of the diamond, which is hard and cutting, and although it may be bright outside of the setting, when it is set and bound in gold, it seems dark and brown; and yet its virtue, which is exceedingly great, does not diminish. The second is the cameo in which several faces and different figures are printed; and its base is brown and the imprint white. The third is like the precious ruby—bright, radiant, and unclouded—which has the property of pleasing one more the more one gazes upon it.[100]

Here ends the book of Christine's *Vision*
Deo Gracias

---

[99] See Exod. 16:14–27.

[100] See Liliane Dulac. "Travail allégorique et ruptures du sens chez Christine de Pizan: *L'Epistre Othéa*" in *Continuités et ruptures dans l'histoire et la littérature: Colloque Franco-Polonais, 9–4 février 1987 Montpellier*, ed. Michèle Weil and Dominique Triaire (Paris: Champion-Slatkine, 1988) 24–32. There she suggests that the three jewels might refer to the three levels of allegorical meaning suggested in Christine's preface.

Interpretive Essay

Glenda McLeod

The last of Christine de Pizan's major allegorical texts, the *Vision* can be especially puzzling to modern readers. As it traces Christine's journey from Chaos and uncertainty to Dame Philosophy and eternal verity, it blends political and intellectual commentary with a woman author's consideration of her life and role. As usual for medieval allegories, the problem lies in bringing these disparate strands of text together. To do so, it is helpful to consider the context in which Christine wrote her vision.

Composed in 1405–1406, the *Vision* came at a critical juncture in the life of both Christine and France. As an author, Christine was effecting a significant change in style. She had written five long allegories in the five to six preceding years (*The Epistle of Othea, The Mutation of Fortune, The City of Ladies, The Book of Three Virtues,* and *The Long Road of Learning*) as well as contributing to an important literary debate on the French allegory, the *Romance of the Rose*. In the years after *Vision*'s composition, she addressed many of the same themes but in other forms, notably the public epistle, learned treatise, book of instruction, and public commentary.[1]

In 1405 France also found itself at a crossroads. Beginning with his first psychotic episode in 1392, intermittent insanity had incapacitated its king, Charles VI, and often left his kingdom virtually without leadership. In the ensuing vacuum, Charles' brother, uncles, and cousin schemed for power and control. As detailed in Bernard Guenée's study, the main rivalry pitted supporters of the King's brother, the Duke of Orleans, against supporters of the King's cousin, the Duke of Burgundy. In August 1405, the year of the *Vision*'s composition, armed forces from both houses were fighting

---

[1] For the dates and dedications to Christine's works, see Laidlaw, "Christine and the Manuscript Tradition" 243–45 and *Advision* 180, n. X/50–55. Among those written after the *Vision* are *Epistre de la prison de vie humaine, Lamentacion sur les maux de la France, Livre de la paix, Livre des fais d'ames et de chevalerie,* and *Livre du corps de policie.*

around a besieged Paris, squabbling over control of the capital and the government. While a fragile peace was established later in October, it proved unlasting. The *Vision* records Christine's response to this critical juncture; as several scholars have argued, she employs the allegorical form one last time not only to present her advice to the rulers of France but also to validate her authority to speak in her own voice on this crisis.[2]

The connection between these two concerns, however, is not always easy to discern. Book I clearly deals with the political crisis but has little to say about the narrator. Book II has more to say on the narrator but, apart from comments on the factionalism of France, little to say on the political struggle. Book III seems to focus exclusively on the narrator. Yet the book's presentation of Christine's evolution as a writer offers a key to France's political quandary: this narrator (and her spiritual and intellectual itinerary) are *exempla* for her audience's emulation. In *The City of Ladies* Christine had similarly used her allegorical narrative to model a psychological process, there of a woman battling the destructive influence of misogynistic authority.[3] In the *Vision*, Christine likewise models a reorientation to wisdom through misfortune and crisis for the leaders of France. While writing the story of her education, she is also tracing a path for political renewal. As Christine Reno and Liliane Dulac have pointed out, the narrator's life, her experiences, and her quest represent "une expérience morale et intellectuelle implicitement proposée en modèle" ("a moral and intellectual experience implicitly proposed as a model") (*Advision* xxiii, translation my own).

In applying such political commentary to a personal dream vision, Christine is following a pattern common in fifteenth-century French literature, as shown in Marchello-Nizia's study of the genre. Christine's vision, however, as Reno and Dulac have noted, is unusual for the prominence of its narrator and the wealth of its autobiographical detail (*Advision* xxiii). As Dulac has pointed out, this Christine narrator also differs from her earlier incarnations by being

---

2   Christine's use of autobiographical narrative as a justification for political commentary in the *Vision* was first discussed in Reno, "Self and Society". See also *Advision* xxiii–xxiv and, for another approach to this interrelationship with special attention to gender issues, Brown-Grant, *Christine de Pizan and the Moral Defence of Women* 89–127 and Paupert," 'La Narracion de mes aventures' " 70–71.

3   See Glenda McLeod, *Virtue and Venom: Catalogs of Women from Antiquity to the Renaissance* (Ann Arbor: University of Michigan Press, 1991) especially 118–36.

the "heroine" rather than merely the "witness" of this book's adventure (Thèmes et variations" 83). Thus, while the *Vision* is not simply an autobiography in the modern sense of the term, as several scholars have suggested,[4] the narrator's importance to the book's unity and political message and the clear links between the narrator and Christine the writer make the Christine protagonist particularly intriguing and important.[5] She has often been the focus of critical commentary, beginning with the book's first editor, Sister Mary Towner, who interpreted the vision as Christine's ascent from material to spiritual concerns (47). Later Margaret Slattery Durley argued the three books showed the itinerary of Christine's life—from the court to the university to the cloister—as a process mediated through the "mother" figures of the three Crowned Ladies. However, when considering the evolution of the narrative voice as an instrument of political, philosophical, and theological commentary, it is useful to keep in mind the professional ascent Christine also enacts in this work, an ascent suggested by three opening self-referential *exempla*.

In the first paragraph of her *Vision*, Christine tells her audience, "I am not Nebuchadnezzar, Scipio, or Joseph, but the secrets of the Almighty are not denied the truly simple" (I.1). Her assertion conforms to the familiar humility *topos* often used by medieval writers, but as usual with medieval women writers, the rhetorical connotations

---

[4]   See, for example, *Advision* xvii–xxiv; chapter three of Brown-Grant, *Christine de Pizan and the Moral Defence of Women*; and Krueger 16. However, Blumenfeld-Kosinski, "Christine de Pizan et L'AutoBiographie Féminine;" Breaulieu; Le Brun-Gouanvic; Paupert, "Christine et Boèce;" and Skemp have argued that Christine's construction of a self-portrait does conform to widely accepted understandings of autobiography. Perhaps the most sensible approach to this question can be found in Dulac and Reno, "The *Livre de l'advision Cristine*" which reviews the different claims made for *Advision*'s genre and concludes that autobiographical and political aspects are intertwined.

[5]   On the subject of Christine's authorization of her role as a writer in this and other works, see, for example, Dulac, "La figure de l'écrivain dans quelques traités en prose de Christine de Pizan" in *Figures de l'Écrivain au Moyen Age: Actes du Colloque du Centre d'Études Médiévales de l'Université de Picardie, Amiens 18–20 mars 1988*. Ed. Danielle Buschinger. (Goppingen: Kümmerle Verlag, 1991) 113–23; Huot; Brownlee, "Le projet «Autobiographique» de Christine de Pizan" and "Widowhood, Sexuality, and Gender in Christine de Pizan;" Semple, "The Consolation of a Woman Writer;" and Chance, "Speaking in *propria persona*". Paupert's " 'La Narracion de mes aventures' " argues that the *Vision* crowns a long process of self-education and a quest for identity throughout Christine's work. She concludes, as I do from other evidence, that Christine uses the autobiography as a justification and legitimation of her claim to be an *auctor*.

are far from humble.[6] Its echo of Canto II of Dante's *Inferno* elevates rather than limits Christine's literary ambitions. Moreover, as Benjamen Semple has demonstrated, Christine's identification as one of the "simple" is itself a type of elevation ("The Critique of Knowledge as Power" 125–26), one drawing from the Biblical motif bestowing grace on the least likely recipient.[7]

Perhaps more interesting, however, claiming authority by declaring inadequacy as well as defining who Christine is by stating who she *isn't* also characterizes the statement as antiphrastic. *Antiphrasis*, a rhetorical figure in which one states the opposite of one's meaning, receives particular attention in the preface to the *Vision* as well as in the opening of the *City of Ladies* (Richards, *City of Ladies* 7; Brown-Grant, *City of Ladies* 8). It was usually classified as a technique of allegory in classical and medieval rhetorics and was often associated with negation.[8] In the *Ad Herennium*, an immensely popular rhetorical text, several of the examples discussed under allegory would be, by Christine's definition, antiphrastic, as, for example, calling "a spendthrift and voluptuary frugal and thrifty;" moreover, the discussion extends antiphrastic description to the use of specifically named *exempla* as in Christine's opening identification.[9] This tri-partite identification by opposites, consistent with allegorical form, invites us to ponder exactly who and what the narrator is. If she is not Nebuchadnezzar, Scipio, or Joseph, who are the models? Following the statement antiphrastically, that is by seeking the opposites of these characters in their respective texts, we can arrive at three fruitful possibilities: not the mad King Nebuchadnezzar but his courtier and advisor, the prophet Daniel; not the author and political exile Scipio but his scholarly and philosophic commentator Macrobius; and finally not the son Joseph, whose life and dreams divided his

6   On this topic, see also Semple, "The Consolation of a Woman Writer" 46. On the general use of this *topos* by medieval women writers see Joan Ferrante, "Public Postures and Private Maneuvers: Roles Medieval Women Play" in *Women and Power in the Middle Ages*, eds. Mary Erler and Maryanne Kowaleski (Athens, Ga: University of Georgia Press, 1988) 213–29.
7   Christ's application of this Biblical motif to himself can be found in Matt. 21:42. On the reversal of apparent values in *Vision*, see Brown-Grant, *Christine de Pizan and the Moral Defence of Women* 116–18.
8   See Rollinson 19 and 116. One ancient Greek rhetorician of the first century BC, Trypho, explicitly specifies that in presenting the opposite by the opposite, *antiphrasis* often expresses the opposite by negation. See Spengel, *Rhetores Graeci*, Vol. 3. 1853–56 (Frankfurt, 1966) 204, 3–18.
9   See *Ad C. Herennium: De Ratione Dicendi*, transl. Harry Caplan. Loeb Classical Library (Cambridge, Mass: Harvard University Press, 1964) 345–47.

family, but the father Jacob, whose dreams and experiences laid the foundation for Israel's national identity.[10]

While not the only authoritative figures behind Christine's text, this series provides what none of the others do alone: a general, over-arching insight into both the narrator's evolution as a writer/thinker and an understanding of what medieval commentators would call Christine's *modus tractandi* or mode of proceeding, the rhetorical and stylistic features (such as a book's organization) that help pro-mote and realize its didactic qualities. In Book I, Daniel governs a discussion of royal politics in the voice of an apocalyptic prophet; in Book II, Macrobius points to a consideration of the methods of philosophical inquiry conducted by a scholarly commentator; in Book III, Jacob prepares us for a personal tale of exile, suffering and redemption applied to the broader problems of the sufferer's people.

This three-part division reflects the influence not only of Dante's *Divine Comedy* but also of Petrarch's autobiographical *Secretum*, which, like the *Vision,* is organized into three parts that proceed through dialogue. In Petrarch's case, the conversation in the presence of Truth occurs between himself and St. Augustine rather than three interlocutors as in the *Vision.* However, both authors mix a literary model of consolation (Boethius' *Consolation of Philosophy*) with aspects of St. Augustine's *Confessions.* Both also inherit Augustine's Neo-Platonic slant, particularly in the importance accorded desire and will in philosophical inquiry. Like Petrarch, Christine revisits, challenges, and upholds previous works, accords herself equal status with other writers she cites and explores, and adopts *Confessions'* innovations as an intellectual autobiography. Like Petrarch, she also insists on the morally efficacious powers of books, particularly the books of the ancients,[11] and speculates on her literary legacy, although she is less wary of the worth of literary glory than Petrarch, for whom literary ambition constitutes a major temptation and theme. The last difference suggests a more central divergence between the two: Petrarch's *Secretum* is subtitled "A private conversation," but

---

[10] Other male models for Christine also appear in the *Vision.* See Blumenfeld–Kosinski, "Christine de Pizan et L'AutoBiographie Féminine" 23–24.

[11] For a discussion of the *Secretum* as a reading of Augustine's texts, see Quillen especially 190–92, 218. A discussion of the *Secretum* as an exploration and ques-tioning of the Humanist approach to the texts of the ancients can also be found in Quillen's introduction to her translation of *The Secret*; see Petrarch 26–43. On the influence of Petrarch in Christine's work see Walters, "The 'Humanist Saint' "and Le Brun-Gouanvic, "Christine de Pizan et l'édification" *Études françaises* 37(2001): 51–66.

the *Vision* seems intended for a public audience, even though only three manuscripts exist today. It does not end, as the *Secretum* does, in dialogue form. A single, firm and positive voice proposes a solution to Christine's dilemma. Like Dante, Christine reveals sources of absolute truth at the end and, like Dante's narrator, hers must grow in stature, understanding, and status to do so.

Christine manages this transformation partly by crafting a narrator who assumes different authorial roles with increasing responsibility and authority as the three examples of Daniel, Macrobius, and Jacob suggest. Libera's title for Christine in Book I, "antygraph," was often applied to a sovereign's secretary, but it also places her at the lowest level of an authorial hierarchy well defined by the scholastic community in relation first to Scripture, then to pagan writers, and finally by the fifteenth century—at times playfully, at times seriously—to living authors.[12] Each role was based on the author's degree of authority and responsibility for the text. The highest level, the *auctor*, was usually reserved for writers of antiquity and carried the greatest responsibility. The others (in descending levels of independence) included commentator, compiler, and scribe (Minnis 94). Both Daniel and Macrobius represent levels at which authority is not personally grounded. In medieval exegesis, a prophet, like Daniel, was traditionally seen as a "scribe" of God, the true *auctor* (Minnis 101–02). Similarly, the Christine narrator is Dame Libera's *antygraph*, a neologism from the Latin for scribe.[13] While a commentator such as Macrobius contributes his own explanations of a text, the focus is still on the words of others. So with Dame Opinion, the narrator in Book II interprets various texts and commentaries, including Christine's own.

These first two roles split voice and authority between scribe and author or commentator and author, but in Book III the narrator attains the summit of the authorial hierarchy as an *auctor*. Medieval commentators described the *auctor* as one who "writes *de suo* but draws upon the statements of other men to support his own views" (Minnis 95). Here the model is Jacob, whose story, experiences, and connections to allegory have many ties with Christine's self-presentation in

---

[12] For a discussion of the development and application of this theory see Minnis. For a discussion of Christine's choice of the word *antygraph*, see Reno and Dulac, "The *Livre de l'advision-Christine*" 213, n. 29.

[13] For a discussion of the word *antigraph* in Christine's work see *Advision* 147, n. V/11–VI/11, which points out that by calling herself a "scribe," Christine follows a tradition also followed by Dante. For other views, see Laennec.

Book III. Jacob was famed as a liar and teller of tales, and his lie to
his father Isaac became an occasion for St. Augustine's expounding
on the nature of personal history as sacred allegory in *Contra mendacium*, a link that Christine, following Dante, extends from the treatment of Biblical figures to her contemporary, personal history.[14] His
exiles made him early on a model of the Christian *viator*, a role
Christine also follows in her pilgrimages. His dream of the ladder
often represents the mystical ascent of the soul to union with God, an
ascent realized in Book III which opens with the image of Christine
climbing a stairs and closes with her identification with God. Finally,
his personal tribulations – especially his wrestling bout with an angel –
often made him a type of redeemed Israel, in the same way that
Christine's struggles with the lessons of Providence position her as a
model for a redeemed France. In his story, theme, and associations
with problems of literary and social authority, Jacob sets the stage for
Book III's presentation of the narrator's position, journey, and authorial role as well as its linkage via allegory to larger themes.

In making this journey from scribe to author, the narrator also
traces an itinerary from fragmentation to integration with obvious
applications for a society riven by civil strife.[15] The fragmentation
of the narrative voice across several characters in Books I and II is
an inner correlative of the political and cultural diffusions Books I
and II attack. By contrast, in Book III, where the narrator's quest
ends in the unity and completion of the Trinity, the third *exemplum*
evokes a drama of reintegration and salvation, a process of ongoing
re-description made necessary, even possible, by the experience of
suffering and loss. This process of re-description reintegrates the
author and guide with the voice of the protagonist, who is painstak-
ingly reconstituted as a female *auctor*. Her quest for a personal

---

[14] In *Contra mendacium*, Augustine sees Jacob's disguise of goatskins as prefigur-
ing allegorically Christ's bearing the sins of others; similarly, his appropriation
of Esau's birthright is allegorically interpreted as the passing of God's choice to
the Christian Church. Such allegorical statements cannot lie, Augustine maintains in X.24 and XII.26–XIII.28, because their significance is true. Thus
Augustine maintains that while Jacob is lying with the intent to deceive, the lie
itself falls under the providential ordering of God, for whom history is a form of
divine allegory. Rollinson 62–63 discusses this explication. Reeves 34–40 discusses Dante's important modification that Christine also adapts: the view of the
author's personal and private history as divine allegory.
[15] Brown–Grant, *Christine de Pizan and the Moral Defence of Women* 93–100 discusses at length how the preface to the *Vision* sets up an interrelationship
between the individual and society.

identity finds its highest realization not in a discovery of its uniqueness but in its self-discovery as an expression of the divine will that underwrites, informs, and shapes creation. This reintegration helps validate Christine's authority to dispense advice to the princes, grounding her authority in her faith and her "readings" of her personal experiences as providential ordering, readings formed by her familiarity with the methods and texts of written authority. She thus models a process of reintegration for the rulers of the realm, becoming, like Jacob, a foreshadowing of the savior whose arrival is predicted by Dame Libera in I.19 and I.20 and Dame Opinion in II.22.

The Dantesque metaphor that united this narrative and the three *exempla*—life as a journey—casts the Christine protagonist as an exile, a "foreign traveler" (III.1).[16] The wandering sojourner especially haunts Book III, contextualized by the story of Jacob, whose last exile to Egypt sets the stage for Exodus' epic exile and return. However, the author Christine also resembles Daniel, an exile at a foreign court, gingerly administering prophecy to an intermittently mad king,[17] while Macrobius wrote of Scipio Africanus Major's self-exile from Rome and life as an exile from man's true home. Throughout, exile implies endurance, fragmentation, factionalism: a loss of autonomy that threatens to strip life of meaning. In the highly charged atmosphere of 1405, these nuances carried personal, political and cultural overtones. All three aspects intertwine across the *Vision*, but Christine begins appropriately enough with the world as Chaos and the voice of an apocalyptic prophet. She begins, then, as a Daniel come to judgment.

Book One: The Prophet and the Scribe

As the first of her three self-referential figures, Daniel not only characterizes the authorial stance of Book I but also indicates themes that will run the course of the book. The description of Chaos, which Brown-Grant identifies as a "threshold image," implicitly refers to several passages from Daniel (*"L'Avision-Christine:* Autobiographical Narrative or Mirror for the Prince?" 97). In his height and span over three realms of creation, Chaos recalls Nebuchadnezzar's dream of the

---

16 For a discussion of this theme in Christine's poetry, see Cerquiglini.
17 This connection between Charles VI and Nebuchadnezzar was not uncommon. See *Advision* xiv, n. 17 and Millet 30.

composite statue (Dan. 2:31–37), which, as in Dante's *Inferno* Canto XIV, suggests historical regression and the fickleness and unreliability of the material world. These nuances reappear in Libera's descriptions of history, as well as Dame Opinion's characterizations of human intelligence, and Philosophy's answer to the instability and misfortune in Christine's life.

The description of the humans cooked within the furnace of Chaos' mouth points to the fiery furnace testing Shadrach, Meshach and Abednego's spiritual purity (Dan. 3). The fire—an image of trial, tribulation, but also purification—occurs in all three books: in Book I's destructive fires sweeping across France, in Book II's alchemical fires destructive of human reason, and in Book III's purging (and finally redemptive) fires of God the goldsmith (Brown-Grant, "*L' Avision-Christine:* Autobiographical Narrative or Mirror for the Prince?" 102, 106). All invoke the often mutually inclusive processes of creation, destruction, and purgation, which are most profoundly explicated in Dame Philosophy's characterization of the narrator's hardships as instruments of education and transformation.

The feeding of Chaos by Nature introduces the importance of nurture in the *Vision* and evokes the feeding references in Daniel, which begins with a food test comparing systems of education. Daniel abstains from the rich fare at court for a religiously proper diet of water and vegetables (Dan. 1), and, after a period of trial, proves the diet superior to Babylonian fare by his superior wisdom and insight. A similar connection between food and education runs throughout the *Vision*, partly in imitation of Boethius' *Consolation of Philosophy*. In Book I the dynamic and reciprocal nature of nurture is highlighted: when properly functioning, Libera nourishes her children and is nourished by them. False nourishment (and instruction) are evoked by the vision of the woman inserting lead in her mouth in I.18, a creative rewriting of a prophecy from Zechariah (*Advision* 157, n. XVIII/9–19). In Book III, references to Christine's ingestion of Philosophy's instruction as well as her description of life as "sober widow's fare" clearly recall the opening pattern from Daniel, for this nourishment serves as a metaphor not only for education but also (through its final association with the Eucharist) for transformation.

Finally Chaos' location by a stream recalls Daniel's vision on the banks of the Tigris predicting a universal time of retribution and a universal savior (Dan. 11–12). These themes evoke France's political crisis in 1405–1406 and Christine's hopes for its resolution. The same narrative arc of retribution and salvation marks Libera's discussion which, much like Daniel's vision, establishes the prophetic significance of history as an expression of God's will.

While Book I has often been described as an allegorical history of France, that history is cited to convey this apocalyptic warning. As in the closing vision of Daniel, Libera's account presents history from both the human perspective of gain and loss and the divine one of providential order. An outer story concerns, at least on the literal level, the narrator: her birth, her travels to France, her ongoing journey, and her relationship with Dame Libera, whose scribe she becomes. The inner story consists of Dame Libera's recitation, which the Christine narrator obediently transcribes. A brief history of France traces the kingdom back to the Trojans. A discussion of the first Christian king Clovis is immediately followed by a description of his degenerate Merovingean descendents, ruled by Fraud, Lust, and Avarice. The same pattern of rise and fall characterizes the story of Charlemagne and his descendants and in more recent history the Jacquerie rebellion, the felicitous reign of Charles V, and the ill-fated history of Charles' sons.

Christine's chronology is not accurate, but chronology is not so much the point as is matching adversity and prosperity with public vice and virtue. When chapters I.15–16 implicitly compare present history with Libera's recently evoked past, a moral causation underlies this decline: Reason, Justice, and Chivalry are held prisoner by Fraud, Lust, and Avarice. Throughout prophecies of catastrophe and hopes for a savior in chapters I.17–26, Libera presents misfortune as proof of moral failure. The last reference to Daniel, the feast of Belshazzar, explicitly warns the proud and arrogant leaders of the land while Libera's hope, that her children will heed her as the King of Ninevah heeded Jonah, presents prophecy as potentially remedial.

This mixture of threat and consolation, voiced in the prophet's double-edged tone, addresses the 1405's spreading political crisis. Indeed, Christine may well be making common cause with Jean Gerson, Chancellor of the University of Paris and one of her allies from the *querelle de la rose*, whose sermon, *Vivat Rex*, she often appears to follow.[18] If so, the choice of Daniel is an especially appropriate one since medieval commentators often equated the mode of prophecy with the mode of preaching (Minnis 136–37).

[18]   *Vivat Rex* (Gerson 7:1137–185) was delivered to the royal court on Nov. 7, 1405. Also cited in *Advision* xiv, n. 16 and Willard, *Christine de Pizan: Her Life and Works* 156–57.

While it provides a powerful vehicle for political commentary, the choice of Daniel also directs our attention to the author's role in the French court.[19] Christine focuses on the interaction between Daniel and Nebuchadnezzar in two ways: as in I.17, she sometimes directly applies Nebuchadnezzar's visions to France (and by interpreting them through Libera presents herself as a Daniel). She also uses Daniel's situation to characterize the French court and her position. Nebuchadnezzar's madness evokes Charles VI's (I.24) while the ill-fated feast of Belshazzar implicitly evokes the corruption of those who have assumed power in Charles' illness (I.27). In a regime dogged by madness and corruption, the author is characterized as a Daniel: a prophet and interpreter from another land serving a stricken king, who, though laid low, is not inured to truth nor incapable of being God's tool (see I.26). From a purely social point of view, the identification with Daniel celebrates Christine's promotion through merit rather than birth or inheritance; however, she is not only prophet and interpreter. She is an exile and isolated courtier as well, endangered by envy but often drawing her power and discernment from her position outside usual sources of influence. Like the diplomatic outsider Daniel, Christine the author (as opposed to the narrator) is a figure of both wit and sophistication, but also and always vulnerability, who comments on the woes of her adopted kingdom and links those woes implicitly to the universal history revealed in her vision.

As a prophet and scribe, Daniel also points to Christine as a writer, characterizing the narrator as the first stage in that career: a simple scribe recording Libera's words. While both characters are creations of the author, it is significant that Christine associates her name with the recorder not the originator of the text. Pragmatically speaking, distancing herself from the blunt criticism of powerful men was probably a prudent strategy. However, as the vision traces Christine's emergence and validation as a voice in the French court, it is also quite logical to start at the bottom of the ladder. Libera's battered body provides an image of the assaulted integrity of the body politic, but the choice of Daniel as a governing image suggests that Christine's authorial integrity is also breeched: she lays no claim through her namesake to the political commentary she writes. As the prophet was often held merely to recite God's word, so Christine's critique belongs to another within the fiction of her allegory.

[19] See Tarnowski, "Le geste prophétique" on Christine's role as a prophet. For a general discussion of the prophecy in political commentary and discussions of the Great Schism, see Millet.

Book II: Shadow or Light: The Dilemma of the Commentator

In Book II, the narrator and author move beyond this level of authorial visibility, for the narrator engages more actively with Dame Opinion and the historical Christine de Pizan's books become a point in the discussion. The interaction begins at the University of Paris where the narrator glimpses Opinion and her daughters influencing the course of a scholarly *disputatio*. Opinion addresses and characterizes the narrator as a "school girl," an appropriate appellation for a commentator working from the traditions of the schools. When the narrator professes ignorance of Opinion's nature, the central issue of Book II is set: who is this odd creature, whose physical manifestation confuses the narrator at the start of Book II, and what is the nature of her equally confusing operations within the human mind? The dialog between Opinion and Christine answers those questions and in the process explores issues of right and wrong interpretive practice.

Opinion begins by discussing the tricky relationship between Opinion and Philosophy. In II.4, she discusses the prophets, the authorial stance of Book I, whose statements are true but open to misinterpretation. In II.6–12, Aristotle's discussion of the errors of early Greek philosophers—taken from Thomas Aquinas' commentary on the *Metaphysics* (*Advision* xxxii–xxxiii)—illustrates interpretation and refutation of texts by two supreme commentators, Aristotle and Aquinas. In II.14–17, Opinion uses their methods and conclusions to disprove Christine's attribution of historical causation to Fortune in the *Mutation of Fortune*. When the narrator still proves confused, Opinion discusses France's current political quandary and key examples of misinterpretations of texts by alchemists (II.18) and knightly combatants (II.19–20). Finally, the narrator fully understands Dame Opinion by her personal experience of misinterpretations in and of the works by the historical Christine herself (II.21–22).

Throughout this struggle to identify and understand Opinion, the narrator as a student and commentator explores the proper exercise of her authorial role. Appropriately, the controlling figure is Macrobius, a late classical Neo-Platonic scholar, whose commentary on the *The Dream of Scipio* exerted a long, extensive influence on medieval writers of all kinds. The reference to Macrobius helps contextualize the relationship between Christine and the knowledge of the schools, characterizing the narrator as a reader whose ability to interpret and judge grows over the course of Book II. Although Christine shares many minor themes with Macrobius—civic health, number lore, the virtues, the nature of the soul, cosmography—his most powerful influence may be felt in his exemplification of the interpreter's art.[20] Like Macrobius, who brought a mystical and aesthetic philosophy to Cicero's discussion of civic vices and virtues, in Book II Christine turns from political commentary to understanding that commentary within a reasoned discussion of first causes: the nature of the human soul and human understanding. She focuses on an intellectual process and its effects on real-world problems, specifically Opinion's divisiveness and potential for abuse. Her question is both simple and important: if Opinion can be both false and true, how does an interpreter/commentator distinguish between the two?

Macrobius also addresses this issue in two sections of his influential commentary. The most celebrated classifies dreams by their powers of divination (Macrobius I.3, 87–92). Before his analysis of dreams, however, Macrobius had taken up Plato's old question of whether a fictional story (such as Scipio's dream) can be the vehicle of philosophic discussion (Macrobius I.2, 83–87). He responds by classifying different types of *figmenta* on much the same basis as his classification of dreams: their ability to reveal the truth. While some do not (his example is Menander's comedies) and are of no use to the philosopher, others, described as allegories, hide the knowledge of holy things under a pious veil of figments, a definition of allegory referenced in Christine's preface.[21] Whether one is interpreting dreams or *figmenta*, the problem then is essentially a literary one of interpretation. For Christine in Book II, the movement from opinion to certainty is not merely an academic exercise. It has tangible consequences in the real world, as indeed it does for Macrobius whose discussion of fiction centers on its appropriateness in a treatise on the ideal state. Thus, the alchemists who misread their texts impoverish their patrons. More sinisterly, the nobility of France who misinterpret legal, theoretical, and even literary texts fail in their duties as combatants.

By far, Book II's longest example of interpretation is the narrator's ongoing "reading" of Dame Opinion. Even more interesting, the real world application of this reading is directed toward Christine's work

---

[20] *Advision* 162–63, n. I–II identifies Macrobius' *Commentary on the Dream of Scipio* (I.12.9) as an important source for the figure of Opinion. For a translation of this passage, see Macrobius 135.

[21] See I.2.9 in Macrobius 85. Macrobius never uses the word "allegory" itself but, as Rollinson notes, his writings in *Commentary* and the *Saturnalia* "constitute a full and important introduction to the development of theories of the allegory of literature in the Latin West." (11).

as an interpreter and commentator in *The Mutation of Fortune* and the *Epistles on* The Romance of the Rose. In this endeavor, Christine the *narrator* functions as a commentator on the works of Christine the *author*. She exerts more personal power in this role than as a scribe. Moreover, she draws closer than in Book I to an identification with Christine the writer. Unlike Libera, Opinion exists within as well as without the narrator, thus blurring the line between the narrative voices Christine the author assumes. Furthermore, the narrator lays claim to Christine's past work as a commentator and interpreter, bridging the gap between the author and her namesake. The merging of the two reinforces an important theme in Book II. Any scrupulous interpretation of a text involves the interpreter's self-scrutiny and analysis, a process that helps validate insightful applications of written authority to personal experience. This process will be the subject of Book III but it also occurs in II.14, where Christine's *Mutation of Fortune*, a long verse poem exploring Fortune's role in history, is reinterpreted under Opinion's direction. When the narrator correctly untangles the argument as to whose influence comes first, Opinion or Fortune, she correctly applies Aristotle's ideas on first causes to her historical causal analysis in *Mutation*, correctly completes Opinion's Aristotelian syllogism, and imitates the master commentators Aquinas and Aristotle in her commentary and critique of Christine's works. Through such reinterpretations and accompanying introspections, the narrator begins to understand the nature of her guide and by extension the interpretive methodologies of a commentator.

How such a critique unfolds within the mind is made clearest in II.21. There Opinion reminds the narrator of the various misinterpretations surrounding Christine's commentary on *The Romance of the Rose*. The narrator ponders how a "doubtful thing [such as Dame Opinion] can bear witness to the unadulterated truth" (II.21); Opinion shows that while her studies have bought material to her intelligence, the intelligence itself has tested its certainty by means of reason. This example clinches the identification: Christine can now furnish a full definition of Opinion from both experience and authoritative citation, validating the mingling of both experience and acquired knowledge in the process of right reading.

For narrator and author, both power *and* vulnerability spring from this knowledge. As a commentator, Christine the narrator gains a greater voice, a greater responsibility, a greater share in Book II. Moreover, she gets the lesson of Book II right by developing a sophisticated understanding of Opinion and her troubled relationship to Philosophy. That understanding, however, raises doubts about her own work to which Opinion alone responds (II.22). If the narrator triumphantly acquires just the interpretive skills and understanding that a commentator needs, the *writer* Christine is left in a vulnerable position akin to Libera and Dame Opinion herself. Just as Opinion has been misinterpreted by the narrator (and by Christine), just as Libera presents herself as a Cassandra whose fate is to be misinterpreted, so Christine, author and text, are at the mercy of misinterpretations maliciously and honestly conceived. While Opinion reassures the Christine narrator that her works contain no errors, she also warns her in II.22 that, like her past books, the *Vision* will be misread. In Book III, the voices of the narrative will be resolved into one voice, that of the *auctor* Christine, who speaks from her own authority. This single tone, to become a mark of integration in Book III, threatens at the end of Book II to become simply another path to fragmentation. It opens the text and the author to the source of Libera's wounds and Book I and II's factional struggles: the perils of interpretation.[22]

Book III: Tribulation, Consolation, and Transformation: the Spiritual Matriarch

Book III tells how to guard oneself from these perils. As we have been tracking the progress of the narrator, the narrative has also been following a clear itinerary. Dame Libera begins by warning her children (and France's rulers) to change their ways. Dame Opinion characterizes that change as internal by discussing the problems of interpretation. In Book III, Dame Philosophy finishes the argument by reinterpreting human affairs in the light of certain (that is, Christian) wisdom. Instead of simply interpreting written authorities, Christine dramatizes the reinterpretation through her narrator's confrontation with her own history, as outlined in III.3–14. In III.15–21, Philosophy helps reinterpret that history by applying the wisdom of Boethius and other authorities. In III.22–25, she moves to a more general discussion of the true nature of good and bad Fortune and identifies the source of genuine happiness, broadening the discussion from Christine in particular to humankind in general. In III.26, she reveals the true source of identity, the Trinity, and in

---

[22] For a discussion of Christine's linkage between misogyny and misreadings of allegories, see Brown-Grant, "Christine de Pizan as a Defender of Women" in *Christine de Pizan: A Casebook* 86–87.

III.27, Christine ends the book by explaining Theology's relevance to the transformation of individuals, institutions, and societies.

In this discussion, Christine sensitively intertwines different strands of influence. At times, she simply imitates, at times transforms, these sources. Philosophy herself indicates the most obvious one: Boethius' *Consolation of Philosophy*. In narrative and argument, Book III owes a great deal to Boethius' seminal work. Many of these debts have been acknowledged before: both writers picture Philosophy as a physician who feeds them a "diet" of wholesome wisdom to heal them, both narrators complain of Fortune's role in their adversities, both are led to a larger view of those misfortunes by Philosophy's counsel, and both end their search for happiness in God.[23] Christine's narrator also strongly resembles Boethius': both are courtier/scholars at the end of long runs of misfortune serving foreign kings. Like Boethius, Christine complains of exile, financial destitution, distraction from her studies, harm to her family, and, perhaps most cutting, undeserved loss of reputation. Philosophy's reinterpretation of Christine's life story in III.15-III.22 follows in spirit and sometimes letter Philosophy's response to Boethius' complaint: Christine has failed to use her reason to rise above her excessive partiality to herself (III.15). She should consider her blessings, for not events but interpretations of them have made her unhappy (III.21). Although in Book III Christine directly quotes 13 long sections practically verbatim, the longest transcriptions occur in III.23, where Philosophy discusses the true nature of Fortune's gifts, and III.25, where she identifies true felicity as God. In these passages, Christine follows Boethius by proving that happiness consists of self-mastery and lies within, also the terminus of the Augustinian quest for God.

When Christine turns to the subject of God, however, her model enlarges. Although Philosophy refuses to use the harsher diet of philosophy for the narrator, Christine does often appropriate the methods of philosophy in Book III.[24] One of her greatest debts to Boethius is the characterization of the narrator as a philosopher

---

[23] Cropp was the first to study in detail Christine's debt to Boethius and to identify the French translation that Christine consulted for *Advision*. For different studies of how Christine used and changed her source, see, for example, Blanchard, "Artefact littéraire et problematisation morale;" *Advision* xxviii–xxxi; Semple, "The Consolation of a Woman Writer;" and Paupert, "Christine et Boèce."

[24] See, however, Blanchard, "Artefact littéraire et problematisation morale" for another view.

seeking consolation through wisdom. However, Boethius ends his book by demonstrating the differences between human and divine intelligence while Christine insists on the presence of the divine within the human psyche. Concomitantly, she reveals that her Philosophy, unlike Boethius', has appeared in the guise of Theology. The distinction is not an idle one. Boethius, whose consolation is famous for its near-exclusion of overtly Christian elements, offers little help for a theological consolation. Book III's ongoing reassessment of Christine's life in the light of eternal truths and its ending union of individual and God within the hidden mystery of the human mind make it likely that, as in the *City of Ladies*, Christine is mixing her Boethian subtext with an Augustinian one, here the *Confessions* (Skemp 20–21, 25, 28, and 30–31).

Like the *Vision*, Augustine's *Confessions* provides a personal reassessment and an ending exposition of the Trinity alluded to in the *Vision* III.26. This exposition integrates the Trinity within the human mind.[25] As Augustine's model also influenced two of Christine's inspirations for her *Vision*—Dante's *Divine Comedy* and Petrarch's *Secretum*—it is not all that surprising to find it in her own work. Indeed, she cites Augustine in Book III more than any other Church Father. He is especially prominent in the last two chapters, which end in a discussion of the Trinity attributed to three sources: his *Book of the Trinity*, rebuttal of Arian, and an unnamed sermon.[26]

Since Augustine was the principal architect of the medieval understanding of the Trinity, these references are not exceptional in and of themselves; however, their appearance after the reappraisal

---

[25]   See Augustine, *De Trinitate* especially section 10.12 in column 984 and sections 11.1–12.15 in columns 983–1012. For a translation, see *On the Trinity*, transl. Stephen McKenna, The Fathers of the Church 45 (Washington: Catholic University Press, 1963). Section 10.12 is found on pages 312–13; sections 11.1–12.15 on 315–68.

[26]   As with other quotations from church authorities, Christine is citing not from the original but from Thomas Hibernicus' *Le Manipulus florum*, a handbook of quotations for preachers that she often used in her works. This compilation of edifying citations, organized by topic, was a great favorite in the late Middle Ages. Campbell first identified it as a source of Christine's; in *Advision* xxxiii–xxxv, Dulac and Reno discuss its use in the *Vision*. In *Le Manipulus florum*, the unnamed sermon is attributed to St. Bernard of Clairvaux, but its internalization of the Trinity is Augustinian in import and similar to passages found in both *The Book of the Trinity* and the end of the *Confessions*. See, for example, *De Trinitate* 10.12 (col. 984) and 11.1–12.15 (columns 983–1012); XIII.11 of the *Confessions* 1:187–88 in O'Donnell's Latin edition and 318–19 of the English translation.

of Christine's personal history suggests she was drawing from the structure as well as the themes of the *Confessions*. As Augustine's biographer Garry Wills has noted, the *Confessions* are marked by the preoccupations of Augustine's middle period: the twin mysteries of the Trinity and the human mind (Wills 91). Although Christine does not cite the *Confessions* specifically, it makes the same connection she makes between autobiography and theology: the investigation of her life also concludes in a revelation of the Divine because, unlike the modern search for uniqueness, Christine's search for identity ends in the universal that underwrites and informs all creation. As in the *Confessions*, self is recovered through reintegration and finally transcendence. This process has been ongoing throughout the *Vision* and, again, the process is often depicted in Augustinian terms. For example, in III.26, Christine mentions one of Augustine's succession of internal triunes by discussing how the reasonable trinity of memory, understanding, and will become, when unmade, the miserable trinity of impotence, ignorance, and concupiscence. Indeed, Libera's evocation of the lost lessons of history describes such a fall of memory into impotence (Skemp 30) as Opinion's anatomy of misinterpretation analyses the fall of understanding into ignorance. But in Book III, as at the end of the *Confessions*, the process flows in the opposite direction, rising from concupiscence to right will through the correction of the author's judgment, the basis of an *auctor*'s authority. In Book III, therefore, the narrator moves to full prominence as a writer and a person, but always within the Augustinian sense of identity as an extension of the Divine.

In medieval commentaries, concern for "the integrity of the individual *auctor*" (Minnis 117) often led to just such increased scrutiny of an author's life and virtue, as when thirteenth-century exegetes pondered how a sinful Solomon or David could become a writer of authority (Minnis 103–12). By the fourteenth century, Petrarch and Boccaccio resolved this difference by simply separating an *auctor*'s power and authority from the failings of his private life, effectively humanizing the author (Minnis 214–15). Christine takes another approach as mediated by her use of Boethian and Augustinian subtexts. By virtue of her struggle to overcome her failings and by virtue of her ability to re-interpret them correctly by applying to them the lessons of her education they become an important *source* of her authority. Only by experiencing and understanding the crisis of her personal life is she empowered to speak to the political crisis in France.

This provocative strategy is aligned with the last of her controlling *exempla*: the long-suffering Jacob. Interestingly, Jacob's inclusion also references the *Confessions*, which discusses Genesis in its ending chapters. The exegetical discourse, which often seems a puzzling departure from autobiography, is actually an important step in Augustine's interpretation of his life. As Wills asserts in his brief life of the saint, Augustine discovers in his personal history a reenactment of the opening book of God; he discusses Genesis because he believes in the universal applicability of its patterns to all human lives (Wills 92–93; Augustine, *The Confessions* 1:xl–xli). Christine's choice of Jacob also affirms her connection with the universal patterns his story reveals, but on the surface, at least, this choice seems both risky and bold.[27] Jacob's history as a liar had exercised exegetes from Augustine onwards while his life of redeemed suffering made him a type of redemption for such early fathers as St. Irenaeus, St. Augustine, and St. Ambrose. Like the Boethian and Augustinian subtexts, his story attempts to master a personal history, to recover and reintegrate a soul fragmented by life's hardships. While Augustine and Boethius supply arguments and organizational and narrative structures for Book III, however, Jacob addresses a much more personal aspect of Book III: specific doubts about Christine's legitimacy, how a woman's life can be universally applicable, even to the affairs of a kingdom, and how a woman can be an *auctor* who speaks with the highest authority in her own voice and from her own experience.

Like Christine, Jacob is a teller of tales whose wisdom and authority are paradoxically authenticated by personal experience. In exploring this validation, his story focuses the reader on three motifs common to both: imposture, exile, and a delicate dance of dispersal and re-collection. As in the Genesis story, exile in Book III is not simply an estrangement from power (as in Book I) but a world of ambiguities and impostures that gives rise to a fuller, more complex, but finally integrated sense of self. Jacob poses as his older twin Esau and illegitimately claims his father's legacy. Similarly, Christine poses as the "son" and heir of her father, a learned counselor to France's royal family. Like Jacob, she must struggle against the taint of inauthenticity to make this claim, but like Jacob her background proves an asset that enriches the legacy. As the quiet, studious Jacob pretends to be his manly, athletic brother, so the woman Christine

---

[27]   In the following comments, I am heavily indebted to the stimulating and rich discussion of Jacob's story in Avivah Zornberg's *Genesis: The Beginning of Desire* (Philadelphia: Jewish Publications Society, 1995) especially 144–263.

adopts the "masculine" roles of writer, scholar and counselor. Yet mysteriously, like Jacob who is somehow the right one, Christine, though not a son, is "naturally and from . . . birth inclined" (III.8) to a life of books and study, the path which her own nature "and the stars" (III.10) have chosen for her. And just as Jacob in his ensuing exile comes to incorporate elements of his rugged outdoorsman brother, so Christine in her struggles after her husband's death not only absorbs and appropriates the "male" roles of scholar, courtier, and counselor but also integrates them within her gender.[28] Nature's metaphors for Christine's literary activity include both the male forge and the female childbirth, with emphasis given the latter by its inclusion after the forge image as Christine's final comparison.[29] As we shall see later, she will in fact use the travails stemming from her gender to validate the narrator's claim to the highest level of authorship.

As Book III explains in great detail, such an enriched sense of self arises not from prosperity but adversity. The world of exile that Jacob enters with his lie and that Christine enters with her husband's death bring both a larger life, but neither recognizes the enhancement. Doubling for both is a problem: the twin Jacob who marries two sisters and submits to two exiles lives a life that is never pure and simple, but, in his desire to return and settle at one point, he longs for it. Similarly, the Christine protagonist lives a life full of complications: the early loss of her homeland, the death of a series of male protectors, the unending lawsuits and financial ruin, the gossip about her love affairs, the absence and recovery of her son, the fight to find him a position, the fear and anxiety over her mother, the concern for her brothers and niece—all divide and plague her. She is, she tells one person, "six times myself" (III.6). Like Jacob, she wishes to flee this unpredictable, complicated existence with its multiplying frustrations and bids on her time and attention for the privacy and solipsism of her study: a life of surety, predictability, simplicity. But like him, circumstances have "exiled" her from that

---

[28] Richards has argued that Christine rejects essentialism, often uses images of androgyny to combat misogynist stereotypes, and reverses standard practice to make the feminine stand for the universal. See Richards, "Rejecting Essentialism and Gendered Writing" and a similar argument in Brown-Grant, *Christine de Pizan and the Moral Defence of Women* 120–22. For another approach, see Thelma Fenster, "Possible Odds: Christine de Pizan and the Paradoxes of Women" in *Contexts and Continuities* 2: 355–66.

[29] This important series of metaphors has drawn a great deal of commentary. See, for example, Huot 367; Brownlee, "Widowhood, Sexuality, and Gender in Christine de Pizan" 353; and Chance, "Speaking *in propria persona*" 280–81.

possibility. A "foreign traveler" (III.1) halted midway on the road (III.10), she describes herself and her fellow widows as exiles in flight (III.6).

Like Jacob, then, she has misread the ways this experience has enriched and empowered her: dispersion (universal applicability) is not fragmentation. In his first dream, God promises Jacob precisely this fate of multiplication as the bedrock of his eventual identity as a patriarch.[30] His seed will be dispersed to all corners of the earth, uniting the identity of Israel with the identity of Jacob (Gen. 28:14). In Jacob's second dream, his struggles with a mysterious angel confirm this enrichment while legitimating his inheritance not in Esau's name but his own (Gen. 32:23–33). Asked again who he is, Jacob responds truthfully and earns the name Israel, which weds his fate to that of the Hebrew nation through an etymological invocation of his struggles and relationship with God.[31] In similar fashion, the narrator's claim to be an *auctor* in Book III arises from her life of exile and struggle as reassessed in the light of Theology's revelation. Like Jacob, she finally claims that life and status in her own name, as a woman. She stresses the "limitations" of her gender throughout Book III—her weak body, ignorant mind, natural timidity. But in III.6, she significantly changes *Mutation of Fortune*'s depiction of her assumption of control after her husband's death. She is still figured as the pilot of a ship now lost at sea, but unlike the portrait in *Mutation*, where she must change gender to meet her obligations, she remains a woman: she lays claim to her father and husband's legacy as herself. [32] It is important to note, however, that just as Jacob does not abandon Esau's skills, so Christine does not reject the male for the female in this change. Rather, she integrates the two realms of experience. She implies both are open to her when she tells Philosophy that she would not willingly exchange her life for that of anyone else—male or female (III.21). Moreover,

---

[30] See Zornberg, *Genesis: The Beginning of Desire* (details cited above) 192–202 on this theme.

[31] St. Augustine, for example, in *Sermo* 122.3 interprets the name Israel as "seeing God." See *Sermo CXXII. PL* 5: col. 682.

[32] This gender change in *Mutation* has excited a great deal of critical commentary. For a sample, see Benkov; Brown-Grant, *Christine de Pizan and the Moral Defence of Women*, especially 120–22; and Richards "Rejecting Essentialism and Gendered Writing" and "Somewhere between Destructive Glosses and Chaos" 48–50. Kelly 605–08 discusses Christine's rewriting of her transformation into a man as part of an evolving conception of herself developed over the course of several works, an argument closest to my position here.

Christine's mother, who figured in *City of Ladies* as an obstacle to Christine's education,[33] becomes a co-nurturer with her father in Book III since she teaches Philosophy's lessons of patience and faith to her daughter. Male and female, paternal and maternal legacies validate the narrator's enhanced experience of life, underwriting her address to France's feuding lords as well as conjuring the full humanity of the speaker beyond the limits imposed by gender definitions. While both Boethius and Augustine also reassess their life stories, only Jacob's draws out these dynamics and tensions between experience and authority, gender and authenticity; and as Jacob's troubles lead to his unique position as Israel's last patriarch, so Christine's gender and the troubles it raises become the basis of her identity as a spiritual matriarch to France.[34]

Within the context of Christine's ultimate expansion of her identity to God, whose Augustinian features have already been suggested, Jacob's tale highlights the link that adversities forge between Christine and the kingdom. Just as Jacob's story of exile and trouble becomes Israel's, so Christine's years in the wilderness and her renewed appraisal of this time as an opportunity for growth model an important way for France's rulers to reinterpret their current political crisis. While Book III begins with the image of exile, its closing imagery expands the Boethian metaphor of nourishment from education to transformation. In III.27, Christine compares Theology's teachings to the manna showered upon the Israelites as they returned from the exile begun by Jacob's journey to regain his son. As Jane Chance has noted, manna is rich in Eucharistic implications ("Speaking *in propria persona*" 282–83). *Eucharist* itself derives from the Greek *eucharistia* or gratitude, which theologians held actualized God's grace within the celebrant and made the offering

---

[33] See II.36 of *The City of Ladies*: Richards 154–55 or Brown-Grant 141. On Christine's contradictory portraits of her mother in earlier works, see Tarnowski, "Maternity and Paternity in *La Mutacion de Fortune*" in *City of Scholars: New Approaches to Christine de Pizan*, ed. Margarete Zimmermann and Dina de Rentiis (Berlin: Walter de Gruyter, 1994) 116–26; chapter one of Quilligan; and Heather Arden, "Her Mother's Daughter: Empowerment and Maternity in the Works of Christine de Pizan" in *Contexts and Continuities* 1: 31–42. In her positive picture of her mother in the *Vision*, Christine may also be evoking Augustine's re-estimation of his own mother, Monica, in the *Confessions*.

[34] On the strategies Christine employs to validate her ability to speak as a political counselor, see also Dulac, "Authority in the Prose Treatises of Christine de Pizan."

real. In III.27, Christine responds to Theology in a profuse expression of gratitude, dramatizing just such a transformation. The ending chapter suggests the mental reorientation that marks such a transformation as well as characterizing Book III's consolation—compared throughout to a feeding—as a Eucharistic celebration that reenacts the fusion of human and divine, individual and God through an act of nourishment that defines and strengthens community.[35] If Christine's readers can "ingest" her book as her narrator has incorporated her readings into her life, then such a transformation is possible; and if such a transformation is possible, then true community can be established.

Obviously, then, this climax to the *Vision*'s imagery of nourishment is meant to celebrate the triumph of the universal over the particular. As such it unites numerous aspects of Christine's text. It brings the reader into the cycle of nurture since the narrator is both a character nourished by Philosophy and a *text* nourishing the reader—an example for his or her edification. As Theology and the narrator become one within the divine ground of being, narrator and text (in the person of the allegorical guide) are also united—a measure of the deeper interpretive process involved in integrating readings into one's life experiences. Book III, unlike I and II, also concludes in the narrator's single voice, which is all but impossible to disentangle from the author's as narrator and author merge. The common ground for all the sciences, God, becomes the common ground that unites reader, text and the different characters assumed by Christine de Pizan in the *Vision*. Moreover, like Jacob, Christine can testify to this universality in the legal sense of the term—through personal experience. As suggested by her closing comparison between her book and various precious jewels, this universality places *Chrisine's Vision* in the treasure chests found in III.1 on the ascent to Philosophy's tower. Able to speak in her own voice and her own name, worthy not merely to be read but also to be interpreted, she has become an *auctor* of a text that can not merely inform but transform the reader.[36] This application of Christine's story to the

---

[35] Book X, the central chapter of Augustine's *Confessions*, is also saturated with Eucharist imagery. See O'Donnell's commentary on *The Confessions* 1:xxxvii.

[36] See also Paupert, " 'La Narracion de mes aventures' " for a similar argument. Brownlee, "Le projet «Autobiographique»" traces a similar evolution in authorial roles across several of Christine's works and situates a similar validation in *Livre des trois vertus*. Richards, "Somewhere between Destructive Glosses and Chaos" 44–45 and Walters, "The 'Humanist Saint' " 875–76 discuss much the same transformation and describe the role that Christine finally aspires to as that of poet-theologian, a term alluded to in the *Vision* II.7.

woes of the kingdom may assimilate and appropriate rather than actively resist male tradition; however, by inserting herself within that tradition, by treating power and identity as a paradox, and making that paradox the method for asserting her own authority, she renews both herself and tradition and extends the hope of renewal to her audience.

Select Bibliography

Old French Editions of *Le Livre de l'advision Cristine*

Reno, Christine and Liliane Dulac, eds. *Le Livre de l'advision Cristine.* Études Christiniennes 4. Paris: Champion, 2001. Based on the ex-Phillipps 128 manuscript, this new edition has an extremely useful introduction, glossary, and bibliography. The endnotes are essential for a serious study of this text.

Towner, Sister Mary L., ed. *Lavision Christine.* 1932. New York: AMS Press, 1969. The first published old French edition of *Avision* based on B.N. f. fr. 1176 and Bibliothèque royale 10309, the text is sometimes difficult to read because of the lack of punctuation; the ex-Phillipps manuscript, which had not come to light in 1932, is not considered in the edition. There is thus no introductory preface.

A Selection of Modern Editions and Translations from Other Works of Christine de Pisan

Baird, Joseph L. and John R. Kane, ed. and trans. *La Querelle de la Rose: Letters and Documents.* University of North Carolina Studies in the Romance Languages and Literatures 199. Chapel Hill: University of North Carolina, Department of Romance Languages, 1978.

Blumenfeld-Kosinski, Renate and Kevin Brownlee, ed. *Selected Writings of Christine de Pizan.* Norton Critical Edition: Texts and Criticism. New York: Norton, 1997.

Brown-Grant, Rosalind, trans. *The Book of the City of Ladies.* Harmondsworth: Penguin, 1999.

Chance, Jane, trans. *Christine de Pizan's Letter of Othea to Hector.* Focus Library of Medieval Women. Newburyport: Focus Information Group, 1990.

Fenster, Thelma, and Mary Carpenter Erler, ed. and trans. *Poems of Cupid, God of Love: Christine de Pizan's "Epistre au dieu d'Amours" and "Dit de la Rose"; Thomas Hoccleve's "The Letter of Cupid"; with George Sewell's "The Proclamation of Cupid".* New York: E. J. Brill, 1990.

Fornhan, Katie Langdon, trans. *The Book of the Body Politic*. Cambridge: Cambridge University Press, 1994.

Kennedy, Arthur, ed. "Christine de Pizan's *Epistre à la reine* (1405)." *Revues des langues romanes* 92 (1988): 253–64.

——, ed. *Christine de Pizan's Epistre de la prison de vie humaine*. Glasgow: University of Glasgow, 1984.

——, ed. "*La Lamentacion sur les maux de la France de Christine de Pizan*." *Mélanges de langue et littérature françaises du Moyen Âge et de la Renaissance offerts à Charles Foulon*. Vol. I. Rennes: Institut de Français, Université de Haute Bretagne, 1980. 177–85.

——, ed. *Le Livre du corps de policie*. Études Christiniennes 1. Paris: Champion, 1998.

——, and Kenneth Varty, ed and trans. *Ditié de Jehanne d'Arc*. Medium Aevum Monographs, New Series IX. Oxford: Society for the Study of Mediaeval Languages and Literature, 1977.

Lawson, Sarah, trans. *The Treasure of the City of Ladies*. New York: Penguin, 1985.

Parussa, Gabrielle, ed. *L'Epistre Othea*. Genève: Droz, 1999.

Paupert, Anne, trans. *La Vision de Christine* in *Le Moyen Âge et la femme: voix politiques, utopiques et amoureuses*. Paris: Robert Laffont. coll. Bouquins. To Appear.

Richards, Earl Jeffrey, trans. *The Book of the City of Ladies*. New York: Persea, 1982.

Roy, Maurice, ed. *Oeuvres poétiques de Christine de Pisan*. 3 vol. SATF 24. 1886–1896. New York: Johnson Reprint Corp., 1965.

Solente, Suzanne, ed. *Le Livre de la mutacion de Fortune*. 4 vol. SATF. Paris: Picard, 1959–1966.

——, ed. *Le Livre des faits et bonnes mœurs du sage roi Charles V*. 2 vols. 1936–40. Reprtd. 1 vol. Genève: Slatkine-Mégariotis, 1977.

Tarnowski, Andrea, ed. and trans. *Le Chemin de longue étude*. Lettres gothiques. Paris: Le Livre de poche, 2000.

Willard, Charity Cannon, ed. *The "Livre de la Paix" of Christine de Pizan: A Critical Edition with Introduction and Notes*. The Hague: Mouton, 1958.

——, ed. *The Writings of Christine de Pizan*. New York: Persea Books, 1994.

——, and Eric Hicks. *Christine de Pizan: Le Livre des trois vertus. Edition critique*. Bibliothèque du XVe siècle. Paris: Champion, 1989.

——, and Madeleine Pelner Cosman, trans. *A Medieval Woman's Mirror of Honor: The Treasury of the City of Ladies*. New York: Persea Books, 1989.

Willard, Charity Cannon, ed. and Sumner Willard, trans. *Le Livre des Fais d'Armes et de Chevalerie*. University Park, Pa: Pennsylvania State University, 1999.

Wisman, Josette, ed. and trans. *The Epistle of the Prison of Human Life, with an Epistle to the Queen of France and Lament on the Evils of the Civil War*. Garland Library of Medieval Literature A21. New York: Garland, 1984.

A Selection of Christine's Major Sources in the *Vision*

Aristotle. *The Metaphysics*. Ed. and trans. Hugh Tredennick. Loeb Classical Library. Vols. 271 and 287. Cambridge, Mass.: Harvard University Press, 1936.

Augustine. *The Confessions*. Ed. James J. O'Donnell. 3 volumes. 1992. Clarendon: Oxford, 1997.

——. *The Confessions*. Trans. R.S. Pine-Coffin. Harmondsworth: Penguin, 1987.

——. *De Trinitate*. In *PL*. Vol. 42, col. 815–1098. Paris: 1844–1864.

Boethius. *The Consolation of Philosophy*. Trans. Victor Watts. London: Penguin, 1999.

Dante Alighieri, *The Divine Comedy of Dante Alighieri*. Ed. and trans. Robert M. Durling. New York: Oxford University Press, 1996.

Guillaume de Lorris and Jean de Meun. *The Romance of the Rose*. Trans. Charles Dahlberg. 3rd edition. Princeton: Princeton University Press, 1995.

Les Grandes Chroniques de France. Ed. Jules Viard. 10 vols. Paris: Société de l'Histoire de France. Champion, Klincksieck, 1920–1953.

Jacquis de Voragine. *The Golden Legend: Selections*. Ed. and transl. Christopher Stace. London: Penquin, 1998.

Jean Gerson. *Oeuvres complètes*. Ed. Palémon Glorieux. 10 vols. New York: Desclée, 1960–1973.

Macrobius. *Commentary on the Dream of Scipio*. Trans. W. H. Stahl. Records of Civilization, Sources and Studies 48. New York: Columbia University Press, 1990.

Petrarch, Francesco. *The Secret by Francesco Petrarch with Related Documents*. Trans. Carol E. Quillen. The Bedford Series in History and Culture. Boston: Bedford St. Martin's, 2003.

Thomas Aquinas. *Commentary on the Metaphysics of Aristotle*. Trans. John P. Rowan. Library of Living Catholic Thought. 2 vols. Chicago: Regnery, 1961.

Critical Studies

Autrand, Françoise. *Charles VI*. Paris: Fayard, 1986.
This accessible biography of Charles VI provides a good basic background to the political problems that surround the composition of *Christine's Vision* and to courtly life in general. Autrand often quotes Christine's works, particularly her eye-witness testimony to Charles' education and illness.

Beaune, Colette. *Naissance de la nation France*. Paris: Gallimard, 1985.
This book discusses Christine's use of the myth of France's Trojan origins in several of her works, including the *Vision*.

Benkov, Edith Joyce. "The Coming to Writing: *Auctoritas* and Authority in Christine de Pizan." *Le Moyen français* 35–36 (1996): 33–48.
While this essay focuses primarily on the *Ditié de Jehanne d'Arc*, Benkov's observations on Christine's strategies for legitimating her stance as author are pertinent to the *Vision*, particularly the discussion of Christine's transformation into a man in the *Mutation of Fortune*.

Blanchard, Joel. "Artefact littéraire et problematisation morale au XVe siècle." *Le Moyen français* 17 (1985):7–47.
This article discusses Christine's use and remodeling of Boethius' *Consolation of Philosophy* in the *Vision*. Blanchard argues that Christine does not use philosophical methods in her reworking.

—— " 'Vox poetica, vox politica': l'entrée du poéte dans le champ politique au XVe siècle." *Actes du Ve colloque international sur le moyen français Milan 6–8 mai 1985*. Vol. III, *Études littèraires sur le XVe siècle*. Milan: Vita e Pensiero, 1986. 39–51. Rpt. in translation by Renate Blumenfeld-Kosinski in Blumenfeld-Kosinski and Kevin Brownlee, *Selected Writings of Christine de Pizan* 362–71. Blanchard discusses how Christine justifies her role as political commentator in her own writings in light of the emergence of the poet as political commentator in the fifteenth century; in the *Vision*, he argues, she does so partly through the autobiographical section.

——. "Christine de Pizan: les raisons de l'histoire." *Le Moyen Âge* 42 (1986): 417–436.
Drawing primarily on *Advision-Cristine, Mutacion de Fortune* and *Le Chemin du long estude*, Blanchard examines how in these three works Christine turns her back on the lyric in her search for a truth beyond herself. He discusses a number of themes in the *Vision*: Christine's personal and France's more general sufferings, her search for spiritual integration and first principles, and the evolution of her conception of herself as a writer.

Blumenfeld-Kosinski, Renate. "Christine de Pizan and the Misogynist Tradition." *Romanic Review* 81 (1990): 279–92.

Explores Christine's response to written misogynist tradition, discusses the portrait of her mother in her works, and examines her definition of the natural woman; Blumenfeld-Kosinski claims Christine rewrote and reread misogynist tradition by uniting experience with a reasonable critique of written authority.

——. "Christine de Pizan and the Political Life in Late Medieval France." *Christine de Pizan: A Casebook.* 9–24.

This essay discusses Christine's commentary on the major political crisis of her time: the Hundred Years War, the Great Schism, and the Civil War.

——. "Christine de Pizan et L'AutoBiographie Féminine." *Mélanges de l'Ecole française de Rome, Italie et Méditerranée* 113 (2001): 2–28.

A study contrasting Christine's autobiographical passages in various works, including *Advision-Cristine*, with her biographies of female heroines in the *Cité des Dames*. In *Advision*, Christine is seen as using her autobiography as an allegory for humanity in general, but she identifies with male models: Job, Christ, and Boethius. In contrast, the feminine biographies she writes in *Cité des Dames* are seen as feminist in approach and structure. Nevertheless, in relying on models of suffering in her autobiographies, Christine is seen to offer a new model of feminine autobiography.

Breaulieu, Jean-Philippe. "*L'Avision Christine* ou la tentation autobiographique." *Littératures* 18 (1998): 15–30.

An exploration of the autobiographical dimension of *L'Avision* within the constraints of the allegorical dream vision. Breaulieu sees Christine as emphasizing the autobiographical element, a modification that he argues constitutes a sign of modernity or at least proto-modernity.

Brown-Grant, Rosalind. "*L'Avision-Christine*: Autobiographical Narrative or Mirror for the Prince?" *Politics, Gender and Genre: The Political Thought of Christine de Pizan.* Ed. Margaret Brabant. Boulder: Westview Press, 1992. 95–111.

An interesting argument that *Advison-Cristine* is better read as a mirror for princes than autobiography. Included are several insightful readings of imagery patterns in the *Vision*.

——. *Christine de Pizan and the Moral Defence of Women: Reading beyond gender.* Cambridge Studies in Medieval Literature 40. Cambridge: Cambridge University Press, 1999.

An important review of Christine's strategies for defending women shown throughout her works. One chapter devoted to *Advision* shows how Christine's self-examination provides French royalty with an ethical lesson in leadership. This chapter places Christine's arguments within the currents of medieval thought, ties Christine's text to her Preface, and details how Christine makes a female model appropriate for her audience of male nobles.

Brownlee, Kevin. "Le projet «Autobiographique» de Christine de Pizan: histoires et fables du moi." *Au Champ des escriptures: Actes du 3ᵉ Colloque international sur Christine de Pizan, Lausanne, 18–22 juillet 1998.* Ed. Eric Hicks with the collaboration of Diego Gonzales and Philippe Simon. Paris: Champion, 2000. 6–23.

Examines Christine's evolving presentation of herself in a series of works from 1395–1405 as readings, rewritings, and rethinkings of several key canonical works: Jean de Meun's *Romance of the Rose*, Dante's *Divine Comedy*, Ovid's *Metamorphosis*, and Boccaccio's *Of Famous Women*. Brownlee argues that by *The Book of Three Virtues*, Christine was presenting herself as an author in her own right.

——. "Widowhood, Sexuality, and Gender in Christine de Pizan." *Romanic Review* 86 (1995): 339–53. Examines Christine's roles as virtuous widow, caring mother, and female clerk, discussing them as rhetorical strategies for affirming but de-eroticizing the gender of the speaker in Christine's works, among them *Christine's Vision*.

Campbell, P.-G.-C. *L'Épître d'Othéa. Étude sur les sources de Christine de Pisan.* Paris: Champion, 1924.

A very important discussion of Christine's main sources for *The Epistle of Othea*, some of which are also used in *Christine's Vision*.

Cerquiglini, Jacqueline. "L'Etranger." *Revue des langues romanes* 92 (1988): 239–51. Translated as "The Stranger" by Renate Blumenfeld-Kosinski in Blumenfeld-Kosinski and Kevin Brownlee, *Selected Writings of Christine de Pizan* 265–74.

An interesting study of the theme of the outsider or exile in Christine's works, particularly with reference to her self-representation as a writer.

Chance, Jane. "Speaking *in propria persona.*" *New Trends in Feminine Spirituality: The Holy Women of Liège and Their Impact.* Ed. Juliette Dor, Lesley Johnson, and Jocelyn Wogan-Browne. Medieval Women: Texts and Contexts 2. Brepols: 1999. 269–94.

This essay examines how Christine de Pizan in the *Vision* valorizes the use of her own voice within the context of affective spirituality. Among the topics covered are Christine's feminization of aspects of the *planctus* genre, consideration of her feminine allegorical guides, her appropriation of traditional male roles, images, and dictums, and her construction of feminine communities from within which to speak.

Courcelle, Pierre. *La Consolation de philosophie dans la tradition littéraire*. Paris: Études Augustiniennes, 1967.

A thorough discussion of the *Consolation of Philosophy* focusing on Boethius' sources and his influence on medieval thought. It includes informative discussion of Boethius' philosophical arguments and the tradition of commentaries he inspired.

Cropp, Glynnis M. "Boèce et Christine de Pizan." *Le Moyen Âge* 87 (1981): 387–417.

In a very important article, Cropp discusses the influences of Boethius in a number of Christine's works, including *Christine's Vision*; she also establishes Christine used a very popular fourteenth century French translation and gloss, *La Consolacion*, for the *Vision*.

Dulac, Liliane. "Authority in the Prose Treatises of Christine de Pizan: The Writer's Discourse and the Prince's Word." Trans. Earl Jeffrey Richards. *Politics, Gender & Genre: The Political Thought of Christine de Pizan*. Ed. Margaret Brabant. Boulder: Westview Press, 1992. 129–40.

Enlightening discussion of the textual strategies Christine de Pizan employs to acquire the influence and respect needed by a political writer. Dulac comments on Christine's many strategies for personalization, her use of the figure of the wise prince and her interlacing of autobiographical and political themes.

———. "Thèmes et variations du *Chemin de long estude à l'Advision-Christine*: remarques sur un itinéraire." *Sur le chemin de longue étude: Actes du colloque d'Orléans juillet 1995*. Ed. Bernard Ribémont. Paris: Champion, 1998. 77–86.

Dulac examines *Vision* as part of an "itinerary" of literary and intellectual development by comparing it with such works as *Mutacion de Fortune* and *Chemin de longue estude*. Among the themes examined are the relationships between Fortune and Opinion, knowledge and wisdom, the self-presentation of Christine and the links drawn between collective and personal misfortune.

Dulac, Liliane and Christine Reno. "L'humanisme vers 1400, essai d'exploration à partir d'un cas marginal: Christine de Pizan traductrice de Thomas d'Aquin." *Actes du Colloque 'Pratiques de la culture écrite en France au XVe siècle'*. Ed. Monique Omato and Nicole Pons. Louvain-la-Neuve: Fédération Internationale des Instituts d'Études Médiévales, 1994. 161–78.

An important investigation of the evidence for Christine's knowledge of and facility with Latin, this article examines in detail Christine's translation of Thomas Aquinas' commentary on Aristotle's *Metaphysics* in Book II of the *Vision*.

Dulac, Liliane and Christine Reno. "The *Livre de l'advision Cristine.*" *Christine de Pizan: A Casebook.* 199–214.

An accessible and balanced treatment discussing the problems of classifying the genre of *Christine's Vision:* autobiography, mirror for princes, political dream vision. Dulac and Reno argue that the allegorical reading of Book One in *Vision's* Preface shows that personal and political dimensions are deeply intertwined and thus of equal importance.

———. "Traduction et adaptation dans l' *Advision,Cristine* de Christine de Pizan." *Traduction et adaptation en France de la fin du Moyen Âge à la Renaissance: Actes du Colloque organisé par l'Université de Nancy II 23, 25 mars 1995.* Ed. Charles Brucker. Paris: Champion, 1997. 121–31.

An essay that explores Christine's changing and imaginative use of Latin sources in her works, including two works important for *Advision:* Thomas Aquinas' commentary on Aristotle's *Metaphysics* and Thomas of Ireland's *Manipulus florum.*

Durley, Maureen Slattery. "The Crowned Dame, Dame Opinion, and Dame Philosophy: the Female Characteristics of Three Ideals in Christine de Pizan's *Lavision Christine.*" *Ideals for Women in the Works of Christine de Pizan.* Ed. Diane Bornstein. Medieval and Renaissance Monograph Series I. Detroit: Michigan Consortium for Medieval and Early Modern Studies, 1981. 29–50.

Durley discusses the narrator Christine's journey in *Christine's Vision* as an evolution from material to spiritual concerns under the guidance of the three allegorical "mother" figures of the Crowned Ladies.

Famiglietiti, Richard C. *Royal Intrigue: Crisis at the Court of Charles VI 1392–1420.* New York: AMS Press, 1986.

A useful and very readable guide to the political difficulties current at the time Christine wrote her *Vision.*

Forhan, Kate Langdon. *The Political Theory of Christine de Pizan.* Aldershot: Ashgate, 2002.

An overview of Christine's political theory, this book contains several references to Christine's depiction of the just war in Book II of *Vision.*

Gauvard, Claude. "Christine de Pizan et ses contemporains: l'engagement politique des écrivains dans le royaume de France aux XIVe et XVe siècles." *Une femme de lettres au Moyen Âge: Études autour de Christine de Pizan.* Ed. Liliane Dulac and Bernard Ribémont. Orléans: Paradigme, 1995. 105–28.

Discusses Christine in the context of other writers of political commentary in the fourteenth and fifteenth centuries. Among the topics

broached are the mix of commentary on actual events with abstract
reflections on the exercise of sovereign power by the monarch, the
emergence of the poet as arbiter in political struggles, and the interlacing of the themes of self-presentation and political power.

Green, Richard Firth. *Poets and Princepleasers: Literature and the
English Court in the Late Middle Ages.* Buffalo: University of
Toronto Press, 1980.
An exploration of the life led by authors employed in the household
of late medieval kings and princes with special consideration of the
expectations placed upon them.

Guenée, Bernard. *Un Meurtre, une société: l'assassinat du duc
d'Orléans, 23 novembre 1407.* Paris: Gallimard, 1992.
A history of the political rivalry between the Dukes of Orleans and
Burgundy containing detailed summaries and an analysis of events
around the time of Christine's composition of *Advision.*

Huot, Sylvia. "Seduction and Sublimation: Christine de Pizan, Jean de
Meun and Dante." *Romance Notes* 25 (1985): 361–73.
A balanced discussion of Christine's feminism, which is finally seen
as limited since Christine never really explored the implications of a
feminist poetics nor did she call on other women to write. Christine's
metaphorical description of poetical creation found in *Advision-
Cristine* is discussed as a response to Jean de Meun's in the *Roman
de la Rose* and as the climax of a move to a new feminist poetics
traced through the *Mutacion de Fortune* and *Cité des dames.*

Kelly, Douglas. "Les Mutations de Christine de Pizan." *Mélanges de
philologie médiévale offerts à Marc-René Jung.* Volume 11. Torino:
Edizioni dell'Orso, 1996. 599–608.
Starting with the famous gender change in *Mutation of Fortune,*
Kelly traces Christine's evolving sense of her role as writer. He sees
her evolution from courtly elegies to moralizing allegories as medi-
ated by Boethius; in *Advision,* he sees a rectification of *Mutation of
Fortune*'s presentation of virtue as essentially male in character.

Kennedy, Angus J. *Christine de Pizan: A Bibliographical Guide.*
London: Grant & Cutler Ltd., 1984.
An essential bibliographical guide current to 1981. The 502 num-
bered entries—many with citations to critical reviews—are divided
into five parts: Bibliographies and Manuscript Catalogues, General
Surveys of Christine de Pizan's Life and Works, Study of Specific
Topics, Anthologies, Selections and Collected Works, and Individual
Works. The bibliography is easy to use and thorough.

———. *Christine de Pizan: A Bibliographical Guide. Supplement I.*
London: Grant & Cutler Ltd., 1994. Equally useful supplement to the

bibliography above, covering the period from 1981–1991. It contains 331 items, again with citations to critical reviews, some for items in the first bibliography which came to the author's attention too late to be included in that publication.

Kennedy, Angus J. *Christine de Pizan: A Bibliographical Guide. Supplement II.* London: Grant and Cutler, Ltd., 2004.

Essential guide to scholarship on Christine since 1991, this new supplement contains 2147 entries, again with citations to critical reviews, some for items in the first supplement.

Krueger, Roberta. "Christine's Anxious Lessons: Gender, Morality, and the Social Order from the *Enseignemens* to the *Avision.*" *Christine de Pizan and the Categories of Difference.* Ed. Marilynn Desmond. Minneapolis: University of Minnesota Press, 1998. 16–40.

Krueger looks at Christine's ongoing reflections on her own role as a teacher and maintains that these reflections often testify to Christine's uncertainties about her reception and her ability to affect her readers and transform society.

Laennec, Christine Moneera. "Christine Antygrafe: Authorial Ambivalence in the Works of Christine de Pizan." *Anxious Power: Reading, Writing and Ambivalence in Narrative by Women.* Eds. Carol J. Singley and Susan Elizabeth Sweeney. New York: SUNY Press, 1993. 35–49.

Drawing on Christine's description of herself as an "antygraph," Laennec examines what she terms "antygraphie" in Christine's writing—the dismemberment of her signature and name, the disavowal of authority and authorship, the distancing of the narrator from the author, the anxiety of warring against misogynist discourse while conforming to that discourse.

Laidlaw, James C. "Christine and the Manuscript Tradition." *Christine de Pizan: A Casebook.* 231–50. A review of the manuscript tradition with special attention to the autograph manuscripts. Laidlaw helps the reader to understand the difficulties in dating some of Christine's work, the pattern of her development as a writer and as a publisher of her own work, and her practice of writing and rewriting works as she prepared new presentation copies.

——. "Christine de Pizan, the Earl of Salisbury and Henry IV." *French Studies* 36 (1982): 129–43.

An inquiry into Christine de Pizan's meeting with the Earl of Salisbury and the question of which manuscript she presented to him. This relationship is mentioned in Book III of the *Vision.*

Le Brun-Gouanvic, Claire. "L'écriture médecine: une relecture de *L'Avision Christine* 1405." *Les Miroirs de L'Écriture: La réflexivité chez les femmes écrivains d'ancien régime.* Ed. Jean-Philippe

Beaulieu and Diane Desrosiers-Bonin. Montreal: Department of French Studies, University of Montreal, 1998. 9–20.

An study of Christine's self-representation in the *Vision*, focusing on the therapeutic function of Book III's consolation and the network of metaphors by which Christine assigns this function to her book and to her own reading.

Lefèvre, Sylvie. "Christine de Pizan." *Dictionnaire des lettres françaises. Le Moyen Âge.* Ed. Geneviève Hasenohr and Michel Zink. 2nd ed. Paris: Fayard, 1992. 280–87.

An overview of Christine's evolution as a writer with brief descriptions of her works' organizations and themes as well as information on dedications, manuscript translations, diffusion of manuscripts, and modern editions.

Marchello-Nizia, Christine. "Entre l'histoire et la poétique: le 'Songe politique'." *Revue des Sciences humaines* 55 (juillet-sept. 1981): 39–53.

Applicable to an understanding of the *Vision* as political commentary, this essay discusses the use of dream visions for social criticism in the late Middle Ages.

Margolis, Nadia. "Elegant Closures: The Use of the Diminutive in Christine de Pizan and Jean de Meun." *Reinterpreting Christine de Pizan.* Eds. Earl Jeffrey Richards with Joan Williamson, Nadia Margolis and Christine Reno. Athens, GA-London: The University of Georgia Press, 1992. 111–23.

An important discussion of Christine's use of diminutives in both poetical and prose works. Margolis discusses those diminutives that adhere to and depart from stereotype as well as those that become a "vehicle for expressing feminine subjectivity." She also addresses how Christine's use of these diminutives responds to aspects of Jean de Meun's style in the *Roman de la Rose.*

Millet, Hélène. "Écoute et usage des prophéties par les prélats pendant le grand schisme d'Occident." *Les Textes prophétiques et la prophétie en Occident XIIe, XVe siècle.* Ed. André Vauchez. *Mélanges de l'Ecole française de Rome. Moyen Âge* 102. (1990, fasc. 2): 425–55.

Discusses the prelates' use of prophecy in arguments on the Great Schism in the years surrounding Christine's composition of the *Vision.* Millet discusses this use of prophecies in political arguments and the use of prophecy to support an ideal of France as historically orthodox in times of Church Schism.

Minnis, A.J. *Medieval Theory of Authorship: Scholastic Literary Attitudes in the Latter Middle Ages.* 2nd edition. Middle Ages Series. Pittsburg: University of Pennsylvania Press, 1988.

This insightful examination of glosses and commentaries written on Latin writers from the twelfth through the fifteenth century leads to an understanding of how medieval readers conceptualized the act of authorship and how these attitudes in the latter middle ages influenced the emergence of the "author."

Mühlethaler, Jean-Claude. "Le poète et le prophète: littérature et politique au XVe siècle." *Le Moyen français* 13 (1983): 37–57.

Examines the use of the Bible in fifteenth-century texts incorporating political commentary and argues that Christine often situates herself as a prophet in the Old Testament tradition.

——. "Les poètes que de vert on couronne." *Le Moyen français* 30 (1992): 97–112.

An interesting discussion of the fifteenth-century evolution of terms applicable to poetic creation, often citing Christine's use of these terms and thus her contribution to the evolution of the ideas they represent.

Ouy, Guy, and Christine Reno. "Identification des autographes de Christine de Pizan." *Scriptorium* 34 (1980): 221–38.

An important study that led to the identification of Christine's handwriting, this essay focuses on the text of *Advision* in the ex-Phillips MS 128 which was used as the base manuscript in *Advision-Cristine*.

Paupert, Anne. "Christine et Boèce: De la lecture à l'écriture à la réécriture à l'écriture du moi." *Contexts and Continuities*. 3: 645–62.

An insightful consideration of Christine's use of Boethius in a number of texts, including *Advision*. Paupert argues that Christine positions herself as a poet and philosopher and that her use of Boethius extends well beyond citation, which becomes a technique of composition itself. She sees the autobiographical section of *Advision* as indicative of how Christine adopts and surpasses her Boethian model to turn her work into a new form of autobiographical writing.

——. "'La Narracion de mes aventures': Des premiers poèmes à *L'Advision*, l'élaboration d'une écriture autobiographique dans l'oeuvre de Christine de Pizan." *Au Champ des escripture: Actes du 3e Colloque international sur Christine de Pizan, Lausanne, 18–22 juillet 1998*. Ed. Eric Hicks with the collaboration of Diego Gonzales and Philippe Simon. Études Christiniennes 6. Paris: Champion, 2000. 51–71.

A perceptive look at *Advision-Cristine* as an intellectual autobiography that crowns a long process of self-education and a lengthy quest for identity and meaning. Paupert sees the autobiography as a justification and legitimization of Christine's assumption of the role of *auctor* and thus her right to speak in her own voice both here and in the ensuing political works of her later career.

Picherit, Jean-Louis G. "Les Références pathologiques et thérapeutiques dans l'oeuvre de Christine de Pizan." *Une Femme de lettres au Moyen Age*. Ed. L. Dulac and B. Ribémont. Orléans: Paradigme, 1995. 233–44.

A consideration of images of disease and healing in Christine's works, particularly *Advision-Cristine*.

Quillen, Carol Everhart. *Rereading the Renaissance: Petrarch, Augustine, and the Language of Humanism*. Ann Arbor: The University of Michigan Press, 1998.

A study of Petrarch's humanism through his textual practices. Chapter Five examines the *Secretum* in terms of a humanist approach to reading ancient texts. Quillen maintains the book structurally echoes the *Confessions* by St. Augustine and evokes Augustine as a way to authorize and question the reading of both the texts and the interpretive approaches Petrarch valued. Enlightening in regard and in contrast to Christine's own interpretive approaches.

Quilligan, Maureen. *The Allegory of Feminine Authority: Christine de Pizan's Cité des Dames*. Ithaca, NY: Cornell University Press, 1991.

Chapter One on the name of the author and Christine's role as a compiler, prophet, and author is especially interesting in the light of Christine's evolving presentation of herself in the *Vision* as an author.

Reeves, Marjorie. "The Bible and Literary Authority in the Middle Ages." *Reading the Text: Biblical Criticism and Literary Theory*. Ed. Stephen Prickett. Cambridge, Ma: Blackwell, 1991. 12–63.

A review of the development of four-fold allegorical reading of the Scripture and the development of Scholastic commentaries. Special attention is paid to the later application of Biblical figures and figurative exegetical techniques to contemporary history by writers such as Joachin de Fiore (mentioned by Christine in Book I) and Dante (one of Christine's models for the *Vision*).

Reno, Christine. "Self and Society in L'Avision-Christine of Christine de Pizan." Diss.Yale University, 1972. Examines the dialectical unity of the *Vision* and Christine's attempt to resolve the "tension" between herself and society. This is one of the first studies to note the intertwining of autobiographical and political aspects of the *Vision*.

———. "The Preface to the *Avision-Christine* in ex-Phillipps 128." *Reinterpreting Christine de Pizan*. Eds. Earl Jeffrey Richards, with Joan Williamson, Nadia Margolis and Christine Reno. Athens, GA-London: The University of Georgia Press, 1992. 207–27.

Presents the first edition and translation of the preface to the *Vision* that was discovered in the Phillips Ms 128. Reno also argues that while the notion of political allegory is French, the concept of poetry comes from Boccaccio.

Richards, Earl Jeffrey. "Christine de Pizan and Dante: A Reexamination." *Archiv für das Studium der neueren Sprachen und Literaturen* 222 (Band 137 1985): 100–11.

Examining four explicit allusions to Dante in Christine's works including *Advision-Cristine*, Richards argues that Christine's admiration for the *Divine Comedy* is usually presented in the context of her opposition to the *Roman de la Rose*.

Richards, Earl Jeffrey. "Rejecting Essentialism and Gendered Writing: The Case of Christine de Pizan." *Gender and Text in the Later Middle Ages*. Ed. Jane Chance. Gainesville: University Press of Florida, 1996. 96–131. Richards argues that Christine rejects essentialism, or the belief in essential gender differences, uses images of androgyny in her work to combat misogynist representations, and universalizes the figure of woman to stand for humankind. He addresses Christine's response to the Thomist scheme of human essence in Book II of *Advision* and the gender switch in the self-portrait Christine presents in *Mutacion de Fortune*.

——. "Somewhere between Destructive Glosses and Chaos: Christine de Pizan and Medieval Theology." *Christine de Pizan: A Casebook*. 43–56.

A short discussion of the evidence of Christine's use of theology in her works to support her defense of women, touching upon several passages from or of importance to *Advision*. Among important topics are Christine's definition of herself as a poet-theologian and her use of the sex change and her birth in *Mutacion de Fortune* to attack Aquinas' position on the nature of women. In *Advision* II.12, Opinion's discussion of perfection and imperfection is also seen as contributing to this critique of Thomist essentialist doctrine.

Rollinson, Philip. *Classical Theories of Allegory and Christian Culture*. London: Duquesne University Press/ Harvester Press, 1981.

A short but very helpful study of the development of allegorical theory in antiquity and the early Middle Ages with chapters outlining the classical background and the Christian response. Appendices contain annotated translations of passages dealing with the critical understanding of allegory.

Rouse, Richard H, and Mary A. *Preachers, Florilegia and Sermons: Studies on the Manipulus florum of Thomas of Ireland*. Studies and Texts 47. Toronto: Pontifical Institute of Mediaeval Studies, 1979.

A useful study of one of Christine's important sources in *Advision*, the *Manipulus florum*.

Semple, Benjamin. "The Consolation of a Woman Writer: Christine de Pizan's Use of Boethius in *L'Avision-Christine*." *Women, the Book and the Worldly: Selected Proceedings of the St. Hilda's Conference, 1993*. Ed. Lesley Smith and Jane H. M. Taylor. Vol. 2. Cambridge: D. S. Brewer, 1995. 39–48.

A discussion of Christine's use of Boethius in Book III of the *Vision* as a narrative imitation rather than simply a textual imitation. Semple focuses on Christine's refitting the Boethian model to the story of a female seeking philosophical enlightenment.

——— "The Critique of Knowledge as Power: The Limits of Philosophy and Theology in Christine de Pizan." *Christine de Pizan and the Categories of Difference*. Ed. Marilynn Desmond. Minneapolis: University of Minnesota Press, 1998. 108–27.

Semple maintains that in her works, particularly *Advision*, Christine investigates the relationship between philosophy and theology, reflects on the limits of human understanding and explores how revelation is almost always subject to interpretation. He discusses how Christine upholds the value of ways of knowing other than faith and reason, particularly experiential wisdom, and promotes the ideal of the simple and devout person as a cautionary example for professional theologians and intellectuals.

Skemp, Mary L. "Autobiography as Authority in *Lavision-Christine*." *Le Moyen français* 35 (1996): 17–31.

Skemp explores the autobiographical aspects of *Advision*, its emphasis on experience, and its position within the tradition established by the *Confessions*.

Tarnowski, Andrea. "Le geste prophétique chez Christine de Pizan." *Apogée et déclin*. Ed. Claude Thomasset and Michel Zink. Cultures et civilisations médiévales VIII. Paris: Presses de l'Université de Paris-Sorbonne, 1993. 225–36.

An intriguing look at Christine's use of prophecy in many of her works, particularly *Advision-Cristine* where Christine uses poetic prophecy as a way to endow herself with authority. Tarnowski also comments briefly on the use of Daniel in Book I and sees the principle of the truth of prophecy as governing the whole of the *Vision*.

———. "Perspectives on the *Advision*." *Christine de Pizan 2000: Studies on Christine de Pizan in Honour of Angus J. Kennedy*. Ed. John Campbell and Nadia Margolis. Amsterdam: Rodopi, 2000. 105–14.

A study of Christine's use of allegory in the *Vision* as a "principle as well as literary technique," a way of looking at the world and a potent tool to span and link the different approaches taken by critics to the *Vision* – political, autobiographical, and literary.

Walters, Lori. "The 'Humanist Saint': Christine, Augustine, Petrarch, and Louis IX." *Contexts and Continuities*. 3:873–88.

A study of Christine's presentation of herself as a "humanist saint" on the model of Petrarch and Saint Augustine. Walters addresses Christine's role as a theologian poet in the tradition of the Italian Humanists and her use of the *Secretum* as a possible source for her transformation into a man in *Mutacion de Fortune*.

Willard, Charity Cannon. *Christine de Pizan: Her Life and Works*. New York: Persea, 1984.

An important guide to Christine's life and accomplishments set within the cultural context of her life and times. Despite the detail of the information presented, the book is accessible.

Wills, Garry. *Saint Augustine*. Penguin Lives Series. New York: Lipper/Viking, 1999.

A concise, very readable, and insightful biographical essay on St. Augustine with helpful commentaries on both the *Confessions* and Augustine's ideas on the nature of the Trinity.

Zumthor, Paul. "Autobiography in the Middle Ages?" Trans. Sherry Simon. *Genre* 6 (1973): 29–48.

A rewarding examination of how autobiographies were used and conceptualized by medieval writers.

Index

Abednego, 143
Abel, 49
Abraham, 14, 44
Absalom (son of King David), 46
accident (philosophical term), 60, 61, 67, 69
Achaz (12th king of Judea, 8th Century BC), 61
Achilles (legendary hero of the Greek forces at Troy), 77
Ad Herennium (Pseudo-Cicero), 138
Adam, 14, 55
Aeneas (legendary Trojan soldier and founder of Rome), 77
Africa, 25
Aganipus (legendary king of Gaul and husband of Cordelia), 62
Ahijah (Hebrew prophet in the reign of King Jeroboam), 59
air (as principle), 61, 65, 66, 69, 72
alchemy, alchemists, 79–82
Alecto, 35; *see* Furies
Alexander the Great (king of Macedonia, 356–323 BC), 62, 78, 94
allegories, *see* Avarice, Charity, Chivalry, Cruelty, Death, Desire for Knowledge, Envy, Error, Faith, Fortune, Fraud, Gluttony, Greed, Hope, Idleness, Ignorance, Justice, Larceny, Libera, Lust, Malice, Misfortune, Opinion, Philosophy, Pity, Reason, Theology
Alps, 25; *see* mountains

Amalek, King of (Biblical enemy of Saul), 42–3
Ambrose (saint and doctor of the Church, bishop of Milan, ca. 340–397 AD), 124, 126–7, 153
Amnon (son of King David), 46
Anaxagoras of Lampascus (Greek philosopher, ca. 500–428 BC), 66, 69
Anaximander (Greek philosopher and disciple of Thales, ca. 610–547 BC), 65
Anaximenes of Miletus (Greek philosopher and disciple of Anaximander, ca. 585–525 BC), 65
animals, *see* ants, badger, beast, bees, birds, butterfly, chameleon, cows, earth worm, elephant, falcon, fish, griffins, hoopoe, lamb, leech, lionesses, phoenix, sea monster, serpent, sheep, vulture, wasps
Anthixtonan, 67
antiphrasis; *see* poetry (poesy) and rhetoric and rhetorical method
ants, 14, 23; *see also* Greeks
antygraph, 13, 22, 140
Apocalypse (Revelations), 56
Aristaeus (brother of Orpheus, mistakenly referred to as Eurystus by Christine), 63; *see also* Eurystus
Aristotle (384–322 BC), 61, 62, 65–6, 69–73, 74, 86, 103, 125, 146; *Book on the Soul,* 65, 69; *Metaphysics,* 6, 59–73, 146;

Aristotle (*cont.*)
   Physics, 66, 67, 69; *Prior*
   Analytics, 86; *see also Of*
   Good and Bad Fortune
arithmetic, *see* sciences
Arius (Alexandrian father whose
   teachings led to the Aryan
   heresy, ca. 250–336 AD), 59,
   131
arms, 30, 57; arrows, 117, 124;
   men of arms, 45, 82–3; lance;
   33, 34; sword, 28, 31, 39 42, 43
arrogance or arrogant ones, 46,
   49, 74, 104, 125, 128
Assyrians, 104
astrology; *see* sciences
Astyagas (last king of the
   Medians, 584–549 BC), 76
Athens, 21, 32, 53, 61, 63
Augustine (saint and Doctor of
   the Church, 354–430 AD), 15,
   76, 113, 115–16, 117, 118,
   128, 130, 131, 132, 139,
   151–52, 153; *Book of the*
   Trinity, 130–31, 151;
   Confessions, 139, 151–52,
   153; *Contra Mendacium,* 141;
   On the Book of Our Savior's
   Words, 131, 151
authorial roles, *auctor,* 140–1,
   149–58; commentator, 140,
   146–47,148–9; scribe, 140, 145
Avarice, as an allegorical figure,
   35–6, 41–3, 144; *see also*
   Greed, as an allegorical figure

Babylon, 45–6, 48, 49, 50, 66,
   75–6
Babylonian captivity, 62
Bacon, Roger (English
   Franciscan philosopher, ca.
   1214–1294 AD), 64
badger, 30
Basine (wife of Childeric I and
   mother of Clovis), 15, 25

battles, 46, 78, 82–3, 99, 120,
   129; *see also* duels, war
beasts, 11, 37, 41, 45–6, 53, 54,
   55, 117
beatings, 28, 31, 32, 34, 48, 50,
   51, 112, 118, 124; *see also*
   whipping
Beauvais, 3, 96
Bede (English monk and scholar,
   named The Venerable,
   673–735 AD), 126
bees, 41
belly, 10, 12, 20; *see also*
   stomach
Belshazzar (last king of
   Babylon, sixth century BC),
   49–50
Belus (the principal god of the
   Babylonians), 58
Bernard, Master (Bernard of
   Trèves, German alchemist, last
   half of 14th Century), 81
Bernard, (saint, mystic, and
   founder of the Abby of
   Clairvaux, 1090–1153 AD),
   87, 120, 129, 131
Bias of Priene (one of the Seven
   Sages of Greece, sixth century
   BC), 62
Bible, 44; *see* the Book of
   Daniel, the Book of Judges,
   the Book of I Kings, the Book
   of II Kings, Proverbs, Psalms,
   the Gospel of John, the
   Gospel of Matthew, Judith;
   Abel, Abraham, Absalom,
   Adam, Amnon, Belshazzar,
   Cain, Caiaphus, Daniel,
   David, Dinah, Eve, Gad,
   Habakkuk, Herod,
   Holofernes, Jacob, James,
   John, John the Baptist, Jonah,
   Jeroboam, Jesus Christ, Job,
   Joseph, Joshua, King of
   Amalek, King of Shechem,

Matthew, Moses, Noah,
Nebuchadnezzar, Peter,
Solomon, Samuel, Samson,
Saul, Tamar, Zedekiah,
Zechariah; Gospels, Holy
Scriptures, parable of the
vine; Babylon, Egypt, Israel,
Jerusalem, Ninevah,
Philistines, Shinar; manna
bile, 11–12, 19
birds, 30, 37, 38, 53; of prey, 16,
29; *see also* phoenix, falcon,
hoopoe, vulture
blessings, 28, 110–11, 112, 119,
121–22, 130
Boccaccio, Giovanni (Italian
writer, 1313–1375 AD), 2, 6,
152
body, 126, 127; and soul, 11, 16;
of Chaos, 10–12, 18–19; of
Libera, 28, 31, 52, 145; of
Opinion, 53–5; of Christine,
18, 20, 88, 100, 114–15, 117,
121; noncorporeal substances
(in philosophy), 69, 70
Boethius (Ancius Manlius
Severinus, poet, philosopher,
and royal counselor; ca.
480–524 AD), 90, 102, 111,
123, 124, 125, 127–28, 130,
149, 150–51; author and
philosopher, 63, 99;
Consolation of Philosophy, 3,
6, 63, 99, 111, 123, 124–26,
127–28, 130, 139, 143,
150–51; *Music,* 64
Bologna-la-Grasse, 91, 92
Book of Daniel, 36–7, 45–6,
49–50
Book of Judges, 40–1; *see also*
Judges
Book of I Kings, 42–3
Book of II Kings, 45, 48
*Book of the Deeds and Good
Customs of Wise King Charles*

V (by Christine de Pizan),
108–09
Book of the Mutation of Fortunes
(by Christine de Pizan), 74,
75, 78, 135, 146, 148
books, 44, 49, 64, 77, 86, 104,
105, 106, 107, 108
Brittany, 59, 62; *see also* England
Brunehalt (wife of Sigebert I,
king of Austrasia, 561–575
AD), 25
Burgundy, *see* John the Fearless,
Phillip the Bold, Duke of
Burgundy
butterflies, 29

Cabochien Revolt, 7
Caesar (Caius Julius, Roman
general, 100–44 BC), 86
Caiaphas (high priest of
Jerusalem temple in the time
of Jesus), 56
Cain, 49
Cassandra (legendary prophetess
and daughter of King Priam of
Troy), 50–1
Cassiodorus (Flavius Magnus
Aurelius, politician and
Roman writer, ca. 490–585
AD), 118–19, 124
Catholic faith, 11, 12, 15, 21, 27,
58, 131; *see also* Christianity,
Church
Cato (Latin poet of the third
century AD), 104
chalice, 49, 110; *see also*
nourishment
Chambre des comptes, 96, 100
chameleon, 30
Chaos, 10–11, 18–20, 135,
142–44; body of, 10–12,
18–19; feeding of, 11–12,
19–20; Christine's
interpretations of, 10–12
charity, 100, 102, 131

Charity, as allegorical figure, 41, 56, 131
Charlemagne (King of France, 742–814 AD), 16, 144
Charles V (King of France, 1364–1380 AD), 144; and Christine's family, 2, 92–4; death of, 28, 94, 108, 111; restoration of France, 16, 27–8
Charles VI (King of France, 1380–1422 AD), 96; ascension of throne, 29, 32; mental illness of, 16, 29, 135, 144, 145
Charles VII (King of France, 1422–1461 AD), 8
Childeric I (king of France, 457–481 AD), 15, 25, 46
Chilon of Lacedaemon (one of the Seven Sages of Greece, sixth century BC), 62
chivalry, 21, 55, 79, 82; knights, military, 31, 82–3, 101, 120; code of, 82–3
Chivalry, Dame, 33–4, 38, 144
Christianity, 15, 16, 126; see also Catholic faith
Christine de Pizan, as a writer, 3–8, 22, 52, 74–5, 85–6, 100, 102, 105–09, 139, 142, 145, 146, 148–49, 150–58; as an *exemplum*, 136, 156–57; characterization of, 22, 31, 40, 52, 53, 85, 86, 88, 89, 96, 98, 100, 102, 103, 104, 109, 110, 111, 112, 113, 114, 121–22; differences from Christine the narrator, 136–37, 140–42, 148–49, 154, 157–58; falsely slandered, 99, 119; financial difficulties, 3, 96–101, 107–110; lawsuits of, 3, 96–101, 117; her authority and gender 136, 153–54, 155–56; her birth and early childhood, 1–2, 12–3; 20–2; 91–3, 111; her brothers, 3, 110, 115; her daughter, 8, 115; her grandfather, 2, 91; her husband, 2, 93, 95, 96, 100, 102, 115–16; her mother, 91, 109–110, 114, 156; her oldest son, 106–07, 115; her studies, 2, 21, 85, 102–07, 110, 116, 121; her widowhood, 3, 95, 101, 109, 117; in domestic roles, 95, 102, 116; patrons and, 4, 106–08; future reputation of, 86; see also Étienne du Castel, Jean du Castel, and Thomas de Pizan
Church, 12, 15, 16, 37, 49, 59, 82, 115, 131
Cleobulus of Lindos (one of the Seven Sages of Greece, sixth century BC), 62
clerks, 54, 81, 84, 85, 95, 100–01
Clovis (King of France, 481–511 AD), 15, 24, 144
coffers and boxes, 35, 42, 88
colleges, see schools
colors, 88; azures, 54; blue, 53; deep browns, 54; green, 54; gold, 54; red, 53, 54; vermillion, 53; the color of fire, 53; the color of water, 53; white, 53, 54
conquests (military), 75–8
conscience, 12, 16, 43, 50, 97, 100, 119, 121, 127
contemplation, the contemplative life, 13, 114, 115, 116
convent, 88
Cordelia (daughter of King Lear), 62
cows, 45–6
Cruelty, allegorical figure of, 38
cultivators, 15, 26; negligent or false cultivators, 24, 26, 43–4; of Libera's garden, 23–8, 44; see also gardeners
Cyrus the Great (founder of the Persian Empire and conqueror

of Babylon, sixth century BC), 50, 65, 66, 76

Daniel (Hebrew prophet), 36, 140; as model for Christine, 138, 139, 142–46; *see also* Book of Daniel
Dante Alighieri (1265–1361 AD), 35, 140, 141, 143; *Divine Comedy*, 5, 35, 143
Darius I (King of Persia, 522–486 BC), 50
David (Saul's successor as king of the Israelites, 11th to 10th century BC), 43, 45
Death, as an allegorical figure, 39, 95, 107, 108, 115
Decretals, 8
Demetrias (saint; 4th to 5th century AD), 133
Democritus (Greek philosopher, ca. 460–370 BC), 66
Desire for Knowledge, allegorical figure of, 55
Devil, 97; *see also* Enemy and Hell
diet (as medicine), 111, 121
Dinah (daughter of Jacob and Leah), 46
Diogenes (Greek philosopher, fifth century BC), 65, 69
disputation (scholarly), 54, 146
divine punishment, 37–9, 40–1, 42–52, 83–4, 119–20, 123–24
doctor, *see* physician; *see also* medicine and Holy Doctors of the Church
dog, 126
door, figurative, 94, 104; of ivory, 89
dream, 10, 18, 37
dream vision, 136–37
duels, 83; *see also* battles, war

earth (as principle of the nature of things), 61, 71, 72

earth worm, 27, 36
Egypt, 36, 142
elephant, 133
Empedocles (Greek philosopher, 490–430 BC), 66, 69
Enemy, 14, 124; *see also* Devil
England, 27, 106; *see also* Brittany
Envy, as an allegorical figure, 59, 86
Error, as an allegorical figure, 59
ethics, *see* sciences
Étienne du Castel, Christine de Pizan's husband (ca. 1355–1390 AD), career of, 2–3, 93, 95; death of, 3, 95, 115–16; marriage of, 2, 93; qualities of, 93, 95; *see also* Christine de Pizan, husband of
Eucharist, 143, 156–57
Euphrates, 76
Eurydice (wife of Orpheus), 63
Eurystus (mistakenly identified as brother of Orpheus), 63
Eve, 55
exile, 25, 43, 45, 90, 100–01; as fragmentation, 142, 153; as enrichment, 154–55
Exodus, as theological poet, 71
Ezekiel (Biblical book of prophecies), 122, 123

faculty, *see* schools
Faith, as allegorical figure, 12, 56, 131
falcon, 16, 29
fame, 24, 29, 47, 63, 125, 127
Fame, as allegorical figure, 12–13, 21, 22
feathers, 11, 12, 19, 29, 35
field, 30, 31, 40–1, 45–6
fire, 23, 24, 26, 39, 40–1, 42, 50, 59, 80, 105, 111, 115–16, 126, 129, 131, 143; as a principle of nature, 61, 65–6, 69, 71, 72; color of fire, 53; Greek fire, 42

fish, 30
flight, flying, 18, 30
floods, literal, 30, 126; figurative, 98, 109; *see also* water
flowers, 28, 55, 95, 115, 128
fly (the insect), 126
foreigners, 22, 24, 28, 36, 43, 79, 106–08
forest, 21, 29; *see also* woods
forge, 105
form (philosophical sense), 71
Fortune, 16, 23, 27, 28, 29, 47, 74, 75, 77, 78, 86, 91, 93–127
fountains, 24, 32; of Philosophy, 103; *see also* water
foxes, 40–1
France, 100–01, 108, 111, 141; Civil War, 6–7; Kingdom of in Christine's allegorical interpretations, 11–2, 14, 15–6; court of, 2, 92
Francio (legendary hero from whom France supposedly derives her name), 15
Fraud, as allegorical figure, 34–5, 39–41, 47–9, 144
Fredegund (wife of Chilperic I, king of Neustria, ca. 547–597 AD), 25
Frenodaches (Athenian general, 6th century BC), 62
friends, friendship, 22, 26, 30, 31, 32, 33, 35, 36, 38, 39, 40, 42, 43, 45, 46, 48, 50, 51, 52, 69, 108, 110, 111, 116, 117, 119, 128
Fulgentius (Fabius Planciades, Roman grammarian and mythographer, sixth century AD), 63
Furies, the, 35; *see also* Alecto, Megra, Theisphone
furnace, 80, 116; *see also* oven

Gad (Hebrew prophet), 45–6
gardens, 23, 24, 32

gardeners, 24, 26, 28; *see also* cultivators
geometry, *see* sciences
Germany, 25, 81
Gluttony, allegorical figure of, 38
God, 22, 26, 37, 38, 39, 42–52, 53, 58, 63, 73, 82–3, 110–132; and grace, 25, 36, 42, 51, 56; and mercy, 27, 31, 42, 120; as father, 27; God the Father, 33, 131, 132; Holy Spirit, 90, 131; *see also*, divine punishment, Jesus Christ, Trinity
gods, 23; *see also*, Neptune, Ocean, Pelagius
goddess, 35; Philosophy as, 110; Reason as, 78; Wisdom as, 27; *see also* Furies, Persephone, Thetis, and Venus
gold, as metal, 79, 80, 81, 115–16
Golden Age, 13
Golden Calf, 59
Golden Fleece, 77
goldsmith, 81; God as, 116, 117
Gospels, 43, 51, 112, 117, 120, 126
Gospel of St. John, 117, 126, 128
Gospel of St. Matthew, 120
grammar, *see* sciences
Greed, as an allegorical figure, 48, 78; *see also* Avarice
Greeks, 14, 50–1, 76–7
Gregory (saint, Pope Gregory I, the Great, ca. 540–604 AD), 118, 119, 122, 123, 124, 126, 128–29, 130, 133; *Moralia*, 118, 119, 123, 124, 129, 133; *On Ezekiel*, 122, 123–24
griffins, 35

Habakkuk (Hebrew prophet, sixth century BC), 76
Haggai (Hebrew prophet in the time of Darius), 66
Hannibal (General of Carthage, 247–183 BC), 46

Hawk, king of arms, 107
Heaven, 10, 37, 45, 50, 56, 115–16, 117, 120, 124, 126, 129, 130, 133, 134
Hebrews, 62, 104; *see also* Jews
Hector (legendary Trojan hero, son of King Priam), 77
Hecuba (Queen of Troy and wife of King Priam), 77
heirs and heritage, 24, 27, 43–4, 92, 96, 97, 109, 117
Helen (chosen girl, wife of Menelaus), 22; rape of, 46, 63, 77;
Hell, 11, 12, 39, 41, 42, 50, 56, 64, 101; *see also* perdition
Henry IV (King of England, 1399–1413 AD), 4, 106–07
Heraclitus (Greek philosopher, ca. 545–480 BC), 65–6
Hercules, 63, 77
heresies and heretics, 12, 15, 59, 82, 120; *see also* Arius, Mani, Pelagius, Priscillian
Herod Agrippa (King and Tetrarch of Galilee, 37–44 AD), 119
Hippasus (Pythagorian philosopher), 65–6
Hippo (Pythagorian philosopher), 65
Holofernes (Assyrian general killed by Hebrew heroine Judith), 41
Holy Doctors of the Church, 15, 24, 83, 118, 120, 128, 130
Holy Scriptures or Holy Writ, 11, 13, 17, 45, 82, 83, 85, 111, 112, 120, 122, 124, 126, 128; *see also* Bible
honey, 11, 12, 19, 41
Hope, as allegorical figure, 56, 131
hoopoe, 29
Hugh Capet (first Capetian king of France, 987–996 AD), 16, 26

Hugh of St. Victor (French theologian and philosopher, ca. 1096–1141 AD), 123
humility topos, 137–38

Idleness, allegorical figure of, 38
Ignorance, allegorical figure of, 55, 58, 86
illness, 94, 95, 97, 112, 118, 124; fever, 98; pestilence, 30, 45, 106; plague, 16, 36, 106; swellings or swollen ones, 36, 37, 45; *see also* medicine, physician
ink, 22; *see also* parchment and quill
interpretation and misinterpretation, 146–49, 155
invalid, 33, 36, 132
Iraneus (saint, ca. 125–202 BC), 153
Isabeau of Bavaria (wife of Charles VI), 6
Isabelle (daughter of Charles VI, wife of Richard II and later Charles of Orleans), 106
Isidore of Seville (Spanish saint and bishop, ca. 560–636 AD), 47; *Synonyms*, 47
Israel, 13, 40, 41, 44, 58, 63, 139, 141
Italy, 77, 91, 109, 111

Jacob (son of Isaac, Biblical patriarch), 46, 139, 140–42, 153–56
Jacquerie rebellion, 27
Jason (legendary hero of the Golden Fleece), 77
Jean de Meun, disciples of, 4, 84–5
Jean du Castel (oldest son of Christine de Pizan, ca. 1384–1425 AD), 4, 8, 106–07,

Jean du Castel (*cont.*)
    108, 115; *see also* Christine de
    Pizan, her oldest son
Jean Gerson (chancellor of the
    University of Paris, 1363–1429
    AD), 5; *Vivat Rex*, 5, 144
Jeroboam (first king of the
    kingdom of Israel, 931–910
    BC), 59
Jerome (saint and Doctor of the
    Church, ca. 342–420 AD),
    117, 133; *Epistle to Cyprian*,
    117; *Epistle to Demetrias*, 133
Jerusalem, 48, 49, 65
Jesus Christ, 14, 43, 56, 58, 61,
    62, 79, 99, 112, 118, 122, 129
jewels, 49, 125, 157; pearls, 73;
    diamonds, 134; cameo, 134;
    ruby, 134
Jews, 44, 59, 134; *see also*
    Hebrews
Joachim (of Fiore, Italian mystic,
    ca. 1145–1202 AD), 16, 44
Joan of Arc (French saint, ca.
    1412–1431 AD), 8, 9
Job, 97, 119
John (saint and prophet), 16, 56,
    119
John the Baptist (saint), 119
John Chrysostom (saint and
    Doctor of the Church,
    347–407 AD), 120, 123
John II ("the good," King of
    France, 1350–1364 AD), 27
John the Fearless (Duke of
    Burgundy, 1404–1419 AD), 5,
    6, 7, 135
Jonah (Hebrew prophet, eighth
    century BC), 51
Joseph (son of Jacob), 18, 137,
    138
Joshua (Moses' successor), 82
Judges, 83, 101; *see also* Book of
    Judges
Justice, allegorical figure of, 27,
    33, 35, 36, 144; *see also*

measuring cup; scale; ruler;
    Christine de Pizan, lawsuits of

key, 42, 89
knights, *see* chivalry

labor, manual, 55
ladies-in-waiting, of Libera,
    32–6; of Philosophy, 89
lamb, 132
Lancaster, king of arms, 107
Laomedon, (legendary king of
    Troy, father of King Priam),
    77
Larceny, allegorical figure of, 38;
    see also Rapine
Latinus (father of Lavinia,
    Aeneas' wife), 79
law, 13, 55, 75, 82, 83; canon,
    83; civil, 83; the Gospels as
    15, 42, 43, 112
lead, 11, 12, 19, 38
Lear (legendary King of
    Brittany), 62
lectern, 89
leech, 42, 43, 97
Libera, 13, 21–52, 140, 143, 145,
    149; as mother, 30–2, 36, 41,
    44, 50, 52; as a widow, 28, 39;
    body of, 28, 31; name of, 14,
    23; *see also* France
light, 18, 28, 32, 33, 35, 39, 40–1,
    44, 89, 90, 130, 131, 132
Linus of Thebes (musician and
    according to some, master of
    Hercules), 63
lionesses, 25
logic, *see* sciences
Lombardy, 13; clothing of, 92;
    proverb of, 125
Louis (Duke of Orleans, brother
    of Charles VI, 1372–1407
    AD), 3–5, 6, 7, 16, 135
Louis I (the Great, King of
    Hungry, 1342–1382 AD), 2,
    92

Louis VIII (King of France, 1223–1226 AD), 26
Louis IX (King of France and saint, 1226–1270 AD), 16, 26
Louis of Guyenne (Dauphin of France and son of Charles VI, 1397–1415 AD), 5, 6, 7
Louvre, 92
love, foolish, 99, 102; fornication, 25; marital, 93, 95; maternal, 41, 50–1, 114; of parents, 95, 109–110, 114; of study, 22, 88, 89, 103–07, 110, 116, 121
loyalty, 25, 52
Lucretia (Roman lady raped by Tarquin the Proud's son), 56, 65
lust, 15
Lust, Dame, 33–4, 38, 46–7, 144

Macrobius (Ambrosius Theodosius, fl. ca. 400 AD), 138; as model for Christine, 138, 139, 140, 142, 146–47; *Dream of Scipio,* 146–47
Maillotins Revolt, 30
Malachi (Hebrew prophet), 66
Malice, allegorical figure of, 39
Mani (founder of the dualistic heresy of Manicheaism, ca. 216–276 AD), 59
manna, 134, 156
marshes, 29
Mary, Virgin, 14, 37
Matthew (saint), 120
measuring cup, 33; *see also* ruler and scale
mechanical and practical arts, 55
Media, kingdom of, 50, 65
medicine, 32, 111, 113, 118, 132; *see also* physician
Megra, 35; *see* Furies
memory, 21, 25, 105, 131
mercury, 81
Merlin, 16, 44

Meshach, 143
Metaphmorphosis, see Ovid
metaphoric language, *see* poetry
Metaphysics, see Aristotle.
microcosm, 10
Milan, Duke of, *see* Visconti, Jean Galéas
milk, 52, 90; *see also* nourishment
mirror, 33, 35
Misfortune, allegorical figure of, 106
Mohammed (founder of Islam, 570–633 AD), 59
molds, 11, 19–20; *see also* waffle irons
moors, 21
Moses, 58
motion (as a principle), 68–70
mountains, 21, 36
Musaeus (mythical poet and musician), 63
Muses of the poets, 102
music, *see* sciences

Nature, as an allegorical figure, 19–20, 22, 82, 85, 105, 143, 154; Christine's interpretation of, 11–12; crowned shadow, 19–20
nature, of the world (philosophical) 59–73; of thoughts and opinions, 56–8; ungraspable by alchemists, 80–1
Nebuchadnezzar (King of Babylon, 604–562 BC), 18, 37, 45–6, 48, 137, 142, 145
Neptune, 22
Nimrod (the giant, legendary founder of Babylon), 75
Ninevah, 51, 75
Ninus (legendary founder of the Assyrian Empire and of Ninevah), 58
Noah, 47

nourishment, 11, 12, 18, 19–20, 29, 43, 51, 52, 62, 90, 98, 102, 103, 110–11, 112, 116–17, 118, 132, 133–34, 143, 156–57; drink, 20, 118, 132; false nourishment, 38, 39, 143; food, 19, 90; meat, 51, 133, 134; *see also* milk, fountains, manna, chalice, belly, stomach, Eucharist
number (as the principle of the nature of things), 66–8

Ocean (Greek divinity), 64
Of Good and Bad Fortune (Pseudo-Aristotle), 125
One Hundred Ballads (by Christine de Pizan), 102
Opinion, Dame (the shadow), 18, 53–87, 140, 146–49; and Philosophy, 55–6; and Truth, 84, 86; and Envy, 86; and Fortune, 74–6, 85; body of, 53–5; cause of discords, 78–9; nature of, 55–8, 85–7
orchards, 24, 28; *see also* gardens
Orleans, Duke of, *see* Louis (Duke of)
Orosius (5ᵗʰ century AD historian wrongly considered the author of *Ancient History Till Julius Caesar*), 76
Orpheus (legendary poet and musician of ancient Greece), 63–4
Our Lady, *see* Mary
Our Lord, *see* Jesus Christ
oven, 20; *see also* furnace
Ovid (Latin poet, 43 BC-18 AD), 3, 63

pagans, 15, 58
Palace of Justice, 99
parable of the vine, 43–4
parchment, 22; *see also* ink and quill

Paris, capital of France, 19, 92, 136
Paris (son of Priam of Troy), 22, 46, 77
path, *see* road
patience, 99, 113–14, 118, 120, 122–23
patriarchs, 14
Paul (saint), 15
Pelagius (fifth century churchman whose doctrines were declared heretical; d. ca. 430 AD), 59
Pelagus (possibly a god of the seas), 23
Pepin (the Short, King of the Franks, 751–768 AD), 25
perdition, 26, 32, 45, 48, 103; *see also* Hell
Periander of Corinth (one of the Seven Sages of Ancient Greece, 625–585 BC), 62
Persephone, 35
Persians, 14, 50, 65
Peter (saint), 27, 119
Peter of Ravenna (saint and doctor of the Church, 1007–1072 AD), 120–21
Petrarch (Francesco Petrarca, Italian writer, 1304–1374 AD), 2, 139–140
Pharamond (legendary leader of the Franks, descendant of the Trojans), 15, 23–4
Philistines, 40
Phillip the Bold (Duke of Burgundy, 1364–1404 AD), 5, 108–09
philosophers, 59–73, 79, 90, 92, 93, 114
philosophy, ancient and medieval investigators of natural philosophy, 59–73, 75; *see also* sciences; Anaxagoras; Anaximander; Anaximenes; Aristotle; Bacon, Roger;

Boethius; Democritus;
Diogenes; Empedocles;
Heraclitus; Hippasus; Hippo;
Hugh of St. Victor; Plato;
Pythagoras; Seneca; Thales;
Thomas of Pizan
Philosophy, Dame, 6, 18, 56, 88,
80–134, 135, 143, 149–51, 157
phoenix, 29
Phyrgia, 21
physician, 90, 110–11, 113, 121,
132; *see also* illness, medicine
physics, *see* sciences
Picardy, 93
pilgrimage, 10, 18, 122; *see also*
road, travelers, voyage
Pittacus of Mytilene (one of the
Seven Sages of ancient
Greece, 650–569 BC), 62
Pity, allegorical figure of, 41
Plato (427–347 BC), 69
poetry or poesy, 105; ballad, 100;
metaphors, metaphoric
language, 10, 64; meter, 104;
poetic language, 10, 115;
veiled language, 10, 104, 147;
virelai, 102; *see also* rhetoric
and rhetorical method
poison, 25, 39
Poissy, abby of, 8, 115
politics, *see* sciences
popes, 15, 16, 49, 59, 83
poverty, the poor, 49, 81–2, 90,
95, 112–13
Priam of Troy, 14, 50, 77
prince (future, who will value
Christine's work), 86
princes, 21, 78, 93, 101, 106,
107, 109
princess, *see* Libera
principles of the nature of things,
59–73
Priscillian (bishop of Avila,
condemned as a heretic, ca.
300–385 AD), 59
prison, 33–5, 38, 39, 40

prisoner, 33–5, 38
promise, 44, 47, 94, 106
prophecy, 16, 18, 36–41, 44, 47,
50–1, 76
prophets, 14, 17, 36–41, 43, 45,
51, 56–8, 59, 76, 85, 142, 145
Proverbs, 42
proverbs, Christine's use of, 42,
50, 82, 102, 107, 125
Psalms, 113, 115, 118, 122, 124
Pythagoras (Greek philosopher
and mathematician, ca.
560–480 BC), 66–8
Pythagoreans, 66–8

quarrels, 78–9, 85, 86
querelle de la rose, 4, 84–5, 144,
148
quill, 22; *see also* parchment and
ink
quires, 105

Rapine, as allegorical figure, 14;
see also Larceny
Reason, Dame, 14, 33–4, 78, 144
Rectitude, Dame, 13
religion, *see* Babylonian
Captivity, Catholic faith,
Christianity, Church, heresies,
Jews, Hebrews, popes, Schism
revolts, *see* Cabochien, Jacquerie,
and Maillotins
rhetoric and rhetorical method, 74,
115; antiphrasis, 16, 138;
Christine's style, 85–6, 104,
105; commonplace speech, 70;
metaphoric language and poetic
style, 10; obscure language, 10,
80, 85; polished rhetoric, 104;
science of, *see* sciences; *see
also* poetry (poesy)
Richard II (King of England,
1377–1399 AD), 106
riches, 39, 109, 124, 126, 127,
128; *see also* wealth and
treasures

rivers, 29, 133; *see also* water, Euphrates, Styx
road, 18, 21, 23, 25, 50, 80, 99, 101, 104, 121, 122, 129; *see also* pilgrimage, travelers, voyage
Romance of the Rose, 4, 84–5, 135, 148
Romans, 14, 62, 104
Rome, 23, 46, 61, 62, 77, 86
Romulus (legendary founder of Rome), 31, 61
ruler, 33; *see also* measuring cup and scale

Sabines, 31
Salisbury (third count of, John de Montacute or De Montagu, ca. 1350–1400 AD), 4, 106–07
Samson, 40–1
Samuel (Hebrew prophet of the 11ᵗʰ century BC), 43
saplings, 29
Saracens, 59
Saul (first king of the Israelites), 42–3
scale, 33; *see also* measuring cup and ruler
Schism, 16, 49
schools, 11, 53–5, 88, 92
sciences, 11, 75, 82, 88, 115, 116, 132–3; in decline, 86; arithmetic, 54; astrology, 54, 93, 95; dialectics, 54; ethics, 132; geometry, 54; grammar, 54, 115; logic, 132; mathematical, 95; music, 54; philosophy, 54, 55, 56; physics, 132; politics, 132; rhetoric, 104, 115; theology, 54; basic, 122; liberal and forbidden, 54; moral, 61; obscure, 104; speculative, 75, 114
Scipio (Aemilianus Africanus Numantinus, Publius Cornelius, Roman general and public statesman, 185–129 BC), 18, 137, 138, 142
sea monster, 53
second age, 22, 75
secret, secrecy, 22, 44, 80, 90, 111, 114, 133
Secretum, see Petarch
Semiramis (legendary queen of Babylon), 76
Seneca (Lucius Annaeus Seneca, Roman writer and philosopher, 4 BC-65 AD), 127
Sensuality, as an allegorical figure, 12
serpent, 35, 53, 54
servant, 12, 31, 36, 49, 75, 90, 91, 93, 94, 96, 108, 109
Seven Sages of Greece, 61; *see also*, Bias of Priene, Chilon of Lacedaemon, Cleobulus of Lindos, Pittacus of Mytilene, Periander of Corinth, Solon of Athens, Thales the Milesian
Sextus (son of Tarquin the Seventh and the violater of Lucretia), 46, 65
shackles, 28, 46, 47
shadow(s), 11, 12, 18, 23, 24, 30, 53–5, 133
Shadrach, 143
Shechem (son of the king of), 46
sheep, 39
Shinar, 38–9
Sibyls, 16, 44
silver, 80
sin, sinners, 13, 15, 16, 40, 41–52, 83–4, 97, 113, 120
sleep, 18, 33–4, 41, 43
Solomon, 42
Solon of Athens (one of the Seven Sages of ancient Greece, ca. 640–560 BC), 62
song, 22, 23, 28, 34
soul, 10, 14, 58, 65, 104, 117, 121, 124, 128, 130, 132, 133; *see also* body, Holy Spirit

Spain, 25, 29
stairs, 88
stomach, 10, 11; *see also* belly,
nourishment
storms, 44; at sea, 96, 120
study, 11, 56, 84
Styx, river of Hell, 64

Tamar (daughter of David), 46
Tarquin I (fifth king of Rome,
616–579 BC), 62
Tarquin (the Proud, seventh and
last king of Rome, 534–509
BC), 46, 65
tears, 28, 31, 40, 98, 129
Thales the Milesian (one of the
Seven Sages of ancient
Greece, philosopher and
mathematician, ca. 640–546
BC), 61–3, 65
Theisphone, 35; *see* Furies
theological poets, 61, 63–4, 71–2
theology, *see* Sciences
Theology (Holy), 12, 132–4, 157;
see also Philosophy
Theseus (legendary king of
Thebes), 63
Thetis (legendary sea goddess
and the mother of Achilles), 64
thieves and thievery, 23, 26, 27,
35–6, 39, 49, 51; *see also*
Larceny, Rapine
Thomas Aquinas (saint,
philosopher and Doctor of the
Church, 1225–1274 AD),
*Commentary on the
Metaphysics of Aristotle*, 6,
59–72, 146; *see also* Aristotle
Thomas de Pizan (d. ca. 1387
AD), 1, 102, 110, 114; as
Charles V's counselor, 2, 92–3;
financial problems, 93, 94;
illness and death, 3, 94–5,
invitations to foreign courts, 2,
91–2; marriage, 91; reputation
of, 95; with Master Bernard, 81

thorns, 23, 26, 27, 28, 129
towers, 36, 37, 39, 88
traitors and treachery, 25, 39,
40–1, 47–8, 102, 107, 108
travelers, 21, 88, 104, 122, 126,
129, 135, 142, 155; *see also*
pilgrimage, road, voyage
treasures, 21, 73, 74, 88, 89, 113,
125; *see also* riches, wealth
Tree of Gold, 14, 23, 32
tribulations and troubles, of
Chaos, 19; of Christine, 90,
94–103, 106–129; of France
(Libera), 22, 26, 27, 52, 29–36,
39
Trinity, 5, 14, 130–32, 141,
151–52
Trojans, 14, 22–3; *see also*
Aeneas, Hector, Hecuba,
Leomedon, Paris
Troy, 46, 50–1, 63, 77
Turnus (Aeneas' legendary
opponent and rival for the
hand of Lavinia), 77

university, *see* schools
Urban (V, pope) 16
Uzziah (or Ozias, king of Judea,
ca. 789–738 BC), 62

Valerius Maximus (Roman writer;
fl. early first century AD), 47
valley, 18, 21, 22, 36, 47, 115
Venice, 91, 92
Venus, 25
Vespasian (Roman Emperor,
69–79 AD), 15
vessel of water, 38–9
vices, the, 32–6, 38–9, 40, 41–2,
45–51; *see also* sin, Fraud;
Avarice; Greed; Lust, Dame
Virgil, 35
Virgin Mary, *see* Mary
virtues, the, 10, 13, 32–6, 48;
see also Chivalry, Dame;
Reason, Dame; Justice

Visconti, Jean Galéas, (Duke of Milan and father of Valentine Visconti, wife of Louis of Orléans, 1351–1402 AD), 107–09
Visconti, Valentine (wife of Louis, Duke of Orleans), 3
voyage, 28; *see also* pilgrimage, road, traveler
vulture, 27, 38

waffle irons, 19; *see also* molds
war, 46; Civil War, 6–7, 135–6; Charles V's, 93; Hundred Years, 7–8, 27; laws for a just, 82–3; Trojan, 22–3; 77
wasps, 29, 39
water, 15, 24, 38, 39, 80, 102; as principle of nature, 61–5, 66, 69, 72; streams, 18, 24; waterway, 24; waves, 109, 120; *see also* floods, fountains, rivers
way, *see* road
wealth, 44, 109, 116–17, 122, 125; *see also* riches, treasure
weapons, *see* arms
weeping, 27, 31, 98, 117–18; *see also* tears
whipping, 27, 32; *see also* beatings

widows, *see* woman
winds, 18, 29, 36–7, 44, 45, 46, 109, 117, 119, 129
Wisdom, as an allegorical figure, 13, 27; Alternate Name of Philosophy, 90; blessed Wisdom, 13
woman, body of, 88, 100, 121; learned, 22, 85; married, 96, 102; nature of, 40, 88, 100, 110; pregnant, 44, 105; voices of, 30, 31, 89, 91; widowed, 96, 98, 100–01, 109
woods, 40; *see also* forests
world, the, 12, 13, 16, 18, 59, 104, 115, 116–17, 119–20, 126, 127, 128–9, 130
wounds, 27, 28, 31, 32, 36, 39, 90, 109, 120, 123, 129, 132
writing, *see* poetry (poesie), rhetoric and rhetorical method

Xerxes (King of Persia 485–465 BC), 76–7

youth, 94, 102–03

Zechariah (Hebrew prophet), 38–9, 66, 143
Zedekiah (last king of Judea; 597–587 BC), 48, 62

Already published titles in this series

Christine de Pizan's Letter of Othea to Hector, *Jane Chance*, 1990

The Writings of Margaret of Oingt, Medieval Prioress and Mystic, *Renate Blumenfeld-Kosinski*, 1990

Saint Bride and her Book: Birgitta of Sweden's Revelations, *Julia Bolton Holloway*, 1992

The Memoirs of Helene Kottanner (1439–1440), *Maya Bijvoet Williamson*, 1998

The Writings of Teresa de Cartagena, *Dayle Seidenspinner-Núñez*, 1998

Julian of Norwich: *Revelations of Divine Love* and *The Motherhood of God*: an excerpt, *Frances Beer*, 1998

Hrotsvit of Gandersheim: A Florilegium of her Works, *Katharina M. Wilson*, 1998

Hildegard of Bingen: On Natural Philosophy and Medicine: Selections from *Cause et Cure, Margret Berger*, 1999

Women Saints' Lives in Old English Prose, *Leslie A. Donovan*, 1999

Angela of Foligno's Memorial, *Cristina Mazzoni*, 2000

The Letters of the Rožmberk Sisters, *John M. Klassen*, 2001

The Life of Saint Douceline, a Beguine of Provence, *Kathleen Garay and Madeleine Jeay*, 2001

Agnes Blannbekin, Viennese Beguine: Life and Revelations, *Ulrike Wiethaus*, 2002

Women of the *Gilte Legende*: A Selection of Middle English Saints Lives, *Larissa Tracy*, 2003

The Book of Margery Kempe: An Abridged Translation, *Liz Herbert McAvoy*, 2003

Mechthild of Magdeburg: Selections from *The Flowing Light of the Godhead*, *Elizabeth A. Andersen*, 2003

Guidance for Women in Twelfth-Century Convents, *Vera Morton with Jocelyn Wogan-Browne*, 2003

Goscelin of St Bertin: *The Book of Encouragement and Consolation [Liber Confortatorius]*, *Monika Otter*, 2004

Anne of France: *Lessons for my Daughter*, *Sharon L. Jansen*, 2004

Late-Medieval German Women's Poetry: Secular and Religious Songs, *Albrecht Classen*, 2004

The Paston Women: Selected Letters, *Diane Watt*, 2004

The Vision of Christine de Pizan, Glenda McLeod and Charity Cannon Willard, 2005

Caritas Pirckheimer: A Journal of the Reformation Years, 1524-1528, *Paul A. McKenzie*, 2006

Women's Books of Hours in Medieval England, *Charity Scott-Stokes*, 2006

Old Norse Women's Poetry: The Voices of Female Skalds, *Sandra Ballif Straubhaar*, 2011

Printed and bound by CPI Group (UK) Ltd, Croydon, CR0 4YY

19/01/2025

14628468-0001